Dear Mike,

Please accept this small 'tome' as a testimony of our deep respect for you - our friend - and beloved Pastor.

In Faith and Love!

Howard & Charlene

DAY BY DAY WITH JONATHAN EDWARDS

DAY BY DAY
WITH
JONATHAN
EDWARDS

Compiled and Edited by

RANDALL J. PEDERSON

HENDRICKSON PUBLISHERS

© 2005 by Hendrickson Publishers, Inc.
P. O. Box 3473
Peabody, Massachusetts 01961-3473

ISBN 1-56563-388-1

Printed in the United States of America

First Printing — August 2005

Unless otherwise noted, all Scripture quotations are taken from the KING JAMES VERSION OF THE BIBLE.

Selections for the days noted below are taken from the following works, used with the kind permission of Yale University Press.

"Images of Divine Things"
From *The Works of Jonathan Edwards*, Volume 11, *Typological Writings* (edited by Wallace E. Anderson, Mason I. Lowance, Jr., and David Watters; New Haven, Conn.: Yale University Press, 1993); January 13; February 11; May 23.

The "Miscellanies"
From *The Works of Jonathan Edwards*, Volume 13, *The "Miscellanies"* (edited by Thomas A. Schafer; New Haven, Conn.: Yale University Press, 1995); February 16, 17, 23; April 17, 28, 29; August 12, 13, 14; September 17.

A Letter to the Reverend George Whitefield
A Letter to the Rev. Thomas Gillespie
From *The Works of Jonathan Edwards*, Volume 16, *Letters and Personal Writings* (edited by George S. Claghorn; New Haven, Conn.: Yale University Press, 1998); January 21; February 12.

The Dreadful Silence of the Lord
The Preciousness of Time
From *The Works of Jonathan Edwards*, Volume 19, *Sermons and Discourses, 1734–1738* (edited by M. X. Lesser; New Haven, Conn.: Yale University Press, 2001); January 8, 9; June 11; November 8.

"The Pleasantness of Religion"
From *The Sermons of Jonathan Edwards: A Reader* (New Haven: Yale University Press, 1999). March 11, 14; August 30; September 6.

Cover Art: Etching of Jonathan Edwards

Library of Congress Cataloging-in-Publication Data

Edwards, Jonathan, 1703–1758.
    Day by day with Jonathan Edwards / compiled and edited by Randall J. Pederson.
    p. cm.
    Includes bibliographical references.
    ISBN 1-56563-388-1 (alk. paper)
    1. Devotional calendars. I. Pederson, Randall J., 1975–   II. Title.
    BV4811.E28 2005
    242'.2—dc22

                    2005019473

Table of Contents

Preface

onathan Edwards is a colossal figure in early American history. Born at the dawn of the eighteenth century in East Windsor, Connecticut, Edwards grew up in a world on the threshold of change. On a widespread scale, the Puritan God-centered world was being replaced with more formal and rationalist religion. Amidst this complex cultural climate, Edwards promoted a form of heart-piety that was often ignored in the world he lived in. This conviction led Edwards to instigate and sustain the massive colonial revivals known as the First Great Awakening. In these revivals he sought to advance the work of Christ in the sinner's soul, to defend the work of the Spirit from the revival's distracters, and to prove that God had not forgotten New England.

What was true for Edwards over 250 years ago is still relevant today. As you read Edwards, you will be pierced, challenged, and comforted. He will call you to greater awareness of yourself and the things of God. Christianity, for Edwards, is serious business; it concerns life and death. We need Edwards, not only as an example of how mind and faith can (and should) work together, but as a remembrancer. Edwards reminds us that God is in the details—that wherever we are, whatever we do, God is there with us. This must be comforting to those who believe, but horrifying to those who don't.

Recently, I had the privilege of reading Edwards in a class at Calvin Theological Seminary. Our discussions were helpful in grasping Edwards as he was—a man intoxicated with the glory of Christ. I must acknowledge with gratitude Dr. John Bolt, who, more than anyone else, helped to bring Edwards alive to my mind. I also want to acknowledge the great debt I owe to Dr. George M. Marsden, not only for his suggestions for this book, but for his helpful biography *Jonathan Edwards: A Life*. As Marsden shows, Edwards was not only the force behind the Great Awakening, he was also a loving husband, father, and friend.

Thanks are due to Dr. Kenneth P. Minkema, the current editor of Yale's *The Works of Jonathan Edwards,* for providing several unpublished transcripts for this book. My sincere thanks go also to Sara Scott and Dawn Harrell for their invaluable help in making this project a reality; and, as ever, to my wife Sarah, without whom neither this nor so many other things could be done.

My prayer is that you would grow more in the awareness of God's sovereignty and eminent beauty; that, like Edwards, you would be ravished with divine love.

Randall J. Pederson

Introduction

J onathan Edwards as the force behind the First Great Awakening was a champion of religious zeal in his day, so it is no wonder that secular as well as religious scholarship has agreed on his importance in American history. The treasures from Edwards's pen have been mined, pondered, and evaluated down to the present day. His famous sermon "Sinners in the Hands of an Angry God" is read and studied in America's public schools as a specimen of the literature of his day. Students of American history pay much attention to Edwards's scientific, philosophical, and psychological writings; scholars regard Edwards's work on revivals as unexcelled in analysis and scope. Christians continue to read his sermons with great appreciation for their rich doctrine, clear and forceful style, and powerful depiction of the majesty of God, the sinfulness of sin, and Christ's power to save.

Still, not everyone agrees about Edwards's place in the history of Christian thought. Scholars continue to debate his philosophical musings, his fidelity to certain historic Calvinist doctrines, and his influence upon subsequent generations. As Iain H. Murray notes, "Edwards divided men in his lifetime and to no less degree he continues to divide his biographers."[1]

As the huge body of his writings shows, Edwards was intellectually brilliant, multifaceted in his interests, and incredibly creative. Spiritually he was profound, reflective, experiential, and intense. Early on he developed the habit of self-mastery and a capacity for unremitting toil. Though laboring in places far from the cultured centers of his society, Edwards influenced many people while he lived and cast a long shadow across the generations to follow.

Jonathan Edwards was born October 5, 1703, in East Windsor, Connecticut. He was the son of the Rev. Timothy Edwards and Esther Stoddard, daughter of the Rev. Solomon Stoddard of Northampton. Edwards's father and maternal grandfather heavily influenced his education and career. Solomon Stoddard served for sixty years as minister of the parish church of Northampton, Massachusetts. He was a powerful force in the pulpit, a leader in the churches of western Massachusetts and along

---

[1] Iain H. Murray, *Jonathan Edwards: A New Biography* (Edinburgh; Carlisle, Pa.: Banner of Truth Trust, 1987; repr., Edinburgh: Banner of Truth, 2003), p. xix.

the Connecticut River, and a stirring writer. Timothy Edwards was highly educated and also well known as a preacher, and, like Stoddard, no stranger to religious revivals.

As many other ministers did in that day, Timothy Edwards conducted a grammar school in his home, preparing boys for Connecticut's Collegiate School, known as Yale College after 1718. The school was founded in 1701 as an orthodox Congregationalist alternative to Harvard College, where the prevailing parties were hostile to the ideas proposed in John Cotton's "Way of the Churches of Christ in New-England," or at least, favorable to Episcopalianism.

Edwards received his early education in his father's school. At age twelve, he went on to the Collegiate School, which as yet had no permanent home. Several towns were competing for the honor of playing host to the fledgling institution. Edwards went to the nearest location, downriver from Windsor at Wethersfield, to begin his studies with Elisha Williams. When the college finally located in 1716 at New Haven under the rectorship of Timothy Cutler, Edwards went to New Haven. He finished at the top of his class and in 1720 was awarded the Bachelor of Arts degree. Edwards stayed on at Yale to study for a master's degree.

Edwards's spiritual life was influenced by various factors. His parents, vibrant and intelligent Christians, offered a godly example and nurtured Edwards toward godliness. He went through several periods of spiritual convictions in his childhood and youth, which culminated in his conversion in 1721 after being convicted by the words of 1 Timothy 1:17, "Now unto the King eternal, immortal, invisible, the only wise God, be honour and glory for ever and ever, Amen." He later wrote,

> As I read [these] words, there came into my soul . . . a sense of the glory of the Divine Being; a new sense quite different from anything I ever experienced before. . . . I kept saying and as it were singing over those words of Scripture to myself and went to pray to God that I might enjoy Him. . . . From that time I began to have a new kind of apprehensions and ideas of Christ, and the work of redemption, and the glorious way of salvation by him. And my mind was greatly engaged to spend my time in reading and meditating on Christ, in the beauty of his person and the lovely way of salvation by free grace in Him.[2]

Edwards's ministerial career began in 1722 with a brief sojourn of eight months in New York City. Frictions had arisen between the English members of First Presbyterian Church and the Scots-Irish majority, led by Scottish minister James Anderson. The English eventually withdrew and began meeting separately. Edwards accepted their invitation to preach for them. Later he wrote:

> I went to New York to preach and my longings after God and holiness were much increased. I felt a burning desire to be in everything conformed to

---

[2] From Jonathan Edwards, "A Personal Narrative."

the blessed image of Christ . . . how I should be more holy and live more holily . . . the heaven I desired was a heaven of holiness, to be with God and to spend my eternity and holy communion with Christ.[3]

In April 1723, Edwards was persuaded by his father to return to Connecticut. After he had completed work for a master's degree at Yale, he spoke at commencement exercises. The title of his talk was "A Sinner is Not Justified before God except through the Righteousness of Christ obtained by Faith." That November, Edwards took a call to the parish church at Bolton, about fifteen miles east of Hartford.

The following year Edwards returned to New Haven to serve as tutor at the college. Yale was in upheaval due to the decision of rector Timothy Cutler in 1722 to abandon Congregationalism and revert to the Church of England. No suitable candidate would agree to take his place, so the college was in the hands of a temporary rector. Each local minister served for a month in rotation, while the forty or so students were left in the care of two tutors. The students were a disorderly lot, adding discipline to the heavy burden of Edwards's teaching. Edwards remained there until 1726 when he received a summons from the people of Northampton, Massachusetts, to come upriver and serve as assistant to his aged grandfather, Solomon Stoddard. Edwards was installed there on February 15, 1727, and became sole minister of the parish church upon the death of Stoddard in 1729.

While at New Haven, Edwards befriended Sarah Pierrepont, whom he met when he was sixteen and she was only thirteen years old. Friendship blossomed into romance, and the two were wed eight years later in 1727 after Edwards was settled at Northampton. Their eleven children were the beginning of a large progeny that greatly affected the life and history of New England.

Edwards's spiritual life was developed by various testings and difficulties. Sometimes he agonized over decisions; sometimes he suffered spells of exhaustion, depression, and serious illness (one episode was so severe that Edwards afterward said God had taken him and shaken him over the pit of hell); and often he faced problems and challenges in the pastorate as well as in his personal and family life. As a true Puritan, Edwards sought to discern the message of Providence in every event and to improve spiritually on all that befell him, good or bad.

Edwards was caught up in the Great Awakening, which began in 1740, and became one of the ablest defenders and instruments of the revival. He preached "Sinners in the Hand of an Angry God" (Deuteronomy 32:35) at Enfield, Connecticut, on July 8, 1741. The congregation was profoundly moved. A witness wrote, "Before the sermon was done, there was a great moaning and crying out throughout the whole house. What shall I do to be saved? Oh, I am going to hell! Oh, what shall I do for Christ?" Edwards asked for silence, but the tumult increased until

---

[3] From Jonathan Edwards, "A Personal Narrative."

Edwards had to stop preaching. A monument to the sermon stands today on the site of the Enfield meeting house.[4]

Edwards remained in Northampton until 1750, when he became embroiled in controversy over who should partake of the Lord's Supper. Solomon Stoddard had taught that the sacrament could be a "converting ordinance" to which any baptized person of blameless life should be admitted. Edwards opposed this view, saying that only people who professed to be converted and who were bringing forth the fruits of conversion in their lives should be received at the Lord's Table. As a corollary, Edwards said that baptism ought to be administered only to the children of believers who had made a credible profession of faith. That was contrary to the long-established practice of the so-called "Half-Way Covenant," as Stoddard's view was called. The Communion controversy resulted in Edwards being dismissed as minister. The following year Edwards left Northampton with his family, taking refuge in the frontier settlement of Stockbridge as a missionary to the Indians.

In 1758, Edwards agreed to become president of the College of New Jersey at Princeton. He left his family that January, as "affectionately as if he should not come again," one of his daughters wrote; as he departed, he turned back to his wife and said, "I commit you to God."[5]

Edwards preached his inaugural sermon at Princeton on Hebrews 13:8, "Jesus Christ the same yesterday, today, and for ever." The sermon was more than two hours long and made a great impact on its hearers. While at Princeton, Edwards hoped to complete two major treatises, one showing "The Harmony of the Old and New Testaments," and the other, a much-expanded treatise on "The History of the Work of Redemption." However, Edwards did not live to complete these works. On March 22, 1758, after only a few months in Princeton, he died of complications from a smallpox inoculation.

Edwards is often remembered for spending thirteen hours a day in study. Modern readers may be inspired or appalled by that, but we should realize that most workers in those times spent nearly as much time pursuing their calling. Under such circumstances, Edwards would have appeared diligent and faithful to his calling, not overcommitted to study or unbalanced in his use of time. Out of those long hours in the study, and especially from the period of relative isolation at Stockbridge, came the vast body of Edwards' writings.

The effect of this spiritual giant's theological insight on New England Christianity, however, has been hotly debated. Some say Edwards provided the impetus to move New England beyond the primitive thought of its founders. In that sense, Edwards was a true philosopher. Others say

---

[4] "The Diary of Stephen Williams" in Oliver Means, *A Sketch of the Strict Congregation Church of Enfield, Connecticut* (Hartford, 1899).

[5] Carol F. Karlson and Laurie Crumpacker, eds., *The Diary of Esther Edwards Burr: 1754–1757* (Yale University Press, 1984), p. 302.

Edwards was the last representative of Puritan theology and thought in the New World, where Puritanism would later be disdained. A third group finds little fault with Edwards or his theology, but accuses his followers of veering from the truths that inspired Edwards himself. Though Edwards himself stressed godly living, some of his successors discarded the biblically Reformed base which supported that godliness in their attempt to adopt Edwards's more speculative views and methods. That, in turn, fostered a decline of both doctrinal and experiential Calvinism in New England. This group maintains that Edwards was a theologian-philosopher whose vision died with him.

Perhaps the most accurate assessment of Edwards is a combination of these three views. Edwards was a profound theologian, as readers of *The End for Which God Created the World* can attest. Edwards was also a minister with great pastoral sensitivity—consider his *Religious Affections*. Most recent scholarship has focused on Edwards's metaphysics, gleaning primarily from his scientific writings (e.g., Sang Hyun Lee's *The Philosophical Theology of Jonathan Edwards* [2000] and Paul Helm's *Jonathan Edwards: Philosophical Theologian* [2003]). Whatever view one may hold on Edwards, all agree that his writings, specifically his sermons, are profitable specimens of one of America's best and last Puritans.

Randall J. Pederson
Joel R. Beeke

FOR FURTHER READING
The standard biographies are Perry Miller's *Jonathan Edwards* (New York: W. Slone, 1949; repr., Amherst, Mass.: University of Massachusetts Press, 1981), Ola Winslow's *Jonathan Edwards, 1703–1758: A Biography* (New York: Collier, 1940; repr., 1961), and Patricia J. Tracy's *Jonathan Edwards, Pastor: Religion and Society in Eighteenth Century Northampton* (New York: Hill & Wang, 1980). Iain H. Murray filled many gaps in Edwards's biography with *Jonathan Edwards: A New Biography*. George M. Marsden recently produced the definitive work on Edwards in *Jonathan Edwards: A Life* (New Haven: Yale University Press, 2003). One of the easiest introductions to the work of Edwards is Stephen J. Nichols's *Jonathan Edwards: A Guided Tour to His Life and Thought* (Phillipsburgh, N.J.: P&R, 2001).

Jealous for His Glory

Such is Christ's love to a true Christian that he is jealous for his good and welfare, and nothing will ever provoke him more than to see any injure him. "If any offend one of these little ones" (Matthew 18:6). And such is the spirit of a Christian towards Christ that he is jealous for his glory; he has a spirit of zeal for the glory of his Redeemer, and nothing will more grieve and offend him than to see him dishonored and his interest suffering. Christ and the soul of the true Christian have a mutual complacence in each other, and Christ especially has delight in the believer. "As the bridegroom rejoiceth over the bride, so shall thy God rejoice over thee" (Isaiah 62:5). Christ is exceedingly well-pleased and takes sweet delight in the graces and virtues of the Christian, in that beauty and loveliness which he has put upon him; "thou hast ravished my heart" (Song of Solomon 4:9).

For I am jealous over you with godly jealousy: for I have espoused you to one husband, that I may present you as a chaste virgin to Christ.
2 Corinthians 11:2

Christ takes sweet delight in the graces and virtues of the Christian.

Before All Things

Whom have I in heaven but thee? and there is none upon earth that I desire beside thee.

Psalm 73:25

It is the spirit of a godly man to prefer God before all other things on the earth. This is the enjoyment of God, for which he hopes hereafter, which is better than anything in this world. The saints prefer what of God may be obtained in this world before all things in the world. They not only prefer those glorious degrees of the enjoyment of God which are promised hereafter before anything in this world, but even such degrees as may be attained to here in this present state, though they are immensely short of what is to be enjoyed in heaven. There is a great difference in the spiritual attainments of the saints in this world. Some attain to much greater acquaintance and communion with God, and conformity to him, than others. But the highest attainments are very small in comparison with what is future. The saint prefers what he has already of God before anything in the world. That which was infused into his heart at his conversion is more precious to him than anything which the world can afford. The knowledge and acquaintance which he has with God, he would not part with for anything that the world can afford. The views which are sometimes given him of the beauty and excellency of God are more precious to him than all the treasures of the wicked. The image of God stamped on his soul he values more than any earthly ornaments.

> The saint prefers what he has already of God before anything in the world.

Gracious Notices

hrist is of infinite condescension. None are so low or inferior, but Christ's condescension is sufficient to take a gracious notice of them. He condescends not only to the angels, humbling himself to behold the things that are done in heaven, but he also condescends to such poor creatures as men; and that not only so as to take notice of princes and great men, but of those that are of meanest rank and degree, "the poor of the world" (James 2:5). Such as are commonly despised by their fellow creatures, Christ does not despise. "Base things of the world, and things that are despised, hath God chosen" (1 Corinthians 1:28). Christ condescends to take notice of beggars (Luke 16:22) and people of the most despised nations. In Christ Jesus is neither "Barbarian, Scythian, bond nor free" (Colossians 3:11). He that is thus high condescends to take a gracious notice of little children; "suffer little children to come unto me" (Matthew 19:14). Yea, which is more, his condescension is sufficient to take a gracious notice of the most unworthy, sinful creatures, those that deserve no good, and those that deserve infinite ill. Yea, so great is his condescension, that it is not only sufficient to take some gracious notice of such as these, but . . . great enough to become their friend, to become their companion, to unite their souls to him in spiritual marriage.

Like as a father pitieth his children, so the LORD pitieth them that fear him.
Psalm 103:13

Christ condescends to take notice of beggars.

9

God's House

In My Father's house are many mansions.

John 14:2

Heaven is the house where God dwells with his family. God is represented in Scripture as having a family; and though some of this family are now on earth, yet in so being they are abroad and not at home, but all going home. . . . Heaven is the place that God has built for himself and his children. God has many children, and the place designed for them is heaven; therefore the saints, being the children of God, are said to be of the household of God. "Now therefore ye are no more strangers and foreigners, but fellow-citizens with the saints, and of the household of God" (Ephesians 2:19). God is represented as a householder or head of a family and heaven is his house. It is the house not only where God has his throne, but also where he as it were keeps his table, where his children sit down with him and where they are feasted in a royal manner becoming the children of so great a King. "That ye may eat and drink at my table in my kingdom" (Luke 22:30); "But I say unto you, I will not drink henceforth of this fruit of the vine, until that day when I drink it new with you in my Father's kingdom" (Matthew 26:29). God is the King of kings, and heaven is the place where he keeps his court.

God is the King of kings, and heaven is where he keeps his court.

Dreadful Fears

he fears and dangers to which men are subject are of two kinds: temporal and eternal. Men are frequently in distress from fear of temporal evils. We live in an evil world, where we are liable to an abundance of sorrows and calamities. A great part of our lives is spent in sorrowing for present or past evils, and in fearing those which are future. What poor, distressed creatures are we, when God is pleased to send his judgments among us! If he visits a place with mortal and prevailing sickness, what terror seizes our hearts! If any person is taken sick, and trembles for his life, or if our near friends are at the point of death, or in many other dangers, how fearful is our condition! Now there is sufficient foundation for peace and safety to those exercised with such fears, and brought into such dangers. But Christ is a refuge in all trouble; there is a foundation for rational support and peace in him, whatever threatens us. He, whose heart is fixed, trusting in Christ, need not be afraid of any evil tidings. "As the mountains are round about Jerusalem, so Christ is round about them that fear him."

But it is the other kind of fear and danger to which we have a principal respect; the fear and danger of God's wrath. The fears of a terrified conscience, the fearful expectation of the dire fruits of sin, and the resentment of an angry God: these are infinitely the most dreadful. If men are in danger of those things, and are not asleep, they will be more terrified than with the fears of any outward evil. Men are in a most deplorable condition, as they are by nature exposed to God's wrath; and if they are sensible how dismal their case is, will be in dreadful fears and dismal expectations.

And a man shall be as an hiding-place from the wind, and a covert from the tempest; as rivers of water in a dry place, as the shadow of a great rock in a weary land.

Isaiah 32:32

Knowing God

And beside this, giving
all diligence, add to
your faith virtue; and
to virtue knowledge.

2 Peter 1:5

Divine truths not only concern ministers, but are of infinite importance to all Christians. It is not with the doctrine of divinity as it is with the doctrines of philosophy and other sciences. These last are generally speculative points, which are of little concern in human life; and it very little alters the case as to our temporal or spiritual interests, whether we know them or not. Philosophers differ about them, some being of one opinion, and others of another. And while they are engaged in warm disputes about them, others may well leave them to dispute among themselves, without troubling their heads much about them; it being of little concern to them, whether the one or the other is in the right. But it is not thus in matters of divinity. The doctrines of this nearly concern every one. They are about those things which relate to every man's eternal salvation and happiness. The common people cannot say, Let us leave these matters to ministers and divines; let them dispute them out among themselves as they can; they concern not us: for they are of infinite importance to every man. Those doctrines which relate to the essence, attributes, and subsistencies of God, concern all; as it is of infinite importance to common people, as well as to ministers, to know what kind of being God is. For he is a Being who has made us all, "in whom we live, and move, and have our being;" who is the Lord of all; the Being to whom we are all accountable; who is the last end of our being, and the only fountain of our happiness.

Infinite Debtors

t is of God that Christ becomes ours, that we are brought to him, and are united to him. It is of God that we receive faith to be close with him, that we may have an interest in him. "For by grace ye are saved through faith; and that not of yourselves: it is the gift of God" (Ephesians 2:8). It is of God that we actually receive all the benefits that Christ has purchased. It is God that pardons and justifies, and delivers from going down to hell; and into his favor the redeemed are received, when they are justified. So it is God that delivers from the dominion of sin, cleanses us from our filthiness, and changes us from our deformity. It is of God that the redeemed receive all their true excellency, wisdom, and holiness; and that two ways, viz., as the Holy Ghost by whom these things are immediately wrought is from God, proceeds from him, and is sent by him; and also as the Holy Ghost himself is God, by whose operation and indwelling the knowledge of God and divine things, a holy disposition and all grace, are conferred and upheld. And though means are made use of in conferring grace on men's souls, yet it is of God that we have these means of grace, and it is he that makes them effectual. It is of God that we have the Holy Scriptures; they are his word. It is of God that we have ordinances, and their efficacy depends on the immediate influence of his Spirit. The ministers of the gospel are sent of God, and all their sufficiency is of him. "We have this treasure in earthen vessels, that the excellency of the power may be of God, and not of us" (2 Corinthians 4:7). Their success depends entirely and absolutely on the immediate blessing and influence of God.

For it is God which worketh in you both to will and to do of his good pleasure.
Philippians 2:13

Consider the Time

The harvest is past,
the summer is ended,
and we are not saved.
Jeremiah 8:20

You are one to whom God has committed that precious talent. You have had a great deal of time. You have had a great deal of time that is past. And time is as much worth to you as to others whether you are so sensible of the worth of it or no. You are one that has an eternity before you. When God created you and gave you a reasonable soul, he made you for an eternity; and he gave you time here in order to prepare for eternity. And your future eternity depends on the improvement of time. Consider therefore what you have done with your past time. You are not now beginning your time; but a great deal of your time is past and gone, and all the wit and power of the universe can't recover it. How have you spent it? Let your own consciences make answer. There are many of you that may well conclude that half your time is gone. If you should to live to the ordinary age of man, your glass is more than half run, and perhaps there may be but few sands remaining; your sun is past the meridian, and perhaps just a-setting, or going into an everlasting eclipse. Consider therefore what account you can give of your improvement of your past time. How have you let the precious golden sands of your glass run?

Consider therefore what account you can give of your past time.

Longsuffering

od often uses many means with wicked men to bring them to forsake their sins. This is what God declares in his Word, that he has no pleasure in the death of a sinner, but he should forsake his sins, and live. "Have I any pleasure at all that the wicked should die? saith the Lord GOD: and not that he should return from his ways, and live?" (Ezekiel 18:23). And again in the thirty-second verse, "For I have no pleasure in the death of him that dieth, saith the Lord GOD: wherefore turn yourselves, and live ye." And there God swears the same thing: "Say unto them, As I live, saith the Lord GOD, I have no pleasure in the death of the wicked; but that the wicked turn from his way and live: turn ye, turn ye from your evil ways; for why will ye die, Ye house of Israel?" Surely it would be horrid presumption in us to call this in question, after God has sworn by his life to the truth of it. The same we are told in the New Testament by the Apostle. "For this is good and acceptable in the sight of God our Saviour; who will have all men to be saved, and come unto the knowledge of the truth" (1 Timothy 2:3–4); "The Lord is longsuffering to us-ward, not willing that any should perish, but that all should come to repentance" (2 Peter 3:9). And therefore God appears in his providence slow to wrath, and is wont to use many means with sinners to bring them to forsake their sins, before he gives them up. Thus God's Spirit strove long with the old world, before he destroyed them. "My spirit shall not always strive with man, for that he also is flesh: yet his days shall be an hundred and twenty years" (Genesis 6:3). For God sent Lot, a preacher of righteousness, to turn the inhabitants of Sodom from their sins, before he destroyed them. So he did not destroy hardhearted Pharaoh, till he had used many means to make him willing to comply with God's commands.

But thou, O Lord, art a God full of compassion, and gracious, longsuffering, and plenteous in mercy and truth.
Psalm 86:15

The False and the True

Will he always call
upon God?
Job 27:10

ypocrites never had the spirit of prayer given them. They may have been stirred up to the external performance of this duty, and that with a great deal of earnestness and affection, and yet always have been destitute of the true spirit of prayer. The spirit of prayer is an holy spirit, a gracious spirit. . . . Wherever there is a true spirit of supplication, there is the spirit of grace. The true spirit of prayer is no other than God's own Spirit dwelling in the hearts of the saints. And as this spirit comes from God, so it naturally tends to God in holy breathings and pantings. It naturally leads to God, to converse with him by prayer. Therefore the Spirit is said to make intercession for the saints with groanings which cannot be uttered (Romans 8:26).

It is far otherwise with the true convert. His work is not done; but he finds still a great work to do, and great wants to be supplied. He sees himself still to be a poor, empty, helpless creature, and that he still stands in great and continual need of God's help. He is sensible that without God he can do nothing. A false conversion makes a man in his own eyes self-sufficient. He says he is rich, increased with goods, has need of nothing, and knows not that he is wretched, miserable, poor, blind, and naked. But after a true conversion, the soul remains sensible of its own impotence and emptiness, as it is in itself, and its sense of it is rather increased than diminished. It is still sensible of its universal dependence on God for everything. A true convert is sensible that his grace is very imperfect; and he is very far from having all that he desires. Instead of that, by conversion are begotten in him new desires which he never had before. He now finds in him holy appetites, a hungering and thirsting after righteousness, a longing after more acquaintance and communion with God. So that he has business enough still at the throne of grace; yea, his business there, instead of being diminished, is, since his conversion, rather increased.

Greatness of Endeavor

B y pressing into the kingdom of God is signified greatness of endeavor. It is expressed in Ecclesiastes 9:10 by doing what our hand finds to do with our might. . . . Where there is strength of desire and firmness of resolution, there will be answerable endeavors. Persons thus engaged in their hearts will "strive to enter in at the strait gate," and will be violent for heaven; their practice will be agreeable to the counsel of the wise man: "My son, if thou wilt receive my words, and hide my commandments with thee; so that thou incline thine ear unto wisdom, and apply thine heart to understanding; yea, if thou criest after knowledge, and liftest up thy voice for understanding; if thou seekest her as silver, and searchest for her as for hid treasures; then shalt thou understand the fear of the Lord, and find the knowledge of God" (Proverbs 2:1–5). Here the earnestness of desire and strength of resolution is signified by inclining the ear to wisdom, and applying the heart to understanding; and the greatness of endeavor is denoted by crying after knowledge, and lifting up the voice for understanding; seeking her as silver, and searching for her as for hid treasures: such desires and resolutions, and such endeavors go together.

And from the days of John the Baptist until now the kingdom of heaven suffereth violence, and the violent take it by force.
Matthew 11:12

The Crown and the Cross

Thou hast given him his heart's desire, and hast not withholden the request of his lips. Selah.

Psalm 21:12

There is something else in Christianity besides self-denial or restraining our inclination. There is a crown as well as a cross. And though we are so strictly required to restrain and keep within bounds our animal inclinations, yet God does not desire we should set any bounds to spiritual and gracious inclinations, which are the most excellent; he that is truly born again, as he has an animal appetite to meat and drink, so he hungers and thirsts after righteousness. It is his meat and his drink to do the will of his Father which is in heaven. He thirsts for God, for the living God, and sometimes his heart pants after God as the hart pants after the water brook (Psalm 42:1). He has an appetite to Jesus Christ, who is the bread which came down from heaven. His soul lives upon Christ as his spiritual meat and drink. He has an appetite to the Word of God as to the food of his soul, for he lives not by bread alone, but by every word which proceeds out of the mouth of God (Matthew 4:4). He as a newborn babe desires the sincere milk of the word, that he may grow thereby (1 Peter 2:2). He has not only a desire from a rational consideration of the need and benefit of it, but it is a desire immediately flowing from his nature, like the natural appetite.

The Spring Season

The spring season is spoken of in Scripture as representing a season of the outpouring of the Spirit of God. As it is so on many other accounts, so in these:

In the spring, the seed that is sown in stony places sprouts and looks as fair as that in good ground, though in the summer, for want of moisture and deepness of earth, it withers away. In the spring, innumerable flowers and young fruits appear flourishing and bid fair that afterwards drop off and come to nothing.

In the spring, many streams flow high, many from snow water—though not every day, even in the spring, but only in warm days by fits, and are frozen up betweenwhiles, like hypocrites' affections by pangs during a great outpouring of the Spirit. And in the spring also, those streams that flowed from living fountains, and run all winter and summer, are greatly increased. But when the spring is over, all streams are totally dried up but those that are supplied by living springs.

So a shower of rain is like an outpouring of the Spirit. It makes water flow abundantly in the streets, and greatly raises the streams from living fountains, and when the shower is over, the streams in the streets are dried up and the streams from fountains are diminished. So a shower causes mushrooms suddenly to spring up, as well as good plants to grow, and blasts many fruits as well as bring others to perfection.

Who covereth the heaven with clouds, who prepareth rain for the earth, who maketh grass to grow upon the mountains.
Psalm 147:8

See and Be Sensible

*For thy name's sake,
O LORD, pardon mine
iniquity; for it is
great.*
Psalm 25:11

We should see our misery, and be sensible of our need of mercy. They who are not sensible of their misery cannot truly look to God for mercy; for it is the very notion of divine mercy, that it is the goodness and grace of God to the miserable. Without misery in the object, there can be no exercise of mercy. To suppose mercy without supposing misery, or pity without calamity, is a contradiction: therefore men cannot look upon themselves as proper objects of mercy, unless they first know themselves to be miserable; and so, unless this be the case, it is impossible that they should come to God for mercy. They must be sensible that they are the children of wrath; that the law is against them, and that they are exposed to the curse of it: that the wrath of God abideth on them; and that he is angry with them every day while they are under the guilt of sin. They must be sensible that it is a very dreadful thing to be the object of the wrath of God; that it is a very awful thing to have him for their enemy; and that they cannot bear his wrath. They must be sensible that the guilt of sin makes them miserable creatures, whatever temporal enjoyments they have; that they can be no other than miserable, undone creatures, so long as God is angry with them; that they are without strength, and must perish, and that eternally, unless God help them. They must see that their case is utterly desperate, for anything that anyone else can do for them; that they hang over the pit of eternal misery; and that they must necessarily drop into it, if God have not mercy on them.

Mercies' Dam

he wrath of God is like great waters that are dammed for the present; they increase more and more, and rise higher and higher, till an outlet is given; and the longer the stream is stopped, the more rapid and mighty is its course, when once it is let loose. It is true that judgment against your evil works has not been executed hitherto; the floods of God's vengeance have been withheld; but your guilt in the meantime is constantly increasing, and you are every day treasuring up more wrath; the waters are constantly rising, and waxing more and more mighty; and there is nothing but the mere pleasure of God that holds the waters back, that are unwilling to be stopped, and press hard to go forward. If God should only withdraw his hand from the flood-gate, it would immediately fly open, and the fiery floods of the fierceness and wrath of God would rush forth with inconceivable fury, and would come upon you with omnipotent power; and if your strength were ten thousand times greater than it is, yea, ten thousand times greater than the strength of the stoutest, sturdiest devil in hell, it would be nothing to withstand or endure it.

Riches profit not in the day of wrath: but righteousness delivereth from death.
Proverbs 11:4

The wrath of God is like great waters that are dammed for the present.

Greater Intimacy

Beloved, now are we the sons of God, and it doth not yet appear what we shall be: but we know that, when he shall appear, we shall be like him; for we shall see him as he is.

1 John 3:2

The saints' conversation with Christ in heaven shall not only be as intimate, and their access to him as free, as of the disciples on earth, but in many respects much more so; for in heaven, that vital union shall be perfect, which is exceeding imperfect here. While the saints are in this world, there are great remains of sin and darkness, to separate or disunite them from Christ, which shall then all be removed. This is not a time for that full acquaintance, and those glorious manifestations of love, which Christ designs for his people hereafter; which seems to be signified by his speech to Mary Magdalene, when ready to embrace him, when she met him after his resurrection; "Jesus saith unto her, Touch me not; for I am not yet ascended to my Father" (John 20:17).

For in heaven, that vital union shall be perfect, which is exceeding imperfect here.

The Sun's Brilliance

s the sun is an image of Christ upon account of its pleasant light and benign, refreshing, life-giving influences, so it is on account of its extraordinary fierce heart, it being a fire of vastly greater fierceness than any other in the visible world. Hereby is represented the wrath of the Lamb. This is a very great argument of the extremity of the misery of the wicked, for doubtless the substance will be vastly beyond the shadow. As God's brightness and glory is so much beyond the brightness of the sun, his image, thus the sun is but a shade and darkness in comparison of it, so his fierceness and wrath is vastly beyond the sun's heat.

And he had in his right hand seven stars: and out of his mouth went a sharp twoedged sword: and his countenance was as the sun shineth in his strength.
Revelation 1:16

The Highest Mountain

There is a way which seemeth right unto a man, but the end thereof are the ways of death.
Proverbs 14:12

There is nothing here below that reaches heaven, no, not the highest things, but all fall immensely short of it. Many things, before we experience them, seem to reach heaven. The tops of high mountains seem to touch the sky, and when we are in the plain and look up to their tops, it seems to us as though, if we were there, we could touch the sun, moon, and stars; but when we are come, we seem as far off from these heavenly things as ever. So there is nothing here below by which we can attain to happiness, though there be many of the high and great things of the world that seem to others that don't enjoy them as though a happiness was to be reached by them. Yet those that have experience find happiness as far from them as from those that are in a lower state of life.

So there is nothing here below by which we can attain to happiness.

Christ's Sufferings

ence we may learn how dreadful Christ's last sufferings were. We learn it from the dreadful effect which the bare foresight of them had upon him in his agony. His last sufferings were so dreadful, that the view which Christ had of them before overwhelmed him and amazed him, as it is said he began to be sore amazed. The very sight of these last sufferings was so very dreadful as to sink his soul down into the dark shadow of death; yea, so dreadful was it, that in the sore conflict which his nature had with it, he was all in a sweat of blood, his body all over was covered with clotted blood, and not only his body, but the very ground under him with the blood that fell from him, which had been forced through his pores through the violence of his agony. And if only the foresight of the cup was so dreadful, how dreadful was the cup itself, how far beyond all that can be uttered or conceived! Many of the martyrs have endured extreme tortures, but from what has been said, there is all reason to think those all were a mere nothing to the last sufferings of Christ on the cross. And what has been said affords a convincing argument that the sufferings which Christ endured in his body on the cross, though they were very dreadful, were yet the least part of his last sufferings; and that beside those, he endured sufferings in his soul which were vastly greater. For if it had been only the sufferings which he endured in his body, though they were very dreadful, we cannot conceive that the mere anticipation of them would have such an effect on Christ. Many of the martyrs, for aught we know, have endured as severe tortures in their bodies as Christ did. Many of the martyrs have been crucified, as Christ was; and yet their souls have not been so overwhelmed. There has been no appearance of such amazing sorrow and distress of mind either at the anticipation of their sufferings, or in the actual enduring of them.

And being in an agony he prayed more earnestly.
Luke 22:44

As the Bird Cares

Casting all your care upon him; for he careth for you.
1 Peter 5:7

There are many things between the young birds in a nest and a dam, resembling what is between Christ and his saints. The bird shelters them; so Christ shelters his saints, as a bird does her young under her wings. They are brought forth by the dam; so the saints are Christ's children. They are hatched by the broodings of the dam; so the soul is brought forth by the warmth and heat and brooding of Christ, by the Heavenly Dove, the Holy Spirit. They dwell in a nest of the dam's providing on high out of the reach of harm, in some place of safety; so are the saints in the church. They are feeble and helpless, can neither fly nor go, which represents the infant state of the saints in this world. The manner of the dam's feeding the young, giving every one his portion, represents the manner of Christ's feeding his saints. When the dam visits the nest, all open their mouth wide together with a cry, and that is all that they can do. So should the saints do, especially at times when Christ makes special visits to his church by his Spirit. They don't open their mouths in vain. So God says, "Open thy mouth wide and I will fill it" (Psalm 81:10). The birds grow by this nourishment till they fly away into heaven to sing in the firmament. So the saints are nourished up to glory.

Strong Hope

here is a holy hope, a truly Christian hope, which the Scripture reckons among the graces of the Spirit. And I think I should never desire or seek any other hope but such a one; for I believe no other hope has any holy or good tendency. Therefore this hope, this grace of hope only, can properly be called a duty. But it is just as absurd to talk of the exercise of this holy hope, the strong exercise of this grace of the Spirit, in a carnal, stupid, careless frame, such a frame yet remaining, as it would be to talk of the strong exercises of love to God, or heavenly-mindedness, or any other grace, remaining in such a frame to come out of it, in and by the strong exercises of all grace; but I should not think it proper to press a man earnestly to maintain strong hope, notwithstanding the prevailing and continuance of great carnality and stupidity . . . For this is plainly to press people to an unholy hope, a strong hope that is no Christian grace; and that is strong wicked presumption. And the promoting of this has most evidently been the effect of such a method of dealing with souls, in innumerable multitudes of awful instances.

Blessed be the God and Father of our Lord Jesus Christ, which according to his abundant mercy hath begotten us again unto a lively hope by the resurrection of Jesus Christ from the dead.
1 Peter 1:3

Divine Liberty

For he saith to Moses,
I will have mercy on
whom I will have
mercy, and I will have
compassion on whom
I will have
compassion.
Romans 9:15

od can, without prejudice to the glory of any of his attributes, bestow salvation on any of the children of men, except on those who have committed the sin against the Holy Ghost. The case was thus when man fell, and before God revealed his eternal purpose and plan for redeeming men by Jesus Christ. It was probably looked upon by the angels as a thing utterly inconsistent with God's attributes to save any of the children of men. It was utterly inconsistent with the honor of the divine attributes to save any one of the fallen children of men, as they were in themselves. It could not have been done had not God contrived a way consistent with the honor of his holiness, majesty, justice, and truth. But since God in the gospel has revealed that nothing is too hard for him to do, nothing beyond the reach of his power, and wisdom, and sufficiency; and since Christ has wrought out the work of redemption, and fulfilled the law by obeying, there is none of mankind whom he may not save without any prejudice to any of his attributes, excepting those who have committed the sin against the Holy Ghost. And those he might have saved without going contrary to any of his attributes, had he not been pleased to declare that he would not. It was not because he could not have saved them consistently with his justice, and consistently with his law, or because his attribute of mercy was not great enough, or the blood of Christ not sufficient to cleanse from that sin. But it has pleased him for wise reasons to declare that that sin shall never be forgiven in this world, or in the world to come. And so now it is contrary to God's truth to save such. But otherwise there is no sinner, let him be ever so great, but God can save him without prejudice to any attribute; if he has been a murderer, adulterer, or perjurer, or idolater, or blasphemer, God may save him if he pleases, and in no respect injure his glory.

Boldness to Persevere

I n these days, men are with difficulty brought to do or submit to that which makes them the objects of the reproach of all their neighbors. Indeed if while some reproach them, others stand by them and honor them, this will support them. But it is very difficult for a man to go on in a way wherein he makes himself the laughing stock of the whole world, and wherein he can find none who do not despise him. Where is the man that can stand the shock of such a trial for twenty years?

Sow to yourselves in righteousness, reap in mercy; break up your fallow ground: for it is time to seek the LORD, till he come and rain righteousness upon you.
Hosea 10:12

But in such an undertaking as this, Noah at the divine direction, engaged and went through it, that he and his family might be saved from the common destruction which was shortly about to come on the world. He began, and also made an end: "According to all that God commanded him, so did he." Length of time did not weary him: he did not grow weary of his vast expense. He stood the shock of the derision of all his neighbors; and of all the world year after year: he did not grow weary of being their laughing-stock, so as to give over his enterprise; but persevered in it till the ark was finished. After this, he was at the trouble and charge of procuring stores for the maintenance of his family, and of all the various kinds of creatures, for so long a time. Such an undertaking he engaged in and went through in order to a temporal salvation. How great an undertaking then should men be willing to engage in and go through in order to their eternal salvation! A salvation from an eternal deluge; from being overwhelmed with the billows of God's wrath of which Noah's flood was but a shadow.

God's Fiery Judgments

And he cried and said,
Father Abraham, have
mercy on me, and send
Lazarus, that he may
dip the tip of his fin-
ger in water, and cool
my tongue; for I am
tormented in this
flame.
Luke 16:24

When sinners hear of hell torments, they sometimes think with themselves, "Well, if it
shall come to that, that I must go to hell, I
will bear it as well as I can," as if by clothing themselves
with resolution and firmness of mind, they would be
able to support themselves in some measure; when, alas!
they will have no resolution, no courage at all. However
they shall have prepared themselves, and collected their
strength; yet as soon as they shall begin to feel that wrath,
their hearts will melt and be as water. However before
they may seem to harden their hearts, in order to prepare
themselves to bear, yet the first moment they feel it, their
hearts will become like wax before the furnace. Their
courage and resolution will be all gone in an instant; it
will vanish away like a shadow in the twinkling of an eye.
The stoutest and sturdiest will have no more courage
than the feeblest infant: let a man be an infant, or a giant,
it will be all one. They will not be able to keep alive any
courage, any strength, any comfort, any hope at all.

The Saints' Glory

The image of God is the saints' glory, and it may well be called glory, for imperfect as it is, it renders them glorious in the eyes of the angels of heaven. The image of God is a greater beauty in their eyes than the brightness and glory of the sun in the firmament.

Indeed the saints have no excellency, as they are in and of themselves. In them, that is, in their flesh, dwells no good thing. They are in themselves poor, guilty, vile creatures, and see themselves to be so. But they have an excellency and glory in them, because they have Christ dwelling in them. The excellency that is in them, though it be but as a spark, yet it is something ten thousand times more excellent than any ruby, or the most precious pearl that ever was found on the earth; and that because it is something divine, something of God.

This holy heavenly spark is put into the soul in conversion, and God maintains it there. All the powers of hell cannot put it out, for God will keep it alive, and it shall prevail more and more. Though it be but small, yet it is powerful; it has influence over the heart to govern it, and brings forth holy fruits in the life, and will not cease to prevail till it has consumed all the corruption that is left in the heart, and till it has turned the whole soul into a pure, holy, and heavenly flame, till the soul of man becomes like the angels, a flame of fire, and shines as the brightness of the firmament.

The righteous is more excellent than his neighbour: but the way of the wicked seduceth them.

Proverbs 12:26

Spiritual Sight

And he said, I will make all my goodness pass before thee, and I will proclaim the name of the LORD before thee; and will be gracious to whom I will be gracious, and will shew mercy on whom I will shew mercy.
Exodus 33:19

When we are absent from our dear friends, they are out of sight; but when we are with them, we have the opportunity and satisfaction of seeing them. So while the saints are in the body, and are absent from the Lord, he is in several respects out of sight: "Whom having not seen, ye love; in whom, though now ye see him not, yet believing" (1 Peter 1:8). They have indeed, in this world, a spiritual sight of Christ; but they see through a glass darkly, and with great interruption; but in heaven they see him face to face (1 Corinthians 13:12). "Blessed are the pure in heart: for they shall see God" (Matthew 5:8). Their beatifical vision of God is in Christ, who is that brightness or effulgence of God's glory, by which his glory shines forth in heaven, to the view of saints and angels there, as well as here on earth. This is the Sun of righteousness, that is not only the light of this world, but is also the sun that enlightens the heavenly Jerusalem; by whose bright beams it is that the glory of God shines forth there, to the enlightening and making happy all the glorious inhabitants.

The Breath of Life

he breath of man is as it were his life, hereby showing what man's life is, even a blast of wind that goes away and comes not again. To this the Scripture seems to have reference in several places, as Job 7:7, "O remember that my life is wind"; Psalm 78:39, "He remembered that they were but flesh; a wind that passeth away, and cometh not again," alluding to the breath's going forth when a person is dying. And that thin, vanishing vapor that is in the breath, that at some seasons appears but vanishes away as it were in a moment, is a type of the very thing expressed, "What is your life? It is even a vapour, that appeareth for a little time, and then vanisheth away" (James 4:14). While the breath continues warm, the vapor appears, but when that warmth is gone, the vapor disappears. This represents how suddenly our vital heat or warmth, that maintains the life of the body, will be gone, and cold death will succeed.

And the LORD God formed man of the dust of the ground, and breathed into his nostrils the breath of life; and man became a living soul.
Genesis 2:7

False Hopes

The transgression of
the wicked saith
within my heart, that
there is no fear of God
before his eyes.
Psalm 36:1

Some flatter themselves with a secret hope, that there is no such thing as another world. They hear a great deal of preaching, and a great deal of talk about hell, and about the eternal judgment; but those things do not seem to them to be real. They never saw anything of them; they never saw hell, never saw the devils and damned spirits; and therefore are ready to say with themselves, "How do I know that there is any such thing as another world? When the beasts die, there is an end of them, and how do I know but that it will be so with me? Perhaps all these things are nothing but the inventions of men, nothing but cunningly devised fables."

Such thoughts are apt to rise in the minds of sinners, and the devil sets in to enforce them. Such thoughts are an ease to them; therefore they wish they were true, and that makes them the more ready to think that they are indeed true, so that they are hardened in the way of sin, by infidelity and atheistical thoughts. "The fool hath said in his heart, There is no God" (Psalm 14:1); "They slay the widow and the stranger, and murder the fatherless. Yet they say, the LORD shall not see; neither shall the God of Jacob regard it" (Psalm 94:6–7).

Redeeming the Time

od has concealed from us the day of our death, without doubt that we might be excited to be always ready, and might live as those that are always waiting for the coming of their Lord, agreeably to the counsel which Christ gives us. That watchman is not faithful who, being set to defend a house from thieves, or a city from an enemy at hand, will at any hour venture to sleep, trusting that the thief or the enemy will not come. Therefore it is expected of the watchman, that he behave himself every hour of the night, as one who does not depend upon it that the enemy will tarry until the next hour. Now therefore let me, in Christ's name, renew the call and counsel of Jesus Christ to you, to watch as those that know not what hour your Lord will come. Let me call upon you who are hitherto in an unrenewed condition. Depend not upon, that you will not be in hell before tomorrow morning. You have no reason for any such dependence. God has not promised to keep you from it, or to withhold his wrath so long. How can you reasonably be easy or quiet for one day, or one night, in such a condition, when you know not but your Lord will come this night? And if you should then be found, as you now are, unregenerate, how unprepared would you be for his coming, and how fearful would be the consequence! Be exhorted therefore, for your own sakes, immediately to awake from the sleep of sin, out of sleep, and sleep no more, as not depending on any other day.

Walk in wisdom toward them that are without, redeeming the time.
Colossians 4:5

Inner Beauty

But the LORD said unto Samuel, Look not on his countenance, or on the height of his stature; because I have refused him: for the LORD seeth not as man seeth; for man looketh on the outward appearance, but the LORD looketh on the heart.

1 Samuel 16:7

avid's outward appearance was not such as would have recommended him to the esteem and choice of men as a person fit for rule and victory; but on the contrary such as tended to cause men to despise him as a candidate for such things. "Look not on his countenance, or on the height of his stature . . . for man looketh on the outward appearance, but the LORD looketh on the heart" (1 Samuel 16:7); "And when the Philistine looked about, and saw David, he disdained him: for he was but a youth" (1 Samuel 17:42); "Inquire whose son this stripling is" (v. 56). Eliab, his elder brother, thought him fitter to be with the sheep than to come to the army (1 Samuel 17:28); agreeable to Isaiah 53:2, "He shall grow up before him as a tender plant, as a root out of a dry ground: he hath no form nor comeliness; and when we shall see him, there is no beauty that we shall desire him." David appeared unexpectedly. Samuel expected a man of great stature, and appearing outwardly like a man of valor; and therefore when he saw Eliab, David's elder brother, that had such an appearance, he said, "Surely the LORD's anointed is before him" (1 Samuel 16:6). His appearance was astonishing to Goliath and to Saul. So the prophecies represent the Messiah's appearance as unexpected and astonishing, being so mean. "Many were astonished at thee; his visage was so marred more than any man" (Isaiah 52:14).

Pursue Happiness

appiness is the end of the creation, as appears by this, because the creation had as good not be, as not rejoice in its being. For certainly it was the goodness of the Creator that moved him to create; and how can we conceive of another end proposed by goodness, than that he might delight in seeing the creatures he made rejoice in that being that he has given them?

Happy is he that hath the God of Jacob for his help, whose hope is in the LORD his God.
Psalm 146:5

It appears also by this, because the end of the creation is that the creation might glorify him. Now what is glorifying God, but a rejoicing at that glory he has displayed? An understanding of the perfections of God, merely, cannot be the end of the creation; for he had as good not understand it, as see it and not be at all moved with joy at the sight. Neither can the highest end of the creation be the declaring God's glory to others; for the declaring God's glory is good for nothing otherwise than to raise joy in ourselves and others at what is declared.

Wherefore, seeing happiness is the highest end of the creation of the universe, and intelligent beings are that consciousness of the creation that is to be the immediate subject of this happiness, how happy may we conclude will be those intelligent beings that are to be made eternally happy?

Lovely Inhabitants

How beautiful are the feet of them that preach the gospel of peace, and bring glad tidings of good things!
Romans 10:15

All the persons that belong to the blessed society of heaven are lovely. The Father of the family is lovely, and so are all his children; the head of the body lovely, and so are all the members. Among the angels there are none that are unlovely, for they are all holy; and no evil angels are suffered to infest heaven as they do this world, but they are kept forever at a distance by that great gulf which is between them and the glorious world of love. And among all the company of the saints, there are no unlovely persons. There are no false professors or hypocrites there; none that pretend to be saints, and yet are of an unchristian and hateful spirit or behavior, as is often the case in this world; none whose gold has not been purified from its dross; none who are not lovely in themselves and to others. There is no one object there to give offense, or at any time to give occasion for any passion or emotion of hatred or dislike, but every object there shall forever draw forth love.

All the persons that belong to the blessed society of heaven are lovely.

Glimmerings

he great God, who so fully manifests himself in heaven, is perfect with an absolute and infinite perfection. The Son of God, who is the brightness of the Father's glory, appears there in the fullness of his glory, without that garb of outward meanness in which he appeared in this world. The Holy Ghost shall there be poured forth with perfect richness and sweetness, as a pure river of the water of life, clear as crystal, proceeding out of the throne of God and of the Lamb. And every member of that holy and blessed society shall be without any stain of sin, or imperfection, or weakness, or imprudence, or blemish of any kind. The whole church, ransomed and purified, shall there be presented to Christ, as a bride, clothed in fine linen, clean and white, without spot, or wrinkle, or any such thing. Wherever the inhabitants of that blessed world shall turn their eyes, they shall see nothing but dignity, and beauty, and glory. The most stately cities on earth, however magnificent their buildings, yet have their foundations in the dust, and their streets dirty and defiled, and made to be trodden under foot; but the very streets of this heavenly city are of pure gold, like unto transparent glass, and its foundations are of precious stones, and its gates are pearls. And all these are but faint emblems of the purity and perfectness of those that dwell therein.

More to be desired are they than gold, yea, than much fine gold: sweeter also than honey and the honeycomb.
Psalm 19:10

Make Restitution

I exhort those who are conscious in themselves that they have heretofore wronged their neighbor to make restitution. This is a duty the obligation to which is exceedingly plain. If a person was wronged in taking away anything that was his, certainly he is wronged also in detaining it. And all the while that a person, who has been guilty of wronging his neighbor, neglects to make restitution, he lives in that wrong. He not only lives impenitent as to that first wrong of which he was guilty, but he continually wrongs his neighbor. A man who hath gotten anything from another wrongfully, goes on to wrong him every day that he neglects to restore it, when he has opportunity to do it. The person injured did not only suffer wrong from the other when his goods were first taken from him, but he suffers new injustice from him all the while they are unjustly kept from him.

Seeing God

here must be a direct and immediate sense of God's glory and excellency. I say direct and immediate, to distinguish it from a mere perception that God is glorious and excellent by means of speculative and distant argumentation, which is a more indirect way of apprehending things. A true sense of the glory of God is that which can never be obtained by speculative ratiocination. And if men convince themselves by argument that God is holy, that never will give a sense of his amiable and glorious holiness. If they argue that he is very merciful, that will not give a sense of his glorious grace and mercy. It must be a more immediate, sensible discovery that must give the mind a real sense of the excellency and beauty of God. He that sees God, has a direct and immediate view of God's great and awful majesty, of his pure and beauteous holiness, of his wonderful and endearing grace and mercy.

Blessed are the pure in heart: for they shall see God.
Matthew 5:8

> A true sense of the glory of God is that which can never be obtained by speculative ratiocination.

Sin, an Infinite Evil

*There is none greater
in this house than I;
neither hath he kept
back any thing from
me but thee, because
thou art his wife: how
then can I do this
great wickedness, and
sin against God?*

Genesis 39:9

Sin is an infinite evil, because it is committed against an infinitely great and excellent Being, and so a violation of infinite obligation. Therefore however great our care be to avoid sin, it cannot be more than proportional to the evil we would avoid. Our care and endeavor cannot be infinite, as the evil of sin is infinite. We ought to use every method that tends to the avoiding of sin. This is manifest to reason. And not only so, but this is positively required of us in the Word of God. "Take diligent heed to do the commandment and the law, which Moses the servant of the LORD charged you, to love the LORD your God, and to walk in all his ways, and to keep his commandments, and to cleave unto him, and to serve him with all your . . . soul" (Joshua 22:5); "Take ye therefore good heed unto yourselves; . . . lest ye corrupt yourselves" (Deuteronomy 4:15–16); "Take heed to thyself that thou be not snared" (ch. 12:30); "Take heed, and beware of covetousness" (Luke 12:15); "Let him that thinketh he standeth take heed lest he fall" (1 Corinthians 10:12); "Take heed to thyself, and keep thy soul diligently" (Deuteronomy 4:9). These and many other texts of Scripture plainly require of us the utmost possible diligence and caution to avoid sin.

Wise unto Salvation

We ought to be much concerned to know whether we do not live in a *state of sin*. All unregenerate men live in sin. We are born under the power and dominion of sin, are sold under sin. Every unconverted sinner is a devoted servant to sin and Satan. We should look upon it as of the greatest importance to us, to know in what state we are, whether we ever had any change made in our hearts from sin to holiness, or whether we be not still in the gall of bitterness and bond of iniquity; whether ever sin were truly mortified in us; whether we do not live in the sin of unbelief, and in the rejection of the Savior. This is what the apostle insists upon with the Corinthians. "Examine yourselves, whether ye be in the faith; prove your own selves. Know ye not your own selves, how that Jesus Christ is in you, except ye be reprobates?" Those who entertain the opinion and hope of themselves, that they are godly, should take great care to see that their foundation be right. Those that are in doubt should not give themselves rest till the matter is resolved.

Search me, O God, and know my heart: try me, and know my thoughts: and see if there be any wicked way in me, and lead me in the way everlasting.
Psalm 139:23–24

Samson: A Type of Christ

There is no less remarkable agreement between the things said of Samson in his history and the things said of the Messiah in the prophecies of him. His name, *Samson,* signifies *little sun,* well agreeing with a type of the Messiah, that great Sun of Righteousness so often compared in the prophecies to the sun. The antitype is far greater than the type, as being its end. Therefore when the type is called by the name of the antitype, it is fitly with a diminutive termination. Samson and other saviors under the Old Testament, that were types of the great Savior, were but little saviors. The prophets, priests, kings, captains, and deliverers of the Old Testament were indeed images of that great light of the church and the world that was to follow. But they were but images; they were little lights that shone during the night. But when Christ came, the great light arose and introduced the day. Samson's birth was miraculous; it was a great wonder in his case that a woman should compass a man, as the prophecies represent it to be in the case of the birth of the Messiah. Samson was raised up to be a savior to God's people from their enemies, agreeable to prophetical representations of the Messiah. Samson was appointed to this great work by God's special election and designation, and that in an eminent and extraordinary way, agreeable to the prophecies of the Messiah.

When Christ came, the great light arose and introduced the day.

The Supreme Ruler

od is . . . by right the supreme and absolute ruler and disposer of all things, both in the natural and moral world. The rational understanding part of the creation is indeed subject to a different sort of government from that to which irrational creatures are subject. God governs the sun, moon, and stars. He governs even the motes of dust which fly in the air. Not a hair of our heads falls to the ground without our heavenly Father. God also governs the brute creatures. By his providence, he orders, according to his own decrees, all events concerning those creatures. And rational creatures are subject to the same sort of government. All their actions, and all events relating to them, being ordered by superior providence, according to absolute decrees so that no event that relates to them ever happens without the disposal of God, according to his own decrees. The rule of this government is God's wise decree, and nothing else.

But our God is in the heavens: he hath done whatsoever he hath pleased.
Psalm 115:3

The Little Flock

For many are called,
but few are chosen.
Matthew 22:14

The greater parts of the world are sinners. Christ's flock is, and ever has been, but a little flock. And the sinners of the *world* are of two sorts: those who are visibly of Satan's kingdom, who are without the pale of the visible church; and those who do not profess the true religion, nor attend the external ordinances of it. Beside these there are the sinners in *Zion*. Both are the objects of the displeasure and wrath of God. But his wrath is more especially manifested in Scripture against the latter. Sinners in Zion will have by far the lowest place in hell. They are exalted nearest to heaven in this world, and they will be lowest in hell in another. The same is meant by *hypocrites*. Sinners in Zion are all hypocrites. For they make a profession of the true religion. They attend God's ordinances, and make a show of being the worshippers of God. But all is hypocrisy.

False Professors

here were some who seemed to believe in Christ and followed him for a while. But Christ did not commit himself to them, he knew they were of an unstable mind, and would not be consistent with themselves. Some of them were for a while greatly affected with his preaching and with the miracles that he wrought, and it is said of them that the glorified God who had given such power to men, and said, "Never man spake like this man" (John 7:46). And it seems as though some of the same Jews who had their affections so raised when Christ was coming into Jerusalem, and who cried, "Hosanna to the son of David, blessed is he that cometh in the name of the Lord;" did presently after cry, "Crucify him, crucify him!" There are many professors like those, and like the Israelites, that sang God's praise, and soon forgot his works, and waited not for his counsel, that "turned back, and dealt unfaithfully like their fathers. They were turned aside like a deceitful bow." That is, a bow that missed the mark to which it seemed to direct the arrow. The arrow seems to be pointed right, as though it would hit the mark, but yet the bow unexpectedly tends quite another way.

And some fell among thorns, and the thorns grew up, and choked it, and it yielded no fruit.
Mark 4:7

Bread-Corn

While the earth remaineth, seedtime and harvest, and cold and heat, and summer and winter, and day and night shall not cease.

Genesis 8:22

Bread-corn is much used in Scripture to represent the saints. The wicked are presented by the clusters of the vine, but the godly by bread-corn. They are called Christ's wheat, that he will gather into his barn and into his garner, and we are all said to be that one bread. Now this is remarkable of wheat and other bread-corn; that it is sown and grows before winter, and then is as it were killed, and long lies dead in the winter season, and then revives in the spring and grows much taller than before, and comes to perfection and brings forth fruit; which is a lively image of the resurrection of saints—as well as the grain's being first buried in the earth and dying there before it comes up—and that often comes to pass, concerning the saints in this life, that is lively represented by it. After their conversion they have a falling away, and long continue in a cold and dead carnal state, and then revive again and grow much taller than before, and never fall again till they bring fruit to perfection. It is also a lively image of what comes to pass with respect to the Christian church, which after it was planted by the apostles and flourished a while, then fell under a wintry season, a low and very suffering state, for a long while, and so continues till about the time of the destruction of Antichrist, and then revives and grows and comes to a glorious degree of prosperity and fruitfulness, which is what is called in Scripture "the first resurrection" (Revelation 20:5–6). Therefore it is said of Israel, "They shall revive as the corn" (Hosea 14:7). The reviving of the church after a low state and a time of trouble is compared to the reviving of corn from under the earth in the spring in Isaiah 37:30–31.

To the Reverend George Whitefield

ev. and Dear Sir,

I have joyful tidings to send you concerning the state of religion in this place. It has been gradually reviving and prevailing more and more, ever since you were here. Religion has become abundantly more the subject of conversation; other things that seemed to impede it, are for the present laid aside. I have reason to think that a considerable number of our young people, some of them children, have already been savingly brought home to Christ. I hope salvation has come to this house since you were in it, with respect to one, if not more, of my children. The Spirit of God seems to be at work with others of the family. That blessed work seems now to be going on in this place, especially among those that are young.

And as God seems to have succeeded your labors among us, and prayers for us, I desire your fervent prayers for us may yet be continued that God would not be to us as a wayfaring man, that turns aside to tarry but for a night, but that he would more and more pour out his Spirit upon us, and no more depart from us; and for me in particular, that I may be filled with his Spirit, and may become fervent, as a flame of fire in my work, and may be abundantly succeeded, and that is would please God, however unworthy I am, to improve me as an instrument of his glory, and advancing the kingdom of Christ.

Iron sharpeneth iron; so a man sharpeneth the countenance of his friend.
Proverbs 27:17

The Spirit of Meekness

Blessed are the meek:
for they shall inherit
the earth.
Matthew 5:5

eekness is a great part of the Christian spirit. Christ, in that earnest and touching call and invitation of his that we have in the eleventh chapter of Matthew, in which he invites all that labor and are heavy laden to come to himself for rest, particularly mentions that he would have them come to learn of him; for he adds, "I am meek and lowly in heart." And meekness, as it respects injuries received from men, is called longsuffering in the Scriptures, and is often mentioned as an exercise, or fruit of the Christian spirit, "The fruit of the Spirit is love, joy, peace, longsuffering" (Galatians 5:22), and "I therefore, the prisoner of the Lord, beseech you that ye walk worthy of the vocation wherewith ye are called, with all lowliness and meekness, with longsuffering" (Ephesians 4:1–2, etc.) and "Put on therefore, as the elect of God, holy and beloved, bowels of mercies, kindness, humbleness of mind, meekness, longsuffering; forbearing one another, and forgiving one another, if any man have a quarrel against any: even as Christ forgave you, so also do ye" (Colossians 3:12–13).

Bearing Injuries

*L*ove to God disposes us to *imitate* him, and therefore disposes us to such longsuffering as he manifests. Longsuffering is often spoken of as one of the attributes of God. In Exodus 34:6, it is said, "And the Lord passed by before him, and proclaimed, The LORD, The LORD God, merciful and gracious, longsuffering," etc. And in Romans 2:4, the apostle asks, "Despisest thou the riches of his goodness and forbearance and longsuffering?" The longsuffering of God is very wonderfully manifest in his bearing innumerable injuries from men, and injuries that are very great and long-continued. If we consider the wickedness that there is in the world, and then consider how God continues the world in existence, and does not destroy it, but showers upon it innumerable mercies, the bounties of his daily providence and grace, we shall perceive how abundant is his longsuffering toward us. And if we consider his longsuffering to some of the great and populous cities of the world, and think how constantly the gifts of his goodness are bestowed on and consumed by them, and then consider how great the wickedness of these very cities is, it will show us how amazingly great is his longsuffering. And the same longsuffering has been manifest to very many particular persons, in all ages of the world. He is longsuffering to the sinners that he spares, and to whom he offers his mercy, even while they are rebelling against him. And he is longsuffering toward his own elect people, many of whom long lived in sin, and despised alike his goodness and his wrath: and yet he bore long with them, even to the end, till they were brought to repentance, and made, through his grace, vessels of mercy and glory. . . . A child's love to his father disposes him to imitate his father, and especially does the love of God's children dispose them to imitate their heavenly Father. And as he is longsuffering, so they should be.

Be ye therefore followers of God, as dear children.
Ephesians 5:1

Do Not Neglect Salvation

Who, when he had found one pearl of great price, went and sold all that he had, and bought it.
Matthew 13:46

God will not force a man into heaven that doesn't seek to go there. He will not bestow salvation upon them that do not think it worth a praying for and inquiring after. If men choose the world for their portion, and take greater care for earthly riches, and pleasures, and diversions than they do for justification and eternal life, God will give them what they mind most. Indeed, God gives salvation freely and of mere grace and not for any work of ours, but yet he bestows it in that way that glorifies his free grace most, and makes it most esteemed and valued. He won't give it to them that do not desire it, or do not desire it enough to think it worth the seeking, or worth the thinking about, and worth the praying for. This would be the way to have the free grace of God despised and trampled underfoot.

Some are ready to harden themselves by saying, "If I'm elected, I shall be saved; let me do what I will." But in their meddling with God's secret counsels, without going to heaven to coax in the reel of the decrees; I can certainly tell whether such men shall be saved or no; if they for that reason continue to neglect their salvation.

God gives salvation freely and of mere grace and not for any work of ours.

Torments of Hell

I am convinced that the torments of hell are literally as great as they are represented by fire and brimstone, a lake of fire, and the like, and that without any hyperbole, by the greatness of the agonies of Christ in the garden. I am ready to think that such agonies of mind as are sufficient to put nature into such a violent commotion and ferment, so as to cause the blood to strain through the pores of the skin, are as great affliction as one would endure, if they were all over in a fiery furnace. I think the souls of the wicked must endure greater agonies than Christ in the garden, because they have despair and many other dreadful sensations of mind, which it's impossible an innocent person should have.

And whosoever was not found written in the book of life was cast into the lake of fire.

Revelation 20:15

Preparatory Work

I the LORD search the heart, I try the reins, even to give every man according to his ways, and according to the fruit of his doings.

Jeremiah 17:10

As to preparatory work before conversion, there is undoubtedly always, except very extraordinary cases, such a thing. For we have shown that conversion is wrought in a moment. Now who can believe that the Spirit of God takes a man in his career in sin, without any forethought, or foreconcern or any such thing, or any preparatory circumstances to introduce it? We have no instance of such a thing without something preparatory, either preparatory thought or circumstances which prepared in some measure his thoughts. We do not determine how great a difference there may be in this preparatory introduction of Christ into the soul.

God's Way

Why does God require prayer in order to the bestowment of mercies? It is not in order that God may be informed of our wants or desires. He is omniscient, and with respect to his knowledge, unchangeable. God never gains any knowledge by information. He knows what we want a thousand times more perfectly than we do ourselves, before we ask him. For though, speaking after the manner of men, God is sometimes represented as if he were moved and persuaded by the prayers of his people, yet it is not to be thought that God is properly moved or made willing by our prayers. For it is no more possible that there should be any new inclination or will in God than new knowledge. The mercy of God is not moved or drawn by anything in the creature. But the spring of God's beneficence is within himself only. He is self-moved, and whatsoever mercy he bestows, the reason and ground of it is not to be sought for in the creature, but in God's own good pleasure. It is the will of God to bestow mercy in this way, viz., in answer to prayer, when he designs beforehand to bestow mercy, yea, when he has promised it, as Ezekiel 36:36–37, "I the LORD have spoken it, and I will do it. Thus saith the Lord GOD; I will yet for this be enquired of by the house of Israel, to do it for them." God has been pleased to constitute prayer, to be antecedent to the bestowment of mercy. And he is pleased to bestow mercy in consequence of prayer, as though he were prevailed on by prayer. When the people of God are stirred up to prayer, it is the effect of his intention to show mercy. Therefore, he pours out the spirit of grace and supplication.

And call upon me in the day of trouble: I will deliver thee, and thou shalt glorify me. Psalm 50:15

Christ's Compassion

But when he saw the multitudes, he was moved with compassion on them, because they fainted, and were scattered abroad, as sheep having no shepherd.
Matthew 9:36

Christ is one that is ready to pity the afflicted. It is natural for persons that are bereaved of any that are dear to them, and for all under deep sorrow, to seek some that they may declare and lay open their griefs to, that they have good reason to think will pity them, and have a fellow-feeling with them of their distress. The heart that is full of grief wants vent, and desires to pour out its complaint; but it seeks a compassionate friend to pour it out before. Christ is such a one, above all others. He of old, before his incarnation, manifested himself full of compassion towards his people. For that is Jesus that is spoken of in Isaiah 63:9, "In all their affliction he was afflicted; and the angel of his presence saved them . . . ; and he bare them, and carried them all the days of old." And when he was upon earth in his state of humiliation, he was the most wonderful instance of a tender, pitiful, compassionate spirit that ever appeared in the world. How often are we told of his having compassion on one and another! . . . His speeches to his disciples were full of compassion; especially those that he uttered a little before his death, of which we have an account in the 13th, 14th, 15th, and 16th chapters of John. His miracles were almost universally deeds of pity to persons under affliction.

Blissful Nearness

he mutual joy of Christ and his church is like that of bridegroom and bride, in that they rejoice in each other, as those whom they have chosen above others, for their nearest, most intimate, and everlasting friends and companions. The church is Christ's chosen. "I have chosen thee, and not cast thee away" (Isaiah 41:9); "I have chosen thee in the furnace of affliction" (ch. 48:10). How often are God's saints called his elect or chosen ones! He has chosen them, not to be mere servants, but friends. "I call you not servants; . . . but I have called you friends" (John 15:15). And though Christ is the Lord of glory, infinitely above men and angels, yet he has chosen the elect to be his companions, and has taken upon him their nature, and so in some respect, as it were, leveled himself with them, that he might be their brother and companion. Christ, as well as David, calls the saints his brethren and companions. . . . So in the book of Canticles, he calls his church his sister and spouse. Christ has loved and chosen his church as his peculiar friend, above others. . . . As the bridegroom chooses the bride for his peculiar friend above all others in the world, so Christ has chosen his church for a peculiar nearness to him, as his flesh and his bone, and the high honor and dignity of espousal above all others, rather than the fallen angels, yea, rather than the elect angels.

This is a great mystery: but I speak concerning Christ and the church.
Ephesians 5:32

The joy of Christ and his church is like that of bridegroom and bride.

An Invitation

Now the Lord of peace himself give you peace always by all means.
2 Thessalonians 3:16

I invite you now to a better portion. There are better things provided for the sinful miserable children of men. There is a surer comfort and more durable peace: comfort that you may enjoy in a state of safety, and on a sure foundation: a peace and rest that you may enjoy with reason and with your eyes open. You may have all your sins forgiven, your greatest and most aggravated transgressions blotted out as a cloud, and buried as in the depths of the sea, that they may never be found more. And being not only forgiven, but accepted to favor, you become the objects of God's complacence and delight. Being taken into God's family and made his children, you may have good evidence that your names were written on the heart of Christ before the world was made, and that you have an interest in that covenant of grace that is well ordered in all things and sure, wherein is promised no less than life and immortality, an inheritance incorruptible and undefiled, a crown of glory that fades not away. Being in such circumstances, nothing shall be able to prevent your being happy to all eternity, having for the foundation of your hope that love of God which is from eternity to eternity, and his promise and oath, and his omnipotent power: things infinitely firmer than mountains of brass. The mountains shall depart, and the hills be removed, yea, the heavens shall vanish away like smoke, and the earth shall wax old like a garment, yet these things will never be abolished.

I invite you to a better portion.

The Valley of Achor

Souls are wont to be brought into trouble before God bestows true hope and comfort. The corrupt hearts of men naturally incline to stupidity and senselessness before God comes with the awakening influences of his Spirit. They are quiet and secure. They have no true comfort and hope, and yet they are quiet; they are at ease. They are in miserable slavery, and yet seek not a remedy. They say, as the children of Israel did in Egypt to Moses, "Let us alone, that we may serve the Egyptians." But if God has a design of mercy to them, it is his manner before he bestows true hope and comfort on them, to bring them into trouble, to distress them, and spoil their ease and false quietness, and to rouse them out of their old resting and sleeping places, and to bring them into a wilderness. They are brought into great trouble and distress, so that they can take no comfort in those things in which they used to take comfort. Their hearts are pinched and stung, and they can find no ease in anything. They have, as it were, an arrow sticking fast in them, which causes grievous and continual pain, an arrow which they cannot shake off, or pull out. . . . Their worldly enjoyments were a sufficient good before; but they are not now. They wander about with wounded hearts, seeking rest, and finding none; like one wandering in a dry and parched wilderness under the burning, scorching heat of the sun, seeking for some shadow where he may sit down and rest, but finding none. Wherever he goes the beams of the sun scorch him. Or he seeks some fountain of cool water to quench his thirst, but finds not a drop. . . . They call on God, but he does not answer, nor seem to regard them. Sometimes they find something in which they take pleasure for a little time, but it soon vanishes away, and leaves them in greater distress than before. And sometimes they are brought to the very borders of despair. Thus they are brought into the wilderness, and into the valley of Achor, or of trouble.

And I will give her her vineyards from thence, and the valley of Achor for a door of hope: and she shall sing there, as in the days of her youth, and as in the day when she came up out of the land of Egypt.
Hosea 2:15

Heavenly Music

What is it then? I will pray with the spirit, and I will pray with the understanding also: I will sing with the spirit, and I will sing with the understanding also.

1 Corinthians 14:15

The best, most beautiful, and most perfect way that we have of expressing a sweet concord of mind to each other is by music. When I would form in my mind an idea of a society in the highest degree happy, I think of them as expressing their love, their joy, and the inward concord and harmony and spiritual beauty of their souls by sweetly singing to each other. But if in heaven minds will have an immediate view of one another's dispositions without any such intermediate expression, how much sweeter will it be. But to me it is probable that the glorified saints, after they have again received their bodies, will have ways of expressing concord with their minds by some other emanations than sounds, of which we cannot conceive, that will be vastly more proportionate, harmonious, and delightful than the nature of sounds is capable of; and the music they will make will be in a medium capable of modulations in an infinitely more nice, exact, and fine proportion than our gross air, and with organs as much more adapted to such a proportion.

Heaven's Repose

We are not to suppose, when the saints have finished their course and done the works appointed them here in this world, and are got to their journey's end, to their Father's house, that they will have nothing to do. It is true, the saints when they get to heaven, rest from their labors and their works follow them. Heaven is not a place of labor and travail, but a place of rest. . . . But yet the rest of heaven does not consist in idleness, and a cessation of all action, but only a cessation from all the trouble and toil and tediousness of action. The most perfect rest is consistent with being continually employed. So it is in heaven. Though the saints are exceedingly full of action, yet their activity is perfectly free from all labor, or weariness, or unpleasantness. They shall rest from their work, that is, from all work of labor and self-denial, and grief, care, and watchfulness, but they will not cease from action. . . . Perfection of happiness does not consist in idleness, but on the contrary, it very much consists in action. The angels are blessed spirits, and yet they are exceedingly active in serving God. They are as a flame of fire, which is the most active thing that we see in this world. God himself enjoys infinite happiness and perfect bliss, and yet he is not inactive, but is himself in his own nature a perfect act, and is continually at work in bringing to pass his own purposes and ends. That principle of holiness that is in its perfection in the saints in heaven is a most active principle. So that though they enjoy perfect rest, yet they are a great deal more active than they were when in this world. In this world they were exceedingly dull, and heavy, and inactive, but now they are a flame of fire. The saints in heaven are not merely passive in their happiness. They do not merely enjoy God passively, but in an active manner. They are not only acted upon by God, but they mutually act towards him and in this action and re-action consists the heavenly happiness.

There remaineth therefore a rest to the people of God.
Hebrews 4:9

The Way of Holiness

Follow peace with all men, and holiness, without which no man shall see the Lord.

Hebrews 12:14

We ought to seek heaven, by traveling in the way that leads there. This is a way of holiness. We should choose and desire to travel thither in this way and in no other, and part with all those carnal appetites which, as weights, will tend to hinder us. "Let us lay aside every weight, and the sin which doth so easily beset us, and let us run with patience the race that is set before us" (Hebrews 12:1). However pleasant the gratification of any appetite may be, we must lay it aside if it be a hindrance, or a stumbling block, in the way to heaven.

We should travel on in the way of obedience to all God's commands, even the difficult as well as the easy, denying all our sinful inclinations and interests. The way to heaven is ascending. We must be content to travel uphill, though it is hard and tiresome, and contrary to the natural bias of our flesh. We should follow Christ: the path he traveled was the right way to heaven. We should take up our cross and follow him, in meekness and lowliness of heart, obedience and charity, diligence to do good, and patience under afflictions. The way to heaven is a heavenly life, an imitation of those who are in heaven in their holy enjoyments, loving, adoring, serving, and praising God and the Lamb. Even if we could go to heaven with the gratification of our lusts, we should prefer a way of holiness and conformity to the spiritual self-denying rules of the gospel.

> We should travel on in the way of obedience to all God's commands.

Heaven's Treasure

ow, the main reason why the godly man has his heart to heaven is because God is there; that is the palace of the Most High. It is the place where God is gloriously present, where his love is gloriously manifested, where the godly may be with him, see him as he is, and love, serve, praise, and enjoy him perfectly. If God and Christ were not in heaven, he would not be so earnest in seeking it, nor would he take so many pains in a laborious travel through this wilderness, nor would the consideration that he is going to heaven when he dies be such a comfort to him under toils and afflictions. The martyrs would not undergo cruel sufferings from their persecutors, with a cheerful prospect of going to heaven, did they not expect to be with Christ, and to enjoy God there. They would not with that cheerfulness forsake all their earthly possessions, and all their earthly friends, as many thousands of them have done, and wander about in poverty and banishment, being destitute, afflicted, tormented, in hopes of exchanging their earthly for a heavenly inheritance, were it not that they hope to be with their glorious Redeemer and heavenly Father. The believer's heart is in heaven, because his treasure is there.

Whom have I in heaven but thee? and there is none upon earth that I desire beside thee.
Psalm 73:25

The believer's heart is in heaven, because his treasure is there.

Relinquish All

Little children, keep yourselves from idols.

1 John 5:21

Be directed to sacrifice everything to your soul's eternal interest. Let seeking this be so much your bent, and what you are so resolved in, that you will make everything give place to it. Let nothing stand before your resolution of seeking the kingdom of God. Whatever it be that you used to look upon as a convenience, or comfort, or ease, or thing desirable on any account, if it stands in the way of this great concern, let it be dismissed without hesitation; and if it be of that nature that it is likely always to be a hindrance, then wholly have done with it, and never entertain any expectation from it more. . . . Whatever it be that stands in the way of your most advantageously seeking salvation . . . offer up all such things together, as it were, in one sacrifice, to the interest of your soul. . . . The rich young man was considerably concerned for salvation; and accordingly was a very strict liver in many things: but when Christ came to direct him to go and sell all that he had, and give to the poor, and come and follow him, he could not find in his heart to comply with it, but went away sorrowful. He had great possessions, and set his heart much on his estate, and could not bear to part with it. It may be, if Christ had directed him only to give away a considerable part of his estate, he would have done it; yea, perhaps, if he had bid him part with half of it, he would have complied with it: but when he directed him to throw up all, he could not grapple with such a proposal. Herein the straightness of the gate very much consists; and it is on this account that so many seek to enter in, and are not able. There are many that have a great mind to salvation, and spend great part of their time in wishing they had it, but they will not comply with the necessary means.

The Best Society

*T*he people of God are the most excellent and happy society in the world. That God, whom they have chosen for their God, is their Father. He has pardoned all their sins, and they are at peace with him, and he has admitted them to all the privileges of his children. As they have devoted themselves to God, so he has given himself to them. He is become their salvation, and their portion: his power and mercy, and all his attributes are theirs. They are in a safe state, free from all possibility of perishing. Satan has no power to destroy them. God carries them on eagle's wings, far above Satan's reach, and above the reach of all the enemies of their souls. God is with them in this world. They have his gracious presence. God is for them: who then can be against them? As the mountains are round about Jerusalem, so Jehovah is round about them. God is their shield, and their exceeding great reward and their fellowship is with the Father, and with his Son Jesus Christ. They have the divine promise and oath, that in the world to come they shall dwell forever in the glorious presence of God.

Happy is that people, whose God is the LORD.
Psalm 144:15

As the mountains are round about Jerusalem, so Jehovah is round about them.

Majesty and Meekness

Mercy and truth are met together; righteousness and peace have kissed each other.

Psalm 85:10

In the person of Christ do meet together infinite *majesty* and transcendent *meekness*. These again are two qualifications that meet together in no other person but Christ. Meekness, properly so called, is a virtue proper only to the creature. We scarcely ever find meekness mentioned as a divine attribute in Scripture, at least not in the New Testament. . . . But Christ, being both God and man, has both infinite majesty and superlative meekness.

Christ was a person of infinite majesty. It is he that is spoken of, "Gird thy sword upon thy thigh, O most mighty, with thy glory and thy majesty" (Psalm 45:3). It is he that is mighty, that rides on the heavens, and his excellency on the sky. It is he that is terrible out of his holy places, who is mightier than the noise of many waters, yea, than the mighty waves of the sea; before whom a fire goes and burns up his enemies round about; at whose presence the earth quakes and the hills melt; who sits on the circle of the earth and all the inhabitants thereof are as grasshoppers; who rebukes the sea and makes it dry and dries up the rivers; whose eyes are as a flame of fire . . . And yet he was the most marvelous instance of meekness, and humble quietness of spirit, that ever was, agreeable to the prophecies of him, "All this was done, that it might be fulfilled which was spoken by the prophet, saying, Tell ye the daughter of Sion, Behold, thy King cometh unto thee, meek, and sitting upon an ass, and a colt the foal of an ass" (Matthew 21:4–5). And, agreeable to what Christ declares of himself, "I am meek and lowly in heart" (Matthew 11:29). . . . With what meekness did he appear in the ring of soldiers that were condemning and mocking him. He was silent, and opened not his mouth, but went as a lamb to the slaughter. Thus is Christ a Lion in majesty and a Lamb in meekness.

The Necessity of Holiness

any are not sensible enough of the necessity of holiness in order to salvation. Everyone hopes for heaven, but if everyone that hoped for heaven ever got there, heaven by this time would have been full of murderers, adulterers, common swearers, drunkards, thieves, robbers, and licentious debauchers. It would have been full of all manner of wickedness and wicked men, such as the earth abounds with at this day. There would have been those there that are no better than wild beasts, howling wolves, and poisonous serpents; yea, devils incarnate, as Judas was.

The heavens declare his righteousness, and all the people see his glory.
Psalm 97:6

What a wretched place would the highest heavens have been by this time if it were so: that pure, undefiled light and glorious place, the heavenly temple, would be as the temple of Jerusalem was in Christ's time, a den of thieves; and the royal palace of the Most High, the holy metropolis of the creation, would be turned into a mere hell. There would be no happiness there for those that are holy. What a horrible, dreadful confusion would there be if the glorious presence of God the Father; the glorified Lamb of God; and the Heavenly Dove, spirit of all grace and original of all holiness; the spotless, glorified saints; the holy angels; and wicked men, beasts and devils [were] all mixed together!

Therefore, it behooves us all to be sensible of the necessity of holiness in order to salvation; of the necessity of real, hearty and sincere, inward and spiritual holiness, such as will stand by us forever and will not leave us at death.

Obeying the Gospel

Faith is a receiving of Christ into the heart. "If thou shalt confess with thy mouth the Lord Jesus, and shalt believe in thine heart that God hath raised him from the dead, thou shalt be saved" (Romans 10:9–10). A true faith includes more than a mere belief; it is accepting the gospel, and includes all acceptance. "This is a faithful saying, and worthy of all acceptation, that Christ Jesus came into the world to save sinners" (1 Timothy 1:15). It is something more than a mere assent of the understanding, because it is called obeying the gospel. "What shall the end be of them that obey not the gospel" (1 Peter 4:17)? It is obeying the doctrine from the heart (Romans 6:17–18). This expression of obeying the gospel seems to denote the heart's yielding to the gospel in what it proposes to us in its believing the truth of the gospel. "Many believed on him; but because of the Pharisees they did not confess him, lest they should be put out of the synagogue" (John 12:42).

A true faith includes more than a mere belief.

God Reigning

The godly man not only loves that God should reign over others, but that he should reign over him too, and that with an uncontrollable power. He is heartily willing that God should be a sovereign King over him. He had rather be ruled by God and have God for his King, than be in all respects at his own disposal. We are not our own; we "are bought with a price" (1 Corinthians 6:19–20). And the believer had rather have it so than otherwise; he had rather be God's than his own. He had rather that God should have an entire right to him, body and soul, than have a right to himself. He loves to have God for a lawgiver, had rather that God should give him laws than not. He loves to have God dispose of him in his providence. He can delight in thinking that he is in the hands of God; that is the language of his soul, which proceeds from the soul with delight and pleasure: "Lord, I am in thy hands; deal with me as seemeth thee good."

And Thomas answered and said unto him, My Lord and my God.
John 20:28

We are not our own; we are bought with a price.

Things Too High

*The secret things be-
long unto the LORD
our God.*
Deuteronomy
29:29

f we find fault with God's government, we virtually suppose ourselves fit to be God's counselors; whereas it becomes us rather, with great humility and adoration, to cry out with the apostle, "O the depth of the riches both of the wisdom and knowledge of God! How unsearchable are his judgments, and his ways past finding out! For who hath known the mind of the Lord? Or who hath been his counselor? Or who hath first given to him, and it shall be recompensed unto him again? For of him, and through him, and to him, are all things: to whom be glory for ever" (Romans 11:33–36). If little children should rise up and find fault with the supreme legislature of a nation, or quarrel with the mysterious administrations of the sovereign, would it not be looked upon that they meddled with things too high for them? And what are we but babes? Our understandings are infinitely less than those of babes, in comparison with the wisdom of God. It becomes us therefore to be sensible of it, and to behave ourselves accordingly. "Lord, my heart is not haughty, nor mine eyes lofty; neither do I exercise myself in great matters, or in things too high for me. Surely I have behaved and quieted myself, as a child" (Psalm 131:1–2). This consideration alone of the infinite distance between God and us, and between God's understanding and ours, should be enough to still and quiet us concerning all that God does, however mysterious and unintelligible to us. Nor have we any right to expect, that God should particularly explain to us the reason of his dispensations. It is fit that God should not give any account of his matters to us, worms of the dust, that we may be sensible of our distance from him, and adore and submit to him in humble reverence.

Faith without Works

oliness is conformity of the heart and the life unto God. Whatever outward appearances men may make by their external actions, as if they were holy, yet if it proceeds not from a most inward, hearty and sincere holiness within, it is nothing. Amaziah did that which was right in the sight of the Lord, but not with a perfect heart (2 Kings 14:1–20); all that he did was not acceptable to God, who searches the hearts and tries the reins of the children of men, and must be worshipped in spirit and in truth.

For as the body without the spirit is dead, so faith without works is dead also.
James 2:26

And whatever holiness they may pretend to have in their hearts, whatever hypocritical pangs of affection they may have had, it is all to no purpose except it manifest itself in the holiness of their lives and conversations: "If any man among you seem to be religious, and bridleth not his tongue, but deceiveth his own heart, this man's religion is vain. Pure religion and undefiled before God and the Father is this, To visit the fatherless and widows in their affliction, and to keep himself unspotted from the world" (James 1:26–27). And in the second chapter, eighteenth verse: "Yea, a man may say, Thou hast faith, and I have works: shew me thy faith without thy works, and I will shew thee my faith by my works." And in the nineteenth and twentieth verses, "Thou believest that there is one God; thou doest well: the devils also believe, and tremble. But wilt thou know, O vain man, that faith without works is dead?" So that there must be conformity of both heart and life to God, in order to true holiness.

Noticed by Christ

Wherefore he is able also to save them to the uttermost that come unto God by him, seeing he ever liveth to make intercession for them.
Hebrews 7:25

From the unchangeableness of Christ you may learn the unchangeableness of his intercession, how he will never cease to intercede for you. And from this you may learn the unalterableness of your heavenly happiness. When once you have entered on the happiness of heaven, it never shall be taken from you, because Christ, your Savior and friend, who bestows it on you, and in whom you have it, is unchangeable. He will be the same forever and ever, and therefore so will be your happiness in heaven. As Christ is an unchangeable Savior, so he is your unchangeable portion. That may be your rejoicing, that however your earthly enjoyments may be removed, Christ can never fail. Your dear friends may be taken away and you suffer many losses. And at last you must part with all those things. Yet you have a portion, a precious treasure, more worth, ten thousand times, than all these things. That portion cannot fail you, for you have it in him, who is the same yesterday, today, and forever.

Become Like Fools

ow foolish a thing it is for men to lean to their own understanding, and trust their own hearts. If we are so blind, then our own wisdom is not to be depended on, and that advice of the wise man is most reasonable. "Trust in the Lord with all thine heart; and lean not unto thine own understanding" (Proverbs 3:5); "He that trusteth in his own heart is a fool" (Proverbs 28:26). They therefore are fools, who trust to their own wisdom, and will question the mysterious doctrines of religion, because they cannot see through them, and will not trust to the infinite wisdom of God.

We are fools for Christ's sake, but ye are wise in Christ; we are weak, but ye are strong; ye are honourable, but we are despised.

1 Corinthians 4:10

Let us therefore become fools. Be sensible of our own natural blindness and folly. There is a treasure of wisdom contained in that one sentence; "If any man among you seemeth to be wise in this world, let him become a fool, that he may be wise" (1 Corinthians 3:18). Seeing our own ignorance, and blindness, is the first step towards having true knowledge. "If any man think that he knoweth any thing, he knoweth nothing yet as he ought to know" (1 Corinthians 8:2).

Let us ask wisdom of God. If we are so blind in ourselves, then knowledge is not to be sought for out of our own stock, but must be sought from some other source. And we have nowhere else to go for it, but to the fountain of light and wisdom. True wisdom is a precious jewel. And none of our fellow-creatures can give it us, nor can we buy it with any price we have to give. It is the sovereign gift of God. The way to obtain it is to go to him sensible of our weakness, and blindness, and misery on that account. "If any lack wisdom, let him ask of God" (James 1:5).

Follow Paul's Example

We ought to follow the good examples of the apostle Paul. We are to consider that the apostle did not say this of himself from an ambitious spirit, from a desire of being set up as a pattern, and eyed and imitated as an example to other Christians. His writings are not of any private interpretation, but he spoke as he was moved by the Holy Ghost. . . . And when we are directed to follow the good examples of the apostle Paul by the Holy Ghost, it is not merely as we are to imitate whatever we see that is good in anyone, let him be how he may. But there are spiritual obligations that lie on Christians to follow the good examples of this great apostle. And it has pleased the Holy Ghost in an especial manner to set up the apostle Paul, not only as a teacher of the Christian church, but as a pattern to other Christians. . . . Of all mere men, no one is so often particularly set forth in the Scripture, as a pattern for Christians to follow, as the apostle Paul.

Love Superior

he gift of prophecy, of miracles, of tongues, and so on, God gave for this very end, to promote the propagation and establishment of the gospel in the world. And the end of the gospel is to turn men from darkness to light, and from the power of sin and Satan to serve the living God, that is, to make men holy. The end of all the extraordinary gifts of the Spirit is the conversion of sinners, and the building up of saints in that holiness which is the fruit of the ordinary influences of the Holy Ghost. For this, the Holy Spirit was poured out on the apostles after Christ's ascension; and they were enabled to speak with tongues, work miracles, and so on; and for this, very many others, in that age, were endued with the extraordinary gifts of the Holy Ghost: "And he gave some, apostles; and some, prophets; and some, evangelists" (Ephesians 4:11). Here the extraordinary gifts of the Spirit are referred to; and the end of all is expressed in the next words, viz., "For the perfecting of the saints, for the work of the ministry, for the edifying of the body of Christ." And what sort of edifying of the body of Christ this is, we learn from verse 16, "Maketh increase of the body unto the edifying of itself in love." In love, that is, in charity . . . And so it is the same as in 1 Corinthians 8:1: "charity edifieth." But the end is always more excellent than the means: this is a maxim universally allowed; for means have no goodness in them any otherwise than as they are subordinate to the end. The end, therefore, must be considered as superior in excellency to the means.

And now abideth faith, hope, charity, these three; but the greatest of these is charity.
1 Corinthians 13:13

The Beauty of Holiness

O worship the LORD in the beauty of holiness: fear before him, all the earth.

Psalm 96:9

Holiness is a most beautiful, lovely thing. Men are apt to drink in strange notions of holiness from their childhood, as if it were a melancholy, morose, sour, and unpleasant thing: but there is nothing in it but what is sweet and ravishing lovely. It is the highest beauty and amiableness, vastly above all other beauties; it is a divine beauty, makes the soul heavenly and far purer than anything here on earth. This world is like mire and filth and defilement compared to that soul which is sanctified. It is of a sweet, lovely, delightful, serene, calm, and still nature. It is almost too high a beauty for any creature to be adorned with; it makes the soul a little, amiable, and delightful image of the blessed Jehovah. How many angels stand with pleased, delighted, and charmed eyes, and look and look with smiles of pleasure upon that soul that is holy!

Christian holiness is above all the heathen virtue, of a more bright and pure nature, more serene, calm, peaceful, and delightsome. What a sweet calmness, what a calm ecstasy, does it bring to the soul! Of what a meek and humble nature is true holiness; how peaceful and quiet. How it changes the soul, and makes it more pure, more bright, and more excellent than other beings.

Christian holiness is above all heathen virtue.

Live in Control

eligion allows the enjoyment of sensitive delights temperately, moderately, and with reason, but the wicked man gluts himself with them. Any of the delights of this world are abundantly sweeter when taken temperately than when taken immoderately, as he that at a feast feeds with temperance has much greater pleasure of what he eats and drinks than he that gluts himself and vomits it up again. The godly have the prudence to take of earthly delights moderately, but the wicked man, he is unreasonable in it by being so greedy and violent, he presently loses the relish of his pleasure; but the godly takes those things so that the sweet relish of them remains all his lifetime. "Hast thou found honey? eat so much as is sufficient for thee, lest thou be filled therewith, and vomit it" (Proverbs 25:16). The righteous man has the prudence to eat no more honey than he can digest, and that the relish of it may remain.

Meekness, temperance: against such there is no law.
Galatians 5:23

The Prayers of Unbelievers

Seest thou how Ahab humbleth himself before me? because he humbleth himself before me, I will not bring the evil in his days: but in his son's days will I bring the evil upon his house.

1 Kings 21:29

God is pleased sometimes to answer the prayers of unbelievers. Indeed he hears not their prayers for their goodness or acceptableness or because of any true respect to him manifested in them, for there is none. Nor has he obliged himself to answer such prayers. Yet he is pleased sometimes, of his sovereign mercy, to pity wicked men, and hear their cries. Thus he heard the cries of the Ninevites (Jonah 3) and the prayer of Ahab (1 Kings 21:27–28). Though there is no regard to God in their prayers yet he, of his infinite grace, is pleased to have respect to their desires of their own happiness, and to grant their requests. He may, and sometimes does, hear the cries of wicked men, as he hears the hungry ravens when they cry (Psalm 147:9). And as he opens his bountiful hand and satisfies the desires of every living thing (Psalm 145:16). Besides the prayers of sinners, though they have no goodness in them, yet are made a means of a preparation for mercy.

Rulers and Magistrates

hose that are by Divine Providence set in a place of public authority and rule are called "gods, and sons of the Most High." And therefore it is peculiarly unbecoming them to be of a mean spirit, a disposition that will admit of their doing those things that are sordid and vile; as when they are persons of a narrow, private spirit, that may be found in little tricks and intrigues to promote their private interest. Such will shamefully defile their hands to gain a few pounds, . . . and will take advantage of their authority or commission to line their pockets with what is fraudulently taken or withheld from others. When a man in authority is of such a mean spirit, it weakens his authority, and makes him justly contemptible in the eyes of men, and is utterly inconsistent with his being a strong rod.

But on the contrary, it greatly establishes his authority, and causes others to stand in awe of him, when they see him to be a man of greatness of mind, one that abhors those things that are mean and sordid, and not capable of a compliance with them: one that is of a public spirit, and not of a private narrow disposition; a man of honor, and not of mean artifice and clandestine management, for filthy lucre; one that abhors trifling and impertinence, or to waste away his time. . . . God charges the rulers in Israel, which pretended to be their great and mighty men, with being mighty to drink wine, and men of strength to mingle strong drink. There does not seem to be any reference to their being men of strong heads, and able to bear a great deal of strong drink, as some have supposed. There is a severe sarcasm in the words; for the prophet is speaking of the great men, princes, and judges in Israel (as appears by the verse next following), which should be mighty men, strong rods, men of eminent qualifications, excelling in nobleness of spirit, of glorious strength and fortitude of mind. But instead of that, they were mighty or eminent for nothing but gluttony and drunkenness.

I have said, Ye are gods; and all of you are children of the most High.
Psalm 82:6

Living in Fear

There were they in
great fear, where no
fear was: for God hath
scattered the bones of
him that encampeth
against thee: thou hast
put them to shame, be-
cause God hath de-
spised them.
Psalm 53:5

he wicked man, though he has the pleasures of this life, yet he partakes of them with fear. He lives in a slavish fear, all his days, of death and hell. He eats and drinks with fear, in fear, and this takes away much of the delight of what he enjoys. Though he is rich and fares sumptuously, yet if he eats and drinks in fear of his life, this takes away all the comfort of his riches. If one lives in the enjoyment of many good things, yet if he lives so that he is exposed to an enemy continually, a man that dwells in a cottage lives better than he. Feed a malefactor condemned to the gallows with the richest fare, he will not have so much comfort of it as one that eats only bread and water without fear. The wicked man, he takes these things as a thief that is afraid of the shaking of a leaf. "The wicked fleeth when no man pursueth" (Proverbs 28:1). Also Job 24:17. But the Christian, he partakes of his delights in safety and without fear, can eat and drink without terrors, with boldness and confidence.

Treasure Knowledge

onsider yourselves as scholars or disciples, put into the school of Christ; and therefore be diligent to make proficiency in Christian knowledge. Content not yourselves with this, that you have been taught your catechism in your childhood, and that you know as much of the principles of religion as is necessary to salvation. So you will be guilty of what the Apostle warns against, viz., going no further than "laying the foundation of repentance from dead works" (Hebrews 6:1).

Buy the truth, and sell it not.
Proverbs 23:23

You are all called to be Christians, and this is your profession. Endeavor, therefore, to acquire knowledge in things which pertain to your profession. Let not your teachers have cause to complain, that while they spend and are spent, to impart knowledge to you, you take little pains to learn. It is a great encouragement to an instructor, to have such to teach as make a business of learning, bending their minds to it. This makes teaching a pleasure, when otherwise it will be a very heavy and burdensome task.

You all have by you a large treasure of divine knowledge, in that you have the Bible in your hands; therefore be not contented in possessing but little of this treasure. God has spoken much to you in the Scripture; labor to understand as much of what he says as you can. God has made you all reasonable creatures; therefore let not the noble faculty of reason or understanding lie neglected. Content not yourselves with having so much knowledge as is thrown in your way, and as you receive in some sense unavoidably by the frequent inculcation of divine truth in the preaching of the Word, of which you are obliged to be hearers, or as you accidentally gain in conversation; but let it be very much your business to search for it, and that with the same diligence and labor with which men are wont to dig in mines of silver and gold.

More Beloved

*A new commandment
I give unto you, That
ye love one another; as
I have loved you, that
ye also love one
another.*

John 13:34

The love of the saints, one to another, will always be mutual and reciprocated, though we cannot suppose that everyone will, in all respects, be equally beloved. Some of the saints are more beloved of God than others, even on earth. The angel told Daniel that he was a man "greatly beloved" (Daniel 9:23); and Luke is called the "beloved physician" (Colossians 4:14); and John, the "disciple whom Jesus loved" (John 20:2). And so, doubtless, those that have been most eminent in fidelity and holiness, and that are highest in glory, are most beloved by Christ in heaven; and doubtless those saints that are most beloved of Christ, and that are nearest to him in glory, are most beloved by all the other saints. Thus we may conclude that such saints as the apostle Paul and the apostle John are more beloved by the saints in heaven than other saints of lower rank. They are more beloved by lower saints than those of equal rank with themselves. But then there are answerable returns of love in these cases; for as such are more beloved by all other saints, so they are fuller of love to other saints. The heart of Christ, the great Head of all the saints, is more full of love than the heart of any saint can be. He loves all the saints far more than any of them love each other. But the more any saint is loved of him, the more is that saint like him, in this respect, that the fuller his heart is of love.

The heart of Christ is more full of love than the heart of any saint can be.

No More Jealousy

The joy of heavenly love shall never be interrupted or damped by jealousy. Heavenly lovers will have no doubt of the love of each other. They shall have no fear that the declarations and professions of love are hypocritical; but shall be perfectly satisfied of the sincerity and strength of each other's affection, as much as if there were a window in every breast, so that everything in the heart could be seen. There shall be no such thing as flattery or dissimulation in heaven, but there perfect sincerity shall reign through all and in all. Every one will be just what he seems to be, and will really have all the love that he seems to have. It will not be as in this world, where comparatively few things are what they seem to be, and where professions are often made lightly and without meaning; but there every expression of love shall come from the bottom of the heart, and all that is professed shall be really and truly felt. The saints shall know that God loves them, and they shall never doubt the greatness of his love, and they shall have no doubt of the love of all their fellow inhabitants in heaven. And they shall not be jealous of the constancy of each other's love. They shall have no suspicion that the love which others have felt toward them is abated, or in any degree withdrawn from themselves for the sake of some rival, or by reason of anything in themselves which they suspect is disagreeable to others, or through any inconstancy in their own hearts or the hearts of others. Nor will they be in the least afraid that the love of any will ever be abated toward them. There shall be no such thing as inconstancy and unfaithfulness in heaven, to molest and disturb the friendship of that blessed society. The saints shall have no fear that the love of God will ever abate towards them, or that Christ will not continue always to love them with unabated tenderness and affection. And they shall have no jealousy one of another, for they shall know that by divine grace the love of all the saints is also unchangeable.

If we love one another, God dwelleth in us, and his love is perfected in us.
1 John 4:12

The Believer's Support

He that can say, "I know that my Redeemer liveth," he knows that his Redeemer is above all and able to do all things for him. If he is persecuted, he knows that his Redeemer is above his persecutors. If he is tempted by the devil, and he sees that the powers of hell rage against him, he knows that his Redeemer is above all the devils in hell, and that he is able to deliver him from their hands. He knows that his foundation is sure and his refuge strong, and that his Redeemer is round about him as the mountains were round about Jerusalem, and that his name is a strong tower, and his salvation that is appointed for his walls and bulwarks is as mountains of brass.

If he has affliction in the world, and is in the midst of storms, he knows that his Redeemer is above the storms of the world, and can restrain them and quell them when he pleases. It is but for him to say, "Peace, be still," and all is calm. If he is tossed like a vessel on the tempestuous sea, he knows that his Redeemer is in the ship, and therefore knows he can't sink.

If death approaches with its most grim and ghastly countenance, yet he knows that his Redeemer is above death, and therefore is not terrified with it, but can look upon it with a calm, pleasant countenance and say, "O death, where is thy sting? O grave, where is thy victory" (1 Corinthians 15:55)?

Time is Uncertain

ime ought to be esteemed by us very precious because we are uncertain of its continuance. We know that it is very short, but we know not how short. We know not how little of it remains, whether a year, or several years, or only a month, a week, or a day. We are every day uncertain whether that day will not be the last, or whether we are to have the whole day. There is nothing that experience doth more verify than this. If a man had but little provision laid up for a journey or a voyage, and at the same time knew that if his provision should fail, he must perish by the way, he would be the more choice of it. How much more would many men prize their time, if they knew that they had but a few months, or a few days, more to live! And certainly a wise man will prize his time the more, as he knows not but that it will be so as to himself. This is the case with multitudes now in the world, who at present enjoy health, and see no signs of approaching death. Many such, no doubt, are to die the next month, many the next week, yea, many probably tomorrow, and some this night. Yet these same persons know nothing of it, and perhaps think nothing of it, and neither they nor their neighbors can say that they are more likely soon to be taken out of the world than others. This teaches us how we ought to prize our time, and how careful we ought to be, that we lose none of it.

To every thing there is a season, and a time to every purpose under the heaven.
Ecclesiastes 3:1

Shadows and Things

So man lieth down,
and riseth not: till the
heavens be no more.
Job 14:12

This world is not our abiding place. Our continuance here is but very short. Man's days on the earth are as a shadow. It was never designed by God that this world should be our home. Neither did God give us these temporal accommodations for that end. If God has given us ample estates, and children, or other pleasant friends, it is with no such design that we should be furnished here as for a settled abode, but with a design that we should use them for the present, and then leave them in a very little time. When we are called to any secular business, or charged with the care of a family, [and] if we improve our lives to any other purpose than as a journey toward heaven, all our labor will be lost. If we spend our lives in the pursuit of a temporal happiness, as riches or sensual pleasures, credit and esteem from men, delight in our children and the prospect of seeing them well brought up and well settled, etc., all these things will be of little significance to us. Death will blow up all our hopes, and will put an end to these enjoyments. "The places that have known us, will know us no more" and "the eye that has seen us, shall see us no more." We must be taken away forever from all these things, and it is uncertain when: it may be soon after we are put into the possession of them. And then, where will be all our worldly employments and enjoyments, when we are laid in the silent grave!

Toward the Mark

e directed to forget the things that are behind: that is, not to keep thinking and making much of what you have done, but let your mind be wholly intent on what you have to do. In some sense you ought to look back; you should look back to your sins; "See thy way in the valley, know what thou hast done" (Jeremiah 2:23). You should look back on the wretchedness of your religious performances, and consider how you have fallen short in them; how exceedingly polluted all your duties have been, and how justly God might reject and loathe them, and you for them. But you ought not to spend your time in looking back, as many persons do, thinking how much they have done for their salvation; what great pains they have taken, how that they have done what they can, and do not see how they can do more; how long a time they have been seeking, and how much more they have done than others, and even than such and such who have obtained mercy. They think with themselves how hardly God deals with them, that he does not extend mercy to them, but turns a deaf ear to their cries; and hence discourage them, and complain of God. Do not thus spend your time in looking back on what is past, but look forward, and consider what is before you; consider what it is that you can do, and what it is necessary that you should do, and what God calls you still to do, in order to your own salvation. The apostle, in the third chapter to the Philippians, tells us what things he did while a Jew, how much he had to boast of, if any could boast; but he tells us, that he forgot those things, and all other things that were behind, and reached forth towards the things that were before, pressing forwards towards the mark for the prize of the high calling of God in Christ Jesus.

I press toward the mark for the prize of the high calling of God in Christ Jesus.
Philippians 3:14

An Ocean of Love

God is Love.
1 John 4:16

God is a glorious God. There is none like him, who is infinite in glory and excellency. He is the most high God, glorious in holiness, fearful in praises, doing wonders. His Name is excellent in all the earth, and his glory is above the heavens. Among the gods there is none like unto him. There is none in heaven to be compared to him, nor are there any among the sons of the mighty that can be likened unto him. Their God is the fountain of all good, and an inexhaustible fountain. He is an all-sufficient God, able to protect and defend them, and do all things for them. He is the King of glory, the Lord strong and mighty, the Lord mighty in battle: a strong rock, and a high tower. There is none like the God of Jeshurun, who rides on the heaven in their help, and in his excellency on the sky. The eternal God is their refuge, and underneath are everlasting arms. He is a God who has all things in his hands, and does whatsoever he pleases. He kills and makes alive; he brings down to the grave and brings up; he makes poor and makes rich: the pillars of the earth are the Lord's. Their God is an infinitely holy God. There is none holy as the Lord. And he is infinitely good and merciful. Many that others worship and serve as gods are cruel beings, spirits that seek the ruin of souls, but this is a God that delights in mercy. His grace is infinite, and endures forever. He is love itself, and infinite fountain and ocean of it.

More Glorious Enjoyment

y your being united to Christ, you will have a more glorious union with and enjoyment of God the Father than otherwise could be. For hereby the saints' relation to God becomes much nearer: they are the children of God in a higher manner than otherwise could be. For, being members of God's own Son, they are in a sort partakers of his relation to the Father. They are not only sons of God by regeneration, but by a kind of communion in the sonship of the eternal Son. This seems to be intended, "God sent forth his Son, made of a woman, made under the law, to redeem them that are under the law, that we might receive the adoption of sons. And because ye are sons, God hath sent forth the Spirit of his Son into your hearts, crying, Abba, Father" (Galatians 4:4–6). The church is the daughter of God, not only as he has begotten her by his Word and Spirit, but as she is the spouse of his eternal Son.

That they all may be one; as thou, Father, art in me, and I in thee, that they also may be one in us: that the world may believe that thou hast sent me.
John 17:21

Increase Spiritual Appetites

*Seek ye the LORD, all
ye meek of the earth,
which have wrought
his judgment; seek
righteousness, seek
meekness: it may be ye
shall be hid in the day
of the LORD's anger.*

Zephaniah 2:3

Endeavor to increase spiritual appetites by meditating on spiritual objects. We are to restrain lustful appetites all that we can by casting away and avoiding thoughts and meditations upon their objects. We are not allowed by any means to give a lease to our thoughts concerning those things, because that tends to increase lustful desires after them. But 'tis our duty to be much in meditation on the objects of spiritual desire: we should often be thinking upon the glory and grace of God, the excellency and wonderful love of Christ, the beauty of holiness. . . . Endeavor to promote spiritual appetites by laying yourself in the way of allurement. We are to avoid being in the way of temptation with respect to our carnal appetites. Job made a covenant with his eyes (Job 31:1). But we ought to take all opportunities to lay ourselves in the way of enticement with respect to our gracious inclinations. Thus you should be often with God in prayer, and then you will be in the way of having your heart drawn forth to him. We ought to be frequent in reading and constant in hearing the Word. And particularly to this end, we ought carefully and with the utmost seriousness and consideration attend the sacrament of the Lord's Supper: this was appointed for this end, to draw forth the longings of our souls towards Jesus Christ. Here are the glorious objects of spiritual desire by visible signs represented to our view. We have Christ evidently set forth crucified. . . . Here we have that spiritual meat and drink represented and offered to excite our hunger and thirst; here we have all that spiritual feast represented which God has provided for poor souls; and here we may hope in some measure to have our longing souls satisfied in this world by the gracious communications of the Spirit of God.

Adoring God's Sovereignty

et us with the greatest humility adore the awful and absolute sovereignty of God. As we have just shown, it is an eminent attribute of the Divine Being, that he is sovereign over such excellent beings as the souls of men, and that in every respect, even in that of their eternal salvation. The infinite greatness of God, and his exaltation above us, appears in nothing more than in his sovereignty. It is spoken of in Scripture as a great part of his glory; "See now that I, even I, am he, and there is no god with me: I kill, and I make alive; I wound, and I heal: neither is there any that can deliver out of my hand" (Deuteronomy 32:39). . . . Our Lord Jesus Christ praised and glorified the Father for the exercise of his sovereignty in the salvation of men: "I thank thee, O Father, Lord of heaven and earth, because thou hast hid these things from the wise and prudent, and hast revealed them unto babes. Even so, Father: for so it seemed good in thy sight" (Matthew 11:25–26). Let us therefore give God the glory of his sovereignty, as adoring him, whose sovereign will orders all things, beholding ourselves as nothing in comparison with him. Dominion and sovereignty require humble reverence and honor in the subject. The absolute, universal, and unlimited sovereignty of God requires that we should adore him with all possible humility and reverence. It is impossible that we should go to excess in lowliness and reverence of that Being, who may dispose of us to all eternity, as he pleases.

But our God is in the heavens: he hath done whatsoever he hath pleased.
Psalm 115:3

Safety in Christ

*The name of the
LORD is a strong
tower: the righteous
runneth into it, and is
safe.*
Proverbs 18:10

I f we are in Christ Jesus, justice and the law have its course with respect to our sins, without our hurt. The foundation of the sinner's fear and distress is the justice and the law of God; they are against him, and they are unalterable, they must have their course. Every jot and tittle of the law must be fulfilled; heaven and earth shall be destroyed, rather than justice should not take place; there is no possibility of sin's escaping justice. But yet if the distressed trembling soul, who is afraid of justice, would fly to Christ, he would be a safe hiding-place. Justice and the threatening of the law will have their course as fully, while he is safe and untouched, as if he were to be eternally destroyed. Christ bears the stroke of justice, and the curse of the law falls fully upon him; Christ bears all that vengeance that belongs to the sin that has been committed by him, and there is no need of its being borne twice over. His temporal sufferings, by reason of the infinite dignity of his person, are fully equivalent to the eternal sufferings of a mere creature. And then his sufferings answer for him who flees to him as well as if they were his own, for indeed they are his own by virtue of the union between Christ and him. Christ has made himself one with them; he is the head, and they are the members. Therefore, if Christ suffers for the believer, there is no need of his suffering; and why should he be afraid? . . . Therefore if those who are afraid will go to Jesus Christ, they need to fear nothing from the threatening of the law. The threatening of the law has nothing to do with them.

Judge Your Sincerity

f there is a day of judgment appointed, then let all be very strict in trying their own sincerity. God on that day will discover the secrets of all hearts. The judgment of that day will be like the fire, which burns up whatsoever is not true gold. Wood, hay, stubble, and dross shall be all consumed by the scorching fire of that day. The judge will be like a refiner's fire, and fuller's soap, which will cleanse away all filthiness; however it may be colored over. "Who may abide the day of his coming? and who shall stand when he appeareth? for he is like a refiner's fire, and like fuller's soap" (Malachi 3:2); and Malachi 4:1, "For, behold, the day cometh, that shall burn as an oven; and all the proud, yea, and all that do wickedly, shall be stubble: and the day that cometh shall burn them up, saith the Lord of hosts."

And see if there be any wicked way in me, and lead me in the way everlasting.
Psalm 139:24

There are multitudes of men that wear the guise of saints, appear like saints, and their state, both in their own eyes and in the eyes of their neighbors, is good. They have sheep's clothing. But no disguise can hide them from the eyes of the judge of the world. His eyes are as a flame of fire. They search the hearts and try the reins of the children of men. He will see whether they be sound at heart. He will see from what principles they have acted. A fair show will in no degree deceive him, as it does men in the present state. It will signify nothing to say, "Lord, we have eaten and drunk in thy presence; and in thy name have we cast out devils, and in thy name have done many wonderful works." It will signify nothing to pretend to a great deal of comfort and joy, and to the experience of great religious affections, and to your having done many things in religion and morality, unless you have some greater evidences of sincerity. Wherefore let everyone take heed that he be not deceived concerning himself.

Vanishing Dreams

*Will he esteem thy
riches? no, not gold,
nor all the forces of
strength.*
Job 36:19

Earthly riches will certainly in a little time be gone. Such is the nature of earthly wealth, and such is the nature of the possessions of them, and such is the constitution of this world, that riches will be soon gone. They that escape accidents the longest of any, yet they must go in a little while without an accident, only according to a natural course. Riches certainly make themselves wings. Those that are the richest, they shall be stripped of all their wealth; and those that are most loathe to part with their wealth, whose hearts are most upon it and who hold it the surest, yet it will at last slip out of their hands. Let them be never so rich, death will strip them as naked as they were born; "Naked came I out of my mother's womb, and naked shall I return thither" (Job 1:21). The rich, let them be never so rich, will soon be upon a level with the poor. "Be not thou afraid when one is made rich, when the glory of his house is increased; for when he dieth he shall carry nothing away: his glory shall not descend after him" (Psalm 49:16–17). And Ecclesiastes 5:15, "As he came forth of his mother's womb, naked shall he return to go as he came, and shall take nothing of his labour, which he may carry away in his hand." A dream will vanish at last.

Earthly riches will certainly in a little time be gone.

Waters of Wrath

he wrath of God is like great waters that are dammed for the present; they increase more and more, and rise higher and higher, till an outlet is given; and the longer the stream is stopped, the more rapid and mighty is its course, when once it is let loose. It is true that judgment against your evil works has not been executed hitherto; the floods of God's vengeance have been withheld; but your guilt in the meantime is constantly increasing, and you are every day treasuring up more wrath; the waters are constantly rising, and waxing more and more mighty; and there is nothing but the mere pleasure of God that holds the waters back, that are unwilling to be stopped, and press hard to go forward. If God should only withdraw his hand from the flood-gate, it would immediately fly open, and the fiery floods of the fierceness and wrath of God would rush forth with inconceivable fury, and would come upon you with omnipotent power; and if your strength were ten thousand times greater than it is, yea, ten thousand times greater than the strength of the stoutest, sturdiest devil in hell, it would be nothing to withstand or endure it.

Pour out thy wrath upon the heathen that have not known thee, and upon the kingdoms that have not called upon thy name.

Psalm 79:6

Spiritual Sense

O taste and see that the LORD is good: blessed is the man that trusteth in him.

Psalm 34:8

Spiritual light is a true sense of the divine excellency of the things revealed in the Word of God, and a conviction of the truth and reality of them thence arising. This spiritual light primarily consists in the former of these, viz., a real sense and apprehension of the divine excellency of things revealed in the Word of God. A spiritual and saving conviction of the truth and reality of these things arises from such a sight of their divine excellency and glory, so that this conviction of their truth is an effect and natural consequence of this sight of their divine glory. There is therefore in this spiritual light a true sense of the divine and superlative excellency of the things of religion: a real sense of the excellency of God and Jesus Christ, and of the work of redemption, and the ways and works of God revealed in the gospel. There is a divine and superlative glory in these things, an excellency that is of a vastly higher kind and more sublime nature than in other things, [and] a glory greatly distinguishing them from all that is earthly and temporal. He that is spiritually enlightened truly apprehends and sees it, or has a sense of it. He does not merely rationally believe that God is glorious, but he has a sense of the gloriousness of God in his heart. There is not only a rational belief that God is holy, and that holiness is a good thing, but there is a sense of the loveliness of God's holiness. There is not only a speculative judging that God is gracious, but a sense how amiable God is on account of the beauty of this divine attribute.

Exalting God

et us be exhorted to exalt God alone, and ascribe to him all the glory of redemption. Let us endeavor to obtain, and increase in, a sensibleness of our great dependence on God, to have our eye to him alone, to mortify a self-dependent and self-righteous disposition. Man is naturally exceeding prone to exalt himself, and depend on his own power or goodness; as though from himself he must expect happiness. He is prone to have respect to enjoyments alien from God and his Spirit, as those in which happiness is to be found. But this doctrine should teach us to exalt God alone; as by trust and reliance, so by praise. "Let him that glorieth, glory in the Lord." Has any man hope that he is converted, and sanctified, and that his mind is endowed with true excellency and spiritual beauty? That his sins are forgiven, and he received into God's favor, and exalted to the honor and blessedness of being his child, and an heir of eternal life? Let him give God all the glory; who alone makes him to differ from the worst of men in this world, or the most miserable of the damned in hell. Hath any man much comfort and strong hope of eternal life, let not his hope lift him up, but dispose him the more to abase himself, to reflect on his own exceeding unworthiness of such a favor, and to exalt God alone. Is any man eminent in holiness, and abundant in good works, let him take nothing of the glory of it to himself, but ascribe it to him whose "workmanship we are, created in Christ Jesus unto good works."

For by grace are ye saved through faith; and that not of yourselves: it is the gift of God.
Ephesians 2:8

Perpetual Glory

The glory of God is subject to no changes or vicissitudes; it will never cease to shine forth. History gives us an account of the sun's light failing, and becoming more faint and dim for many months together. But the glory of God will never be subject to fade. Of the light of that Sun there never will be any eclipse or dimness, but it will shine eternally in its strength; "The sun shall be no more thy light by day; neither for brightness shall the moon give light unto thee: but the LORD shall be unto thee an everlasting light, and thy God thy glory" (Isaiah 60:19). So the love of God, to those who see his face, will never fail, or be subject to any abatement. He loves his saints with an everlasting love: "The Lord hath appeared of old unto me, saying, Yea, I have loved thee with an everlasting love: therefore with lovingkindness have I drawn thee" (Jeremiah 31:3). Those streams of pleasure which are at God's right hand are never dry, but ever flowing and ever full.

But the glory of God will never be subject to fade.

Loving God

I f a man sincerely loves God it will dispose him to render all proper respect to him; and men need no other incitement to shew each other all the respect that is due, than love. Love to God will dispose a man to honor him, to worship and adore him, and heartily to acknowledge his greatness and glory and dominion. And so it will dispose to all acts of obedience to God; for the servant that loves his master, and the subject that loves his sovereign, will be disposed to proper subjection and obedience. Love will dispose the Christian to behave toward God, as a child to a father; amid difficulties, to resort to him for help, and put all his trust in him; just as it is natural for us, in case of need or affliction, to go to one that we love for pity and help. It will lead us, too, to give credit to his word, and to put confidence in him; for we are not apt to suspect the veracity of those we have entire friendship for. It will dispose us to praise God for the mercies we receive from him, just as we are disposed to gratitude for any kindness we receive from our fellow men that we love. Love, again, will dispose our hearts to submission to the will of God; for we are more willing that the will of those we love should be done, than of others. We naturally desire that those we love should be suited, and that we should be agreeable to them; and true affection and love to God will dispose the heart to acknowledge God's right to govern, and that he is worthy to do it, and so will dispose to submission. Love to God will dispose us to walk humbly with him, for he that loves God will be disposed to acknowledge the vast distance between God and himself. It will be agreeable to such an one, to exalt God, and set him on high above all, and to lie low before him. A true Christian delights to have God exalted on his own abasement, because he loves him. He is willing to own that God is worthy of this, and it is with delight that he casts himself in the dust before the Most High, from his sincere love to him.

And walk in love, as Christ also hath loved us, and hath given himself for us an offering and a sacrifice to God for a sweetsmelling savour.
Ephesians 5:2

Children of God

In this the children of God are manifest, and the children of the devil: whosoever doeth not righteousness is not of God, neither he that loveth not his brother.

1 John 3:10

Christians are the children of God in a more honorable way than the angels themselves; for the angels are the sons of God by virtue of that relation which they have to God, as they are in themselves singly and separately. But Christians are the children of God, as partaking with Christ, the only begotten Son, in his sonship, whose sonship is immensely more honorable than that of the angels. And Christians, being the children of God, are honored of God as such. They are sometimes owned as such by the inward testimony of the Spirit of God. For, as it is found in the verse already cited from Romans, "the Spirit beareth witness with our spirits that we are the children of God." They are treated as such in the great value God puts upon them, for they are his jewels, those which he has set apart for himself; and he is tender of them as of the apple of his eye. He disregards wicked men in comparison of them. He will give kings for them and princes for their life. He is jealous for them. He is very angry with those that hurt them. If any offend them, it were better for them that a millstone were cast about their neck, and they were drowned in the depths of the sea. He loves them with a very great and wonderful love. He pities them as a father pities his children. He will protect them, and defend them and provide for them, as a father provides for his children. This honor have all they that fear and love God, and trust in the Lord Jesus Christ.

Evangelical Humiliation

The gracious soul, when convinced of sin after great declensions, and recovered out of them, is deeply humbled; for it is brought to the dust before God. There is an evangelical repentance. The heart is broken for sin. That sacrifice is offered to God, which David offered rather than burnt offerings after his great fall; "For thou desirest not sacrifice; else would I give it: thou delightest not in burnt offering. The sacrifices of God are a broken spirit: a broken and a contrite heart, O God, thou wilt not despise" (Psalm 51:16–17). They are brought as Job was, after he had sinned, in complaining of God's dealings with him, to abhor themselves (Job 42:6). And they are in a meeker frame, as the Christian Corinthians were, after they had greatly gone out of the way, and had been reproved by the apostle Paul; "For behold this selfsame thing, that ye sorrowed after a godly sort, what carefulness it wrought in you, yea, what clearing of yourselves, yea, what indignation, yea, what fear, yea, what vehement desire, yea, what zeal, yea, what revenge" (2 Corinthians 7:11). . . . When Christians are convinced of their sin after remarkable miscarriages and ill frames, they are commonly convinced of many of the same things of which they were convinced under their first humiliation, but to a greater degree than ever before. They are brought to a new conviction, and a greater conviction than ever before, of their own emptiness, and to be sensible what poor, feeble, helpless creatures, and what sinful, vile, utterly unworthy creatures, they are; how undeserving they are of any mercy, and how much they deserve God's wrath. And this conviction works by a gracious humbling of the soul. The grace of humility is greatly increased by it, and very commonly they are more poor in spirit and lowly of heart during all their future life. They see more what cause there is for them to lay their hands on their mouths, and to walk humbly with God, and lie low before him.

Humble yourselves therefore under the mighty hand of God, that he may exalt you in due time.
1 Peter 5:6

Praising God

I will give thee thanks in the great congregation: I will praise thee among much people.
Psalm 35:18

Let it be considered, that we all of us hope to spend an eternity with the saints in heaven, and in the same work of praising God. There is, it may be, not one of us but who hopes to be a saint in heaven, and there continually to sing praises to God and the Lamb. But how disagreeable will it be with such a hope, to live in the neglect of praising God now! We ought now to begin that work which we intend shall be the work of another world. For this life is given us on purpose that therein we might prepare for a future life. The present state is a state of probation and preparation, a state of preparation for the enjoyments and employment of another, future, and eternal state. And no one is ever admitted to those enjoyments and employments, but those who are prepared for them here. If ever we would go to heaven, we must be fitted for heaven in this world. We must here have our souls molded and fashioned for that work and that happiness. They must be formed for praise, and they must begin their work here. The beginnings of future things are in this world. The seed must be sown here. The foundation must be laid in this world. Here is laid the foundation of future misery, and of future happiness. If it be not begun here, it never will be begun. If our hearts be not in some measure tuned to praise in this world, we shall never do anything at the work hereafter. The light must dawn in this world, or the sun will never rise in the next. As we therefore all of us would be, and hope to be, of that blessed company which praise God in heaven, we should now inure ourselves to the work.

Fleeting Riches

It is from the nature of earthly riches that they are thus fleeting. They are things that are of a flying nature. They naturally incline to have wings and to fly away; as young birds, though for a season they remain in the nest, yet in time their wings will grow and they will be gone. And that for two reasons: both because they are in themselves corruptible things—they are liable to decay and corruption, and [to] be consumed and come utterly to an end—and also because their relation to us is dissoluble. The bonds by which we hold them are easily broken. Their being ours is not as inherent qualities are ours, [as] the endowments of the mind; but our possession of them is only dependent upon some external circumstances that are very changeable. The propriety of these things, even while they last, is easily by providence shifted from one to another.

A little that a righteous man hath is better than the riches of many wicked.
Psalm 37:16

Earthly riches
... are of a
flying nature.

Refreshing Winds

And when he had said this, he breathed on them, and saith unto them, Receive ye the Holy Ghost.
John 20:22

Christ puts strength and a principle of new life into the weary soul that comes to him. The sinner, before he comes to Christ, is as a sick man that is weakened and brought low, and whose nature is consumed by some strong distemper: he is full of pain, and so weak that he cannot walk nor stand. Therefore, Christ is compared to a physician. "But when Jesus heard that, he said unto them, They that be whole need not a physician, but they that are sick" (Matthew 9:12). When he comes and speaks the word, he puts a principle of life into him that was before as dead: he gives a principle of spiritual life and the beginning of eternal life; he invigorates the mind with a communication of his own life and strength, and renews the nature and creates it again, and makes the man to be a new creature, so that the fainting, sinking spirits are now revived, and this principle of spiritual life is a continual spring of refreshment, like a well of living water. "Whosoever drinketh of the water that I shall give him, shall never thirst; but the water that I shall give him shall be in him a well of water springing up into everlasting life." Christ gives his Spirit that calms the mind and is like a refreshing breeze of wind. He gives that strength whereby he lifts up the hands that hang down, and strengthens the feeble knees.

Imputed Righteousness

t is evident that the subject of justification is looked upon as destitute of any righteousness in himself, by that expression *it is counted, or imputed to him for righteousness.* The phrase, as the apostle uses it here and in the context, manifestly imports that God of his sovereign grace is pleased in his dealings with the sinner, so to regard one that has no righteousness, that the consequence shall be the same as if he had. This however may be from the respect it bears to something that is indeed righteous. It is plain that this is the force of the expression in the preceding verses. In the last verse but one, it is manifest, the apostle lays the stress of his argument for the free grace of God, from that text of the Old Testament about Abraham, on the word *counted* or *imputed.* This is the thing that he supposed God to show his grace in, viz., in his counting something for righteousness, in his consequential dealings with Abraham, which was no righteousness in itself. And in the next verse, which immediately precedes the text, "Now to him that worketh is the reward not reckoned of grace, but of debt," the word there translated *reckoned,* is the same that in the other verses is rendered *imputed* and *counted,* and it is as much as if the apostle had said, "As to him that works, there is no need of any gracious reckoning or counting it for righteousness, and causing the reward to follow as if it were a righteousness. For if he has works, he has that which is a righteousness in itself, to which the reward properly belongs." This is further evident by the words that follow, "Even as David also described the blessedness of the man, unto whom God imputeth righteousness without works" (Romans 4:6). What can here be meant by imputing righteousness without works, but imputing righteousness to him that has none of his own?

And therefore it was imputed to him for righteousness.
Romans 4:22

Infinitely Lovely

Honour and majesty
are before him:
strength and beauty
are in his sanctuary.
Psalm 96:6

God is a being infinitely lovely, because he hath infinite excellency and beauty. To have infinite excellency and beauty is the same thing as to have infinite loveliness. He is a being of infinite greatness, majesty, and glory; and therefore he is infinitely honorable. He is infinitely exalted above the greatest potentates of the earth, and highest angels in heaven; and therefore he is infinitely more honorable than they. His authority over us is infinite; and the ground of his right to our obedience is infinitely strong; for he is infinitely worthy to be obeyed himself, and we have an absolute, universal, and infinite dependence upon him.

His authority over us is infinite.

Following Christ

Christians are the followers of Christ, and they should follow him . . . We see from what we have heard, how great the labor and travail of Christ's soul was for others' salvation, and what earnest and strong cries to God accompanied his labors. Here he hath set us an example. Herein he hath set an example for ministers, who should as co-workers with Christ travail in birth with them till Christ be found in them; "My little children, of whom I travail in birth again until Christ be formed in you" (Galatians 4:19). They should be willing to spend and be spent for them. They should not only labor for them, and pray earnestly for them, but should, if occasion required, be ready to suffer for them, and to spend not only their strength, but their blood for them: "And I will very gladly spend and be spent for you; though the more abundantly I love you, the less I be loved" (2 Corinthians 12:15). Here is an example for parents, showing how they ought to labor and cry to God for the spiritual good of their children. You see how Christ labored and strove and cried to God for the salvation of his spiritual children; and will not you earnestly seek and cry to God for your natural children?

And he saith unto them, Follow me, and I will make you fishers of men.
Matthew 4:19

Christ Rejoices

For as a young man marrieth a virgin, so shall thy sons marry thee: and as the bridegroom rejoiceth over the bride, so shall thy God rejoice over thee.
Isaiah 62:5

Christ rejoices over his saints as the bridegroom over the bride at all times. But there are some seasons wherein he does so more especially. Such a season is the time of the soul's conversion. When the good shepherd finds his lost sheep, then he brings it home rejoicing and calls together his friends and neighbors, saying, "Rejoice with me." The day of a sinner's conversion is the day of Christ's espousals, and so is eminently the day of his rejoicing: "Go forth, O ye daughters of Zion, and behold king Solomon with the crown wherewith his mother crowned him in the day of his espousals, and in the day of the gladness of his heart" (Canticles 3:11). And it is oftentimes remarkably the day of the saints' rejoicing in Christ. For then God turns again the captivity of his elect people and, as it were, fills their mouth with laughter and their tongue with singing; as in Psalm 126 at the beginning. We read of the jailer that, when he was converted, he "rejoiced, believing in God with all his house," Acts 16:34. There are other seasons of special communion of the saints with Christ wherein Christ does in a special manner rejoice over his saints, and as their bridegroom brings them into his chambers, that they also may be glad and rejoice in him (Canticles 1:4).

Many Mansions

There are many mansions [in heaven]. The disciples seemed very sorrowful at the news of Christ's going away, but Christ comforts them with that, that in his Father's house where he was going there was not only room for him, but room for them too; there were many mansions. There was not only a mansion there for him, but there were mansions enough for them all. There was room enough in heaven for them. When the disciples perceived that Christ was going away, they manifested a great desire to go with him, and particularly Peter. Peter in the latter part of the foregoing chapter (John 13:36–38) asked him whither he went to that end that he might follow him. Christ told him that whither he went he could not follow him now, but that he should follow him afterwards. But Peter, not content with Christ, seemed to have a great mind to follow him now. "Lord," says he, "why cannot I follow thee now?" So that the disciples had a great mind still to be with Christ, and Christ in the words of the text intimates that they shall be with him. Christ signifies to them that he was going home to his Father's house, and he encourages them that they shall be with him there in due time, in that there were many mansions there. There was a mansion provided not only for him, but for them all (for Judas was not then present), and not only for them, but for all that should ever believe in him to the end of the world; and though he went before, he only went to prepare a place for them that should follow.

In my Father's house are many mansions: if it were not so, I would have told you. I go to prepare a place for you.
John 14:2

Devils Fear and Tremble

*Thou believest that
there is one God; thou
doest well: the devils
also believe, and
tremble.*

James 2:19

*T*he devils know God's almighty *power*. They saw a great manifestation of it when they saw God lay the foundation of the earth, etc., and were much affected with it. They have seen innumerable other great demonstrations of his power, as in the universal deluge, the destruction of Sodom, the wonders in Egypt, at the Red Sea, and in the wilderness, causing the sun to stand still in Joshua's time, and many others. And they had a very affecting manifestation of God's mighty power on themselves in casting all their hosts down from heaven into hell. And have continual affecting experience of it, in God's reserving them in strong chains of darkness, and in the strong pains they feel. They will hereafter have far more affecting experience of it, when they shall be punished from the glory of God's power, with that mighty destruction in expectation of which they now tremble. So the devils have a great knowledge of the *wisdom* of God. They have had unspeakably more opportunity and occasion to observe it in the work of creation, and also in the works of providence, than any mortal man has ever had. And have been themselves the subjects of innumerable affecting manifestations of it, in God's disappointing and confounding them in their most subtle devices, in so wonderful and amazing a manner. So they see and find the infinite purity and *holiness* of the divine nature, in the most affecting manner, as this appears in his infinite hatred of sin, in what they feel of the dreadful effects of that hatred. They know already by what they suffer, and will know hereafter to a greater degree, and far more affecting manner, that such is the opposition of God's nature to sin, that is like a consuming fire, which burns with infinite vehemence against it. They also will see the holiness of God, as exercised in his love to righteousness and holiness, in the glory of Christ and his church, which also will be very affecting to devils and wicked men.

The Fight of Faith

here are many things that do greatly oppose the grace which is in the heart of the Christian. This holy principle has innumerable enemies watching and warring against it. The child of God is encompassed with enemies on every side. He is a pilgrim and stranger passing through an enemy's country, and exposed to attack at any and every moment. There are thousands of devils, artful, intelligent, active, mighty, and implacable, that are bitter enemies to the grace that is in the heart of the Christian, and do all that lies in their power against it. And the world is an enemy to this grace, because it abounds with persons and things that make opposition to it, and with various forms of allurement and temptation, to win or drive us from the path of duty. And the Christian has not only many enemies without, but multitudes within his own breast, that he carries about with him, and from which he cannot get free. Evil thoughts and sinful inclinations cling to him; and many corruptions that still hold their footing in his heart are the worst enemies that grace has, and have the greatest advantage of any in their warfare against it. And these enemies are not only many, but exceeding strong and powerful, and very bitter in their animosity, implacable, irreconcilable, mortal enemies, seeking nothing short of the utter ruin and overthrow of grace. And they are unwearied in their opposition, so that the Christian, while he remains in this world, is represented as being in a state of warfare, and his business is that of the soldier, insomuch that he is often spoken of as a soldier of the cross, and as one whose great duty it is to fight manfully the good fight of faith.

Fight the good fight of faith, lay hold on eternal life, whereunto thou art also called, and hast professed a good profession before many witnesses.

1 Timothy 6:12

Hearty Affections

That they should seek the Lord, if haply they might feel after him, and find him, though he be not far from every one of us.
Acts 17:27

The business of *religion* is from time to time compared to those *exercises*, wherein men are wont to have their hearts and strength greatly exercised and engaged, such as running, wrestling, or agonizing for a great prize or crown, and fighting with strong enemies that seek our lives, and warring as those that by violence take a city or kingdom. And though true grace has various degrees, and there are some that are but babes in Christ, in whom the exercise of the inclination and will, towards divine and heavenly things, is comparatively weak; yet everyone that has the power of godliness in his heart, has his inclinations and heart exercised towards God and divine things, with such strength and vigor that these holy exercises do prevail in him above all carnal or natural affections, and are effectual to overcome them. For every true disciple of Christ "loves him above father or mother, wife and children, brethren and sisters, houses and lands: yea, his own life." From hence it follows, that wherever true religion is, there are vigorous exercises of the inclination and will towards divine objects. But by what was said before, the vigorous, lively, and sensible exercises of the will are no other than the *affections* of the soul.

Common and Saving Graces

uch phrases as *common grace*, and *special* or *saving grace*, may be understood as signifying either diverse kinds of influence of God's Spirit on the hearts of men, or diverse fruits and effects of that influence. The Spirit of God is supposed sometimes to have some influence upon the minds of men that are not true Christians, and [it is supposed] that those dispositions, frames, and exercises of their minds that are of a good tendency, but are common to them with the saints, are in some respect owing to some influence or assistance of God's Spirit. But as there are some things in the hearts of true Christians that are peculiar to them, and that are more excellent than anything that is to be found in others, so it is supposed that there is an operation of the Spirit of God different, and that the value which distinguishes them is owing to a higher influence and assistance than the virtues of others. So that sometimes the phrase *common grace* is used to signify that kind of action or influence of the Spirit of God, to which are owing those religious or moral attainments that are common to both saints and sinners, and so signifies as much as common assistance; and sometimes those moral or religious attainments themselves that are the fruits of this assistance, are intended. So likewise the phrase *special* or *saving grace* is sometimes used to signify that peculiar kind or degree of operation or influence of God's Spirit, whence saving actions and attainments do arise in the godly, or, which is the same thing, special and saving assistance; or else to signify that distinguishing saving virtue itself, which is the fruit of this assistance. These phrases are more frequently understood in the latter sense, viz., not for common and special assistance, but for common and special, or saving, virtue.

That ye may be the children of your Father which is in heaven: for he maketh his sun to rise on the evil and on the good, and sendeth rain on the just and on the unjust.

Matthew 5:45

The Reward of Happiness

Happy art thou, O Is-rael: who is like unto thee, O people saved by the LORD, the shield of thy help, and who is the sword of thy excellency! And thine enemies shall be found liars unto thee; and thou shalt tread upon their high places.
Deuteronomy
33:29

ow is it said that our happiness is the reward of holiness and good works, and yet that we are made happy wholly and solely for the sake of Christ? I answer, it is not solely by Christ that we have holiness and good works given us, but it is only by him that our holiness and good works are capable of a reward. He purchased holiness for us, which is indeed not different from happiness; and he purchased that they should be capable of a reward, and should be rewarded, yea that their good works should be worthy of a reward. So that properly, now, the good works of saints are worthy of being rewarded; the saints are worthy to walk in white (Revelation 3:4).

He purchased holiness for us, which is indeed not different from happiness.

Knowing Heaven

abor to be much acquainted with heaven. If you are not acquainted with it, you will not be likely to spend your life as a journey thither. You will not be sensible of its worth, nor will you long for it. Unless you are much conversant in your mind with a better good, it will be exceeding difficult to you to have your hearts loose from these things, to use them only in subordination to something else, and be ready to part with them for the sake of that better good. Labor therefore to obtain a realizing sense of a heavenly world, to get a firm belief of its reality, and to be very much conversant with it in your thoughts.

Seek heaven only by Jesus Christ. Christ tells us that he is the way, and the truth, and the life (John 14:6). He tells us that he is the door of the sheep, "I am the door: by me if any man enter in, he shall be saved, and go in and out, and find pasture" (John 10:9). If we therefore would improve our lives as a journey towards heaven, we must seek it by him and not by our own righteousness, as expecting to obtain it only for his sake: looking to him and having our dependence on him, who has procured it for us by his merit. And expect that strength to walk in holiness, the way that leads to heaven, only from him.

Jesus saith unto him, I am the way, the truth, and the life: no man cometh unto the Father, but by me.
John 14:6

Honoring God

In this was manifested the love of God toward us, because that God sent his only begotten Son into the world, that we might live through him.
1 John 4:9

If we live in any way of sin, we live in a way whereby God is *dishonored.* But the honor of God ought to be supremely regarded by all. If everyone would make it his great care in all things to obey God, to live justly and holily, to walk in everything according to Christian rules, and would maintain a strict, watchful, and scrutinous eye over himself, to see if there were no wicked way in him, would give diligence to amend whatsoever is amiss, would avoid every unholy, unchristian, and sinful way, and if the practice of all were universally as becomes Christians, how greatly would this be to the glory of God, and of Jesus Christ! How greatly would it be to the credit and honor of religion! How would it tend to excite a high esteem of religion in spectators, and to recommend a holy life! How would it stop the mouths of objectors and opposers! How beautiful and amiable would religion then appear, when exemplified in the lives of Christians, not maimed and mutilated, but whole and entire, as it were in its true shape, having all its parts and its proper beauty! Religion would then appear to be an amiable thing indeed.

Reflected Glory

ence we learn the great privilege we have, who possess such advantages to come to the blessed-ness of seeing God. We have the true God re-vealed to us in the Word of God, who is the Being in the sight of whom this happiness is to be en-joyed. We have the glorious attributes and perfections of God declared to us. The glory of God in the face of Jesus Christ is discovered in the gospel which we enjoy, his beauties and glories are there as it were pointed forth by God's own hand to our view, so that we have those means which God hath provided for our obtaining those begin-nings of this sight of him which the saints have in this world, in that spiritual knowledge which they have of God, which is absolutely necessary in order to our having it perfectly in another world.

The knowledge which believers have of God and his glory, as appearing in the face of Christ, is the imper-fect beginning of this heavenly sight, it is an earnest of it, it is the dawning of the heavenly light. And this beginning must evermore precede, or a perfect vision of God in heaven cannot be obtained. And all those that have this beginning shall obtain that perfection also. Great there-fore is our privilege, that we have the means of this spiri-tual knowledge. We may in this world see God as in a glass darkly, in order to our seeing him hereafter face to face. And surely our privilege is very great, that he has given us that glass from whence God's glory is reflected.

And ye said, Behold, the LORD our God hath shewed us his glory and his great-ness, and we have heard his voice out of the midst of the fire: we have seen this day that God doth talk with man, and he liveth.
Deuteronomy 5:24

Keeping Promises

*I will pay my vows
unto the LORD now in
the presence of all his
people.*
Psalm 116:18

Ordinarily when men promise anything to their neighbor, or enter into engagements by undertaking any business with which their neighbor entrust them, their engagements invest their neighbor with a right to that which is engaged; so that if they withhold it, they usurp that which belongs to their neighbor. So, when men break their promises, because they find them to be inconvenient, and they cannot fulfill them without difficulty and trouble; or merely because they have altered their minds since they promised. They think they have not consulted their own interest in the promise which they have made, and that if they had considered the matter as much before they promised as they have since, they should not have promised. Therefore they take the liberty to set their own promises aside. Besides, sometimes persons violate this command, by neglecting to fulfill their engagements, through a careless, negligent spirit.

118

Sense the World's Vanity

Labor to get a sense of the vanity of this world, on account of the little satisfaction that is to be enjoyed here, its short continuance, and unserviceableness when we most stand in need of help, viz., on a deathbed. All men, that live any considerable time in the world, might see enough to convince them of its vanity, if they would but consider. Be persuaded therefore to exercise consideration when you see and hear, from time to time, of the death of others. Labor to turn your thoughts this way; see the vanity of the world in such a glass.

All the labour of man is for his mouth, and yet the appetite is not filled.
Ecclesiastes 6:7

> Labor to get a sense of the vanity of this world.

Desiring God

Whom have I in heaven but thee? And there is none upon earth that I desire beside thee.

Psalm 73:25

The godly prefer God before anything else that actually is in heaven. Every godly man has his heart in heaven; his affections are mainly set on what is to be had there. Heaven is his chosen country and inheritance. He has respect to heaven, as a traveler, who is in a distant land, has to his own country. The traveler can content himself to be in a strange land for a while, but his own native land is preferred by him to all others; "These all died in faith, not having received the promises, but . . . were persuaded of them, and embraced them, and confessed that they were strangers and pilgrims on the earth. For they that say such things declare plainly that they seek a country. And truly, if they had been mindful of that country from whence they came out, they might have had opportunity to have returned. But now they desire a better country, that is, an heavenly" (Hebrews 11:13–16). The respect which a godly person hath to heaven may be compared to the respect which a child, when he is abroad, has to his father's house. He can be contented abroad for a little while; but the place to which he desires to return, and in which to dwell, is his own home. Heaven is the true saint's Father's house: "In my Father's house are many mansions" (John 14:2); "I ascend unto my Father and your Father" (John 20:17).

Flee Temptation

I t was the manner among the Israelites to build their houses with flat roofs, so that persons might walk on the tops of their houses. And therefore God took care to make it a law among them, that every man should have battlements upon the edges of their roofs; lest any person should fall off and be killed: "When thou buildest a new house, then thou shalt make a battlement for thy roof, that thou bring not blood upon thine house, if any man fall from thence" (Deuteronomy 22:8). And certainly we ought to take the like care that we do not fall into sin; which carries in it eternal death. We should, as it were, fix a battlement, a guard, to keep us from the edge of the precipice. Much more ought we to take care, that we do not go upon a roof that is not only without battlements, but when it is steep, and we shall naturally incline to fall. Men's lusts are like strong enemies, endeavoring to draw them into sin. If a man stood upon a dangerous precipice, and had enemies about him, pulling and drawing him, endeavoring to throw him down; would he, in such a case, choose or dare to stand near the edge? Would he look upon himself safe, close on the brink? Would he not endeavor, for his own safety, to keep at a distance?

But every man is tempted, when he is drawn away of his own lust, and enticed.
James 1:14

Pleasantness of Religion

*The lines are fallen
unto me in pleasant
places; yea, I have a
goodly heritage.*
Psalm 16:6

Religion is not a sour thing that is contrived for nothing but to cross our inclinations and to cut us short of the delights of life. No, it is quite of another nature: it abridges us of no pleasures, but only such as of their own nature (however pleasing for the present) do lay a foundation for woe and misery. They are in their own nature a poison, that though sweet in the mouth, do really as it were destroy the constitution of the soul; "At the last it biteth like a serpent, and stingeth like an adder" (Proverbs 23:32). But as for those delights that better the soul and have a tendency to the future, as well as the present, well-being of it, they are allowed fully and are promoted by religion; yea, true religion is the only source from whence they flow.

How much happier therefore is the man that chooses a holy and a spiritual religious life than he that chooses a carnal, sensual life. Sensual men may be ready to think they should be happy men if there were nothing to restrain their enjoyment of their [appetites], if they might at all time satisfy their appetites, and have their full swing at their pleasures with impunity and without any danger of any succeeding inconvenience. But if it were so, they would be but miserable men in comparison of the godly man who enjoys the pleasures of acquaintance with the glorious God and his Son Jesus Christ, and a communion of the holy and blessed Spirit of God and Christ, and a true peace of conscience and inward testimonies of the favor and acceptance of God and [Christ], and have liberty without restraint to indulge themselves in the enjoyment of those pleasures. "[Wisdom's] ways are ways of pleasantness, and all her paths are peace" (Proverbs 3:17).

The New Birth

When people are born again, and circumcised in heart, when they repent, and are converted, and spiritually raised from the dead, it is the same change which is meant when the Scripture speaks of making the heart and spirit new, or giving a new heart and spirit. It is almost needless to observe, how evidently this is spoken of as necessary to salvation, and as the change in which are attained the habits of true virtue and holiness, and the character of a true saint; as has been observed of regeneration, conversion, and how apparent it is, that the change is the same. Thus repentance, the change of the mind, is the same as being changed to a new mind, or a new heart and spirit. Conversion is the turning of the heart; which is the same thing as changing it so that there shall be another heart, or a new heart, or a new spirit. To be born again, is to be born anew; which implies a becoming new, and is represented as becoming newborn babes. But none supposes it is the body that is immediately and properly new, but the mind, heart, or spirit. And so a spiritual resurrection is the resurrection of the spirit, or rising to begin a new existence and life, as to the mind, heart, or spirit. Thus all these phrases imply having a new heart, and being renewed in the spirit, according to their plain signification.

And I will give them one heart, and I will put a new spirit within you; and I will take the stony heart out of their flesh, and will give them an heart of flesh.
Ezekiel 11:19

The Face of God

And he said, My presence shall go with thee, and I will give thee rest.
Exodus 33:14

Christ is called the face of God. The word in the original signifies face, looks, form or appearance. Now what can be so properly and fitly called so with respect to God as God's own perfect idea of Himself whereby He has every moment a view of His own essence: this idea is that "face of God" which God sees as a man sees his own face in a looking glass. It is of such form or appearance whereby God eternally appears to Himself. The root that the original word comes from signifies to look upon or behold: now what is that which God looks upon or beholds in so eminent a manner as He doth on His own idea or that perfect image of Himself which He has in view. This is what is eminently in God's presence and is therefore called the angel of God's presence or face (Isaiah 63:9). But that the Son of God is God's own eternal and perfect idea is a thing we have yet much more expressly revealed in God's Word. First, in that Christ is called "the wisdom of God." If we are taught in the Scripture that Christ is the same with God's wisdom or knowledge, then it teaches us that He is the same with God's perfect and eternal idea. They are the same as we have already observed and I suppose none will deny. But Christ is said to be the wisdom of God (1 Corinthians 1:24, Luke 11:49, compare with Matthew 23:34); and how much Christ speaks in Proverbs under the name of Wisdom especially in the 8th chapter.

To the Sincere

Why should we suppose that God would make any promises of spiritual and eternal blessings to that which has no goodness in it? Why should he promise his grace to a seeking of it that is not right, or to those that don't truly seek it? Why should he promise that they shall obtain conversion that don't do any right thing, or use any proper means in order to obtain it? For the proper means of obtaining grace is seeking of it truly, with a love and appetite to it, and desire of it, and sense of its excellency and worthiness, and seeking of it of God through Christ; and to such as seek it thus, God has faithfully promised that he will bestow it.

Hearken to me, ye that follow after righteousness, ye that seek the LORD: look unto the rock whence ye are hewn, and to the hole of the pit whence ye are digged.
Isaiah 51:1

For the proper means of obtaining grace is seeking of it truly.

True Kindred

For whosoever shall do
the will of my Father
which is in heaven,
the same is my
brother, and sister,
and mother.
Matthew 12:50

The word "gospel," "glad tidings," seems to be to signify a discovery of salvation after fear and distress, and sense of misery and despair of helping ourselves. In Matthew 18:24ff, the servant that owed ten thousand talents; first his master held him to his debt, and pronounced sentence of the condemnation against him, and ordered him to be sold, and his wife and children, and so humbled him. He fell down and worshipped him, and acknowledged the justice of the debt. "Have patience with me, and I will pay thee all." And then his lord forgave and comforted him. Another thing in Scripture that seems to favor the need of such conviction before conversion is the frequent comparisons made between the church's spiritually bringing forth Christ and a woman in travail, in pain to be delivered. John 16:21, "A woman when she is in travail hath sorrow, because her hour is come: but as soon as she is delivered of the child, she remembreth no more the anguish, for joy that a man is born into the world;" and to the same purpose, Revelation 12:2. Now the conversion of a sinner is also represented by the same thing: it is a bringing forth Christ in the heart. Therefore Christ says that everyone that believes in him is his mother.

Everlasting Love

God's love to his saints has had being from all eternity. God often in his Word is setting forth how great his love is to his saints, how dear they are to him. But this love of his to them he had before ever they had any being. There it was in the heart of God of old. In former ages, thousands of years ago, in the ages before the flood, and when God created the world, there was that love; yea, and before the foundation of the world. And if we look back ever so far, there is no beginning of it. This love that God has to his saints that is thus everlasting, is not only general, as God did from all eternity love saints, i.e., loved their character; the qualifications of saints were what he naturally delighted in. But his love to the particular persons is from eternity. He did as it were know them by name, and set his love in such particular saints. And therefore God is said to have foreknown his saints, i.e., he from all eternity saw them particularly, and knew them as his own.

He brought me to the banqueting house, and his banner over me was love.
Song of Solomon 2:4

> God's love to his saints has had being from all eternity.

Signs from Heaven

Would it be sufficient if you could hear God speak from heaven? How was it in Moses' time, when they heard God speak out of the midst of the fire, and heard the voice of words exceeding loud and full of majesty, so that they exceedingly trembled; when they saw Mount Sinai all covered with smoke and shaking exceedingly? How did they behave themselves? Did they all turn from their sins, and after that walk in the ways of God? It is true, they were very much affected at first, while it was a new and strange thing to them; but how hard-hearted and rebellious were they soon after! They did not scruple to rebel against this same great and glorious God. Yea, they made a golden calf while Moses was in the mount conversing with God, just after they had seen those dreadful appearances of divine majesty. Thus they rebelled against the Lord, although they had seen so many miracles and wonders in Egypt at the Red Sea, and in the wilderness; although they continually saw the pillar of cloud and of fire going before them, were continually fed in a miraculous manner with manna, and in the same miraculous manner made to drink water out of the rock.

The Serpent's Snare

n the manner in which birds and squirrels that are charmed by serpents go into their mouths and are destroyed by them, is a lively representation of the manner in which sinners under the gospel are very often charmed and destroyed by the devil. The animal that is charmed by the serpent seems to be in great exercise and fear, screams and makes ado, but yet don't flee away. It comes nearer to the serpent, and then seems to have its distress increased and goes a little back again, but then comes still nearer than ever, and then appears as if greatly affrighted and runs or flies back again a little way, but yet don't flee quite away, and soon comes a little nearer and a little nearer with seeming fear and distress that drives them a little back between whiles, until at length they come so near that the serpent can lay hold of them, and so they become their prey.

Now the serpent was more subtil than any beast of the field which the LORD God had made.
Genesis 3:1

Just thus, oftentimes sinners under the gospel are bewitched by their lusts. They have considerable fears of destruction and remorse of conscience that makes them hang back, and they have a great deal of exercise between while, and some partial reformations, but yet they don't flee away. They won't wholly forsake their beloved lusts, but return to them again; and so whatever warnings they have, and whatever checks of conscience that may exercise them and make them go back a little and stand off for a while, yet they will keep their beloved sin in sight, and won't utterly break off from it and forsake it, but will return to it again and again, and go a little further and a little further, until Satan remedilessly makes a prey of them. But if anyone comes and kills the serpent, the animal immediately escapes. So the way in which poor souls are delivered from the snare of the devil is by Christ's coming and bruising the serpent's head.

New Nature

And have put on the new man, which is re-newed in knowledge after the image of him that created him.
Colossians 3:10

The new nature that is in the saints is of God, and is a divine nature, and therefore must be an enemy to every degree of that which is against God. Every saint has a new nature in him that is quite diverse from that old nature, the nature he was born with, and is above it; and differs from it, as that which is heavenly differs from that which is earthly; or as that which is angelical does from that which is brutish, or as that which is divine does from that which is devilish.

This new nature is from God, and is something of God; and therefore it tends to God again, and is contented with nothing short of God, and a perfect conformity to him. As long as there is any separation or alienation remaining, it will not be easy; because as long as it is thus, the soul is kept off in some measure from God, whence its new nature is.

This new nature is from God.

A Tender Warning

Some will backslide. They will be unsteady. If now they seem to be pretty much engaged, it will not hold. Times will probably alter by and by, and they having not obtained grace, there will be many temptations to backsliding, with which they will comply. The hearts of men are very unsteady. They are not to be trusted. Men are very short-winded. They cannot tell how to have patience to wait upon God. They are soon discouraged. Some that are now under convictions may lose them. Perhaps they will not leave off seeking salvation at once. But they will come to it by degrees. After a while, they will begin to hearken to excuses, not to be quite so constant in duty. They will begin to think that they need not be quite so strict. They will say to themselves they see no hurt in such and such things. They see into but they may practice them without any great guilt. Thus giving way to temptations, and hearkening to excuses, they will by degrees lose their convictions, and become secure in sin.

And my people are bent to backsliding from me: though they called them to the most High, none at all would exalt him.
Hosea 11:7

Men are very short-winded.

Atheism

There is a spirit of atheism prevailing in the hearts of men; a strange disposition to doubt of the very being of God, and of another world, and of everything which cannot be seen with the bodily eyes. "The fool hath said in his heart, There is no God" (Psalm 14:1). They do not realize that God sees them when they commit sin, and will call them to an account for it. And therefore, if they can hide sin from the eyes of men, they are not concerned, but are bold to commit it. "Yet they say, The Lord shall not see, neither shall the God of Jacob regard it. Understand, ye brutish among the people; and ye fools, when will ye be wise? He that planted the ear, shall he not hear? he that formed the eye, shall he not see" (Psalm 94:7–9)? "They say, How doth God know? and is there knowledge in the Most High" (Psalm 73:11)? So unbelieving are they of future things, of heaven and hell, and will commonly run the venture of damnation sooner than be convinced. They are stupidly senseless to the importance of eternal things. How hard to make them believe, and to give them a real conviction, that to be happy to all eternity is better than all other good; and to be miserable forever under the wrath of God, is worse than all other evil. Men show themselves senseless enough in temporal things; but in spiritual things far more so. "Ye hypocrites, ye can discern the face of the sky and of the earth; but how is it that ye do not discern this time" (Luke 12:56)? They are very subtle in evil designs, but senseless in those things which most concern them. "They are wise to do evil, but to do good they have no knowledge" (Jeremiah 4:22). Wicked men show themselves more foolish and senseless of what is best for them, than the very brutes. "The ox knoweth his owner, and the ass his master's crib; but Israel doth not know, my people doth not consider" (Isaiah 1:3).

The Beatitudes

*he discourse of Christ on the mount seems principally leveled against the false notions, and carnal prejudices, that were at that day embraced by the nation of the Jews. And those benedictions, which we have in the beginning of his sermon, were sayings that were mere paradoxes to them, wholly contrary to the notions which they had received. That he, who was poor in spirit, was blessed, was a doctrine contrary to the received opinion of the world, and especially of that nation, who was exceedingly ambitious of the praise of men, and highly conceited of their own righteousness. And that he was a blessed and happy man, who mourned for sin, and lived mortified to the pleasures and vanities of the world, was contrary to their notions, who placed their highest happiness in worldly and carnal things. So also that they who were meek were blessed, was another doctrine very contrary to their notions, who were a very haughty, proud nation, and very revengeful, and maintained the lawfulness of private revenge, as may be seen in the 38th verse. Equally strange to them was the declaration that they who hungered and thirsted after righteousness were happy, for they placed their happiness, not in possessing a high degree of righteousness, but in having a great share of worldly good. They were wont to labor for the meat that perishes. They had no notion of any such thing as spiritual riches, or of happiness in satisfying a spiritual appetite. The Jews were dreadfully in the dark at that day about spiritual things. The happiness which they expected by the Messiah was a temporal and carnal, and not a spiritual, happiness. Christ also tells them that they were blessed who were merciful and who were peacemakers, which was also a doctrine that the Jews especially stood in need of at that day, for they were generally of a cruel, unmerciful, persecuting spirit.

Blessed are the pure in heart.
Matthew 5:8

True Peace

I will both lay me down in peace, and sleep: for thou, LORD, only makest me dwell in safety.
Psalm 4:8

You that have hitherto spent your time in the pursuit of satisfaction in the profit and glory of the world, or in the pleasures and vanities of youth, have this day an offer of that excellent and everlasting peace and blessedness, which Christ has purchased with the price of his own blood. As long as you continue to reject those offers and invitations of Christ, and continue in a Christless condition, you never will enjoy any true peace or comfort, but will be like the prodigal, that in vain endeavored to be satisfied with the husks that the swine did eat. The wrath of God will abide upon, and misery will attend you, wherever you go, which you never will be able to escape. Christ gives peace to the most sinful and miserable that come to him. He heals the broken in heart and binds up their wounds. But it is impossible that they should have peace while they continue in their sins (Isaiah 57:19–21). There is no peace between God and them. For as they have the guilt of sin remaining in their souls, and are under its dominion, so God's indignation continually burns against them, and therefore there is reason why they should travail in pain all their days. While you continue in such a state, you live in a state of dreadful uncertainty what will become of you, and in continual danger. What reasonable peace can anyone enjoy in such a state as this? What though you clothe him in gorgeous apparel, or to set him on a throne, or at a prince's table, and feed him with the rarest dainties the earth affords? How miserable is the ease and cheerfulness that such have! What a poor kind of comfort and joy is it that such take in their wealth and pleasures for a moment, while they are the prisoners of divine justice, and wretched captives of the devil! They have none to befriend them, being without Christ, aliens from the commonwealth of Israel, strangers from the covenant of promise, having no hope, and without God in the world!

Spiritual Thirst

By the fall, the spiritual appetite was lost, and so the animal appetites were left sole masters, and having no superior principle to restrain them. In regeneration, the spiritual appetites are again in some measure restored, and the sensual appetite is again restrained and kept within bounds by it. And it is our duty, with all possible care, watchfulness, and resolution, to restrain them and to see that they don't go beyond their due bounds.

Ho, every one that thirsteth, come ye to the waters, and he that hath no money; come ye, buy, and eat; yea, come, buy wine and milk without money and without price.
Isaiah 55:1

And this is one main part of the work that a Christian has to do in this militant state: to mortify carnal affections, to subdue his animal appetite, to crucify the flesh with the affections and lusts, to keep under the body and bring it into subjection.

Herein chiefly consists the difficulty of a Christian's work. The animal appetites are very strong and impatient of any restraint. It is a bearing the cross daily and like cutting off of a right hand; and it looks with a frightful countenance to carnal men, and is what makes many afraid indeed to embrace Christianity and a holy life. However, there is something else in Christianity besides self-denial or restraining our inclination. There is a crown as well as a cross. And though we are so strictly required to restrain and keep within bounds our animal inclinations, yet God does not desire we should set any bounds to spiritual and gracious inclinations, which are the most excellent. He that is truly born again, as he has an animal appetite to meat and drink, so he hungers and thirsts after righteousness; it is his meat and his drink to do the will of his Father which is in heaven. He thirsts for God, for the living God, and sometimes his heart pants after God as the hart pants after the water brooks (Psalm 42:1). He has an appetite to Jesus Christ, who is the bread which came down from heaven. His soul lives upon Christ as his spiritual meat and drink.

God in the Midst

he people that have God amongst them, they have the fountain of all good in the midst of them. There is a full fountain, indeed an inexhaustible and infinite fountain, enough for the supply of everyone, under all their circumstances and necessities: whatever anyone wants, he may go to this fountain, and there he may have a supply. Such a people that have this God amongst them, may glory in him, and say, "The Lord is our shepherd, we shall not want," and may say, as in Habakkuk 3:17–18, "Although the fig tree shall not blossom, neither shall fruit be in the vines; the labour of the olive shall fail, and the fields shall yield no meat; the flock shall be cut off from the fold, and there shall be no herd in the stalls: yet I will rejoice in the LORD, I will joy in the God of my salvation."

**Such a people
that have this
God may glory
in him.**

Sacrifice All

Be directed to sacrifice everything to your soul's eternal interest. Let seeking this be so much your bent, and what you are so resolved in, that you will make everything give place to it. Let nothing stand before your resolution of seeking the kingdom of God. Whatever it be that you used to look upon as a convenience, or comfort, or ease, or thing desirable on any account, if it stands in the way of this great concern, let it be dismissed without hesitation; and if it be of that nature that it is likely always to be a hindrance, then wholly have done with it, and never entertain any expectation from it more. If in time past you have, for the sake of worldly gain, involved yourself in more care and business than you find to be consistent with your being so thorough in the business of religion as you ought to be, then get into some other way, though you suffer in your worldly interest by it. Or if you have heretofore been conversant with company that you have reason to think have been and will be a snare to you, and a hindrance to this great design in any wise, break off from their society, however it may expose you to reproach from your old companions, or let what will be the effect of it. Whatever it be that stands in the way of your most advantageously seeking salvation . . . offer up all such things together, as it were, in one sacrifice, to the interest of your soul. Let nothing stand in competition with this, but make everything to fall before it.

I beseech you therefore, brethren, by the mercies of God, that ye present your bodies a living sacrifice, holy, acceptable unto God, which is your reasonable service.
Romans 12:1

Seek the Kingdom

But seek ye first the kingdom of God, and his righteousness; and all these things shall be added unto you.
Matthew 6:33

We should "seek first the kingdom of God" (Matthew 6:33). We ought above all things to desire a heavenly happiness; to be with God and dwell with Jesus Christ. Though surrounded with outward enjoyments, and settled in families with desirable friends and relations; though we have companions whose society is delightful, and children in whom we see many promising qualifications; though we live by good neighbors, and are generally beloved where known; we ought not to take our rest in these things as our portion. We should be so far from resting in them that we should desire to leave them all, in God's due time. We ought to possess, enjoy and use them, with no other view but readily to quit them, whenever we are called to it, and to change them willingly and cheerfully for heaven.

We ought above all things to desire a heavenly happiness.

Give Bountifully

t is the duty of the people of God to give *bountifully* [to the poor]. It is commanded once and again in the text, "Thou shalt open thine hand wide unto thy poor brother." Merely to give something is not sufficient. It answers not the rule, nor comes up to the holy command of God. But we must open our hand wide. What we give, considering our neighbor's wants, and our ability, should be such as may be called a liberal gift. What is meant in the text by opening the hand wide, with respect to those that are able, is explained in Deuteronomy 15:8, "Thou shalt open thine hand wide unto him, and shalt surely lend him sufficient for his need, in that which he wanteth." By lending here, as is evident by the two following verses, and as we have just now shown, is not only meant lending to receive again; [for] the word lend in Scripture is sometimes used for giving; as in Luke 6:35, "Do good, and lend, hoping for nothing again."

I have shewed you all things, how that so labouring ye ought to support the weak, and to remember the words of the Lord Jesus, how he said, It is more blessed to give than to receive.
Acts 20:35

We must open our hand wide.

To the Uttermost

Wherefore he is able also to save them to the uttermost that come unto God by him, seeing he ever liveth to make intercession for them.
Hebrews 7:25

Christ has undertaken to save all such from what they fear, if they come to him. It is his professional business; the work in which he engaged before the foundation of the world. It is what he always had in his thoughts and intentions; he undertook from everlasting to be the refuge of those that are afraid of God's wrath. His wisdom is such, that he would never undertake a work for which he is not sufficient. If there were some in so dreadful a case that he was not able to defend them, or so guilty that it was not fit that he should save them, then he never would have undertaken for them. Those who are in trouble and distressing fear, if they come to Jesus Christ, have this to ease them of their fears, that Christ has promised them that he will protect them; that they come upon his invitation; that Christ has plighted his faith for their security if they will close with him; and that he is engaged by covenant to God the Father that he will save those afflicted and distressed souls that come to him.

He will save those afflicted and distressed souls that come to him.

Lion of the Tribe of Judah

hrist is called a Lion. Behold, the Lion of the tribe of Judah. He seems to be called the Lion of the tribe of Judah, in allusion to what Jacob said in his blessing of the tribe on his deathbed, who when he came to bless Judah, compares him to a lion, "Judah is a lion's whelp: from the prey, my son, thou art gone up: he stooped down, he couched as a lion, and as an old lion; who shall rouse him up?" (Genesis 49:9). And also to the standard of the camp of Judah in the wilderness, on which was displayed a lion, according to the ancient tradition of the Jews. It is much on account of the valiant acts of David that the tribe of Judah, of which David was, is in Jacob's prophetical blessing compared to a lion, but more especially with an eye to Jesus Christ, who also was of that tribe, and was descended of David, and is in our text called "the Root of David." Therefore Christ is here called "the Lion of the tribe of Judah."

And one of the elders saith unto me, Weep not: behold, the Lion of the tribe of Juda, the Root of David, hath prevailed to open the book, and to loose the seven seals thereof.
Revelation 5:5

Ruth's Resolution

*And Ruth said,
Intreat me not to leave
thee, or to return from
following after thee:
for whither thou goest,
I will go; and where
thou lodgest, I will
lodge: thy people shall
be my people, and thy
God my God.
Ruth 1:16*

would particularly observe that wherein the virtuousness of Ruth's resolution consists, viz., that it was for the sake of the God of Israel, and that she might be one of his people, that she was thus resolved to cleave to Naomi: "Thy people shall be my people, and thy God my God." It was for God's sake that she did thus, and therefore her so doing is afterwards spoken of as a virtuous behavior in her, "And Boaz answered and said unto her, It hath fully been shewed me, all that thou hast done unto thy mother in law since the death of thine husband: and how thou has left thy father and thy mother, and the land of thy nativity, and art come unto a people which thou knewest not heretofore. The LORD recompense thy work, and a full reward be given thee of the LORD God of Israel, under whose wings thou art come to trust" (Ruth 2:11–12). She left her father and mother, and the land of her nativity, to come and trust under the shadow of God's wings, and she had indeed a full reward given her, as Boaz wished. For besides immediate spiritual blessings to her own soul, and eternal rewards in another world, she was rewarded with plentiful and prosperous outward circumstances in the family of Boaz. And God raised up David and Solomon of her seed, and established the crown of Israel (the people that she chose before her own people) in her posterity; and, which is much more, of her seed he raised up Jesus Christ, in whom all the families of the earth are blessed.

Above Angels

The wisdom appearing in the way of salvation by Jesus Christ is far above the wisdom of the angels. For here it is mentioned as one end of God in revealing the contrivance of our salvation, that the angels thereby might see and know how great and manifold the wisdom of God is, to hold forth the divine wisdom to the angels' view and admiration. But why is it so, if this wisdom be not higher than their own wisdom? It never would have been mentioned as one end of revealing the contrivance of redemption, that the angels might see how manifold God's wisdom is, if all the wisdom to be seen in it was no greater than their own. It is mentioned as a wisdom such as they had never seen before, not in God, much less in themselves. That *now* might be known how manifold the wisdom of God is, now, four thousand years since the creation. In all that time the angels had always beheld the face of God, and had been studying God's works of creation. Yet they never, till that day, had seen anything like that; never knew how manifold God's wisdom is, as now they knew it by the church.

For unto which of the angels said he at any time, Thou art my Son, this day have I begotten thee? And again, I will be to him a Father, and he shall be to me a Son?

Hebrews 1:5

Song of Songs

The Song of Songs,
which is Solomon's.
Song of Solomon
1:1

he name by which Solomon calls this song con-
firms in me that it is more than an ordinary love
song, and that it was designed for a divine song,
and of divine authority; for we read, 1 Kings 4:32, that
Solomon's "songs were a thousand and five." This he calls
the "song of songs" (Song of Solomon 1:1), that is, the
most excellent of all his songs, which it seems very probable to me to be upon that account, because it was a song
of the most excellent subject, treating of the love, union,
and communion between Christ and his spouse, of which
marriage, and conjugal love was but a shadow. These are
the most excellent lovers, and their love the most excellent love.

Mr. Matthew Henry, in the introduction to his expo-
sition of this book, says, it appears that this book was
"taken in a spiritual sense by the Jewish church, for whose
use it was first composed, as appears by the Chaldee para-
phrase, and the most ancient Jewish expositors." In the
same place he says, "In our belief, both of the church of
the Jews, to whom were committed the oracles of God,
and who never made any doubt of the authority of this
book, and of the Christian church, which happily suc-
ceeds them in that trust and honor."

Not for the World

We are not made for an earthly happiness. God certainly never made man for that sort of happiness which he cannot hold; he was never made for that happiness which, almost as soon as enjoyed, flies from us and leaves us disappointed. If this was the highest happiness we are made for, that happiness that would be unavoidably accompanied with those disappointments and frustrations that do more than counterbalance it, if we were made for this happiness, it would be our greatest wisdom to set our hearts upon it, for it is our wisdom to set our hearts upon what we are made for; but as the case now stands, the more we set our hearts on those things, the more trouble and vexation, and the less satisfaction, do we find in them.

This, the wise heathen plainly saw, and for that reason taught it as a great part of the wisdom of man, to abstract his thoughts and affections from all earthly things. Though they had no other knowledge of a future happiness than what naked reason taught them, even they discovered so much unsatisfactoriness and vexation of these enjoyments, that many of them, of their own choice, sequestered themselves from these things, and denied themselves even the common comforts of life.

There is treasure to be desired and oil in the dwelling of the wise; but a foolish man spendeth it up.
Proverbs 21:20

Dedication to God

The sacrifices of God
are a broken spirit: a
broken and a contrite
heart, O God, thou
wilt not despise.

Psalm 51:17

now it behooves us all to know that God never looks upon us as his, to make us happy, till we have given ourselves entirely to him and look upon ourselves as his, to obey his laws and in all things submit to his will. This giving ourselves to God is the very thing that alone gives us a right to the privilege of the sons of God, and makes us partakers of the benefits purchased by his dear and only Son; for until we have given ourselves to God, and have offered ourselves as a sacrifice to him, we belong to the devil and he claims a right to us. For we have all in effect given ourselves to him by sin, and except we can show another deed whereby we have given ourselves to God, whereby that is disannulled, when we come to die he will certainly stand ready at our deathbeds, and will lay hold of us as his own, as those that are his servants, that have sold and given themselves to him, and will violently hurry us away to hell, his own habitation.

Christ, the Light of the World

here is scarcely anything that is excellent, beautiful, pleasant, or profitable but what is used in the Scripture as an emblem for Christ. He is called a lion for his great power, victory, and glorious conquests. He is called a lamb for his great love, pity, and compassion; for that merciful, compassionate, condescending, lamblike disposition of his; for his humility, meekness, and great patience; and because he was slain like a lamb. He was brought as a lamb to the slaughter, so he opened not his mouth. He is called the bread of life and water of life, for the spiritual refreshment and nourishment he gives to the members, and yields that comfort to the soul that refreshes it as the fruit of the vine does the body. He is called life, for he is the life of the soul. He is called a rose and lily, and other such similitudes, because of his transcendent beauty and fragrancy. He is called the bright and morning star, and the sun of righteousness; and in our text, the light of the world, of which it is our business at present to speak.

I am the light of the world.
John 8:12

He is called a rose and lily, and other such similitudes.

True Life

For if ye live after the flesh, ye shall die: but if ye through the Spirit do mortify the deeds of the body, ye shall live.

Romans 8:13

Those things that precede a living to Christ are these: a dying to sin, to self, and the world. The life of a true Christian whereby he lives to Christ is a new life; it is called a resurrection from the dead, as well as regeneration. It is this sort of resurrection that is spoken of in John 5:25, "Verily, verily, I say unto you, The hour is coming, and now is, when the dead shall hear the voice of the Son of God: and they that hear shall live." It is this sort of resurrection that Ezekiel speaks of in his vision of the valley of dry bones, and the Apostle in the sixth chapter of Romans: "Therefore we are buried with him by baptism into death: that like as Christ was raised up from the dead by the glory of the Father, even so we also should walk in newness of life;" and in Ephesians 2:5–6, "Even when we were dead in sins, hath quickened us together with Christ, (by grace ye are saved;) and hath raised us up together, and made us sit together in heavenly places in Christ Jesus," and frequently elsewhere.

Clothed with Christ

W e, in our fallen state, need garments to hide our nakedness (having lost our primitive glory) which were needless in our state of innocency. And whatsoever God has provided for mankind to clothe themselves with, seems to represent Jesus Christ and his righteousness: whether it be anything made of skin, as the coats of skins that God made our first parents represented the righteousness of Christ; or the fleeces of sheep do represent the righteousness of him who is the Lamb of God, and who was dumb as a sheep before his shearers. And the beautiful clothing from the silkworm, that that worm yields us at his death, represents the glorious clothing we have for our souls by the death of him who became man, who is a worm; and the son of man, who is a worm, and who said he was a worm and no man (Psalm 22:6).

And he said, Who told thee that thou wast naked? Hast thou eaten of the tree, whereof I commanded thee that thou shouldest not eat?
Genesis 3:11

Born in a Manger

And she brought forth her firstborn son, and wrapped him in swaddling clothes, and laid him in a manger; because there was no room for them in the inn.

Luke 2:7

Christ's infinite condescension marvelously appeared in the manner of his birth. He was brought forth in a stable because there was no room for them in the inn. The inn was taken up by others that were looked upon as persons of greater account. The blessed Virgin, being poor and despised, was turned or shut out. Though she was in such necessitous circumstances, yet those that counted themselves her betters would not give place to her. Therefore, in the time of her travail, she was forced to betake herself to a stable, and when the child was born, it was wrapped in swaddling-clothes, and laid in a manger. There Christ lay a little infant, and there he eminently appeared as a lamb. But yet this feeble infant, born thus in a stable, and laid in a manger, was born to conquer and triumph over Satan, that roaring lion. He came to subdue the mighty powers of darkness, and make a show of them openly: so to restore peace on earth, to manifest God's goodwill towards men, and to bring glory to God in the highest. Accordingly the end of his birth was declared by the joyful songs of the glorious hosts of angels, who appeared to the shepherds at the same time that the infant lay in the manger, whereby his divine dignity was manifested.

Looking Back

We ought not to look back when fleeing out of Sodom, because Sodom is a city appointed to destruction. The cry of the city hath reached up to heaven. The earth cannot bear such a burden as her inhabitants are. She will therefore disburden herself of them, and spew them out. God will not suffer such a city to stand; he will consume it. God is holy, and his nature is infinitely opposite to all such uncleanness. He will therefore be a consuming fire to it. The holiness of God will not suffer it to stand, and the majesty and justice of God require that the inhabitants of that city who thus offend and provoke him be destroyed. And God will surely destroy them. It is the immutable and irreversible decree of God. He hath said it, and he will do it. The decree is gone forth, and so sure as there is a God, and he is almighty, and able to fulfill his decrees and threatenings, so surely will he destroy Sodom. Genesis 19:12–13, "Whatsoever thou hast in this city, bring them out of this place; for we will destroy this place, because the cry of them is waxen great before the face of the LORD, and the LORD has sent us to destroy it." And in verse 14, "Up, get you out of this place; for the LORD will destroy this city."

Brethren, I count not myself to have apprehended: but this one thing I do, forgetting those things which are behind, and reaching forth unto those things which are before.
Philippians 3:13

Christ's Divinity

For in him dwelleth all the fulness of the God-head bodily.
Colossians 2:9

As Christ is one of the persons of the Trinity, he is God, and so has the divine nature, or the Godhead dwelling in him, and all the divine attributes belong to him, of which immutability or unchangeableness is one. Christ in his human nature was not absolutely unchangeable, though his human nature, by reason of its union with the divine, was not liable to those changes to which it was liable, as a mere creature. As for instance, it was indestructible and imperishable. Having the divine nature to uphold it, it was not liable to fall and commit sin, as Adam and the fallen angels did, but yet the human nature of Christ, when he was upon earth, was subject to many changes. It had a beginning. It was conceived in the womb of the Virgin Mary. It was in a state of infancy, and afterwards changed from that state to a state of manhood, and this was attended not only with a change on his body, by his increasing in stature, but also on his mind. For we read that he not only increased in stature but also in wisdom (Luke 2:52). And the human nature of Christ was subject to sorrowful changes, though not to sinful ones. He suffered hunger, and thirst, and cold. And at last he suffered dreadful changes by having his body tortured and destroyed, and his soul poured out unto death. And afterwards became subject to a glorious change at his resurrection and ascension. And that his human nature was not liable to sinful changes, as Adam's or the angels', was not owing to anything in his human nature, but to its relation to the divine nature which upheld it. But the divine nature of Christ is absolutely unchangeable, and not liable to the least alteration or variation in any respect. It is the same now as it was before the world was created.

Rejecting Christ

he unbeliever shows the mean and contemptible thoughts that he has of Christ, in refusing to accept of him, and in shutting the door of his heart against him. Christ stands at the door and knocks, and sometimes stands many years knocking at the door of his heart, but he refuses to open to him. Now it certainly shows that men have a very mean thought of a person when they shut him out of their doors. Unbelievers show the mean and dishonorable thoughts they have of Christ, in that they dare not trust him. They believe not what he says to be true. They will not trust the word of Christ, so far as the word of one of their honest neighbors, or of a servant whom they have found to be faithful. It also appears that they have no real honor for Christ in the hearts, in that they refuse to obey his commands. They do nothing from a spirit of obedience to him; and that external obedience which they render is but a forced, feigned obedience, and not from any respect to Christ's authority or worthiness to be obeyed.

Why will ye die, O house of Israel?
Ezekiel 18:31

They believe not what he says to be true.

True Christian Hope

According to my earnest expectation and my hope, that in nothing I shall be ashamed, but that with all boldness, as always, so now also Christ shall be magnified in my body, whether it be by life, or by death.

Philippians 1:20

Paul insists on the blessed nature of hope, in that it enables us to glory in tribulations. This excellent nature of true Christian hope is described in the following words, "And not only so, but we glory in tribulations also: knowing that tribulation worketh patience; and patience, experience; and experience, hope: and hope maketh not ashamed; because the love of God is shed abroad in our hearts by the Holy Ghost which is given unto us" (Romans 5:3–5). As if he had said, through hope of a blessed reward, that will abundantly more than make up for all tribulation, we are enabled to bear tribulation with patience; patiently bearing, and patiently waiting for the reward. And patience works experience; for when we thus bear tribulation with patient waiting for the reward, this brings experience of the earnest of the reward, viz., the earnest of the Spirit, in our feeling the love of God shed abroad in our hearts by the Holy Ghost. So that our hope does not make us ashamed: it is not disappointed; for in the midst of our tribulation, we experience those blessed incomes of the Spirit in our souls, that make even a time of tribulation sweet to us; and is such an earnest abundant confirmation of our hope; and so experience works hope.

Sensible Sinners

hey who are not sensible of their misery cannot truly look to God for mercy; for it is the very notion of divine mercy that it is the goodness and grace of God to the miserable. Without misery in the object, there can be no exercise of mercy. To suppose mercy without supposing misery, or pity without calamity, is a contradiction: therefore men cannot look upon themselves as proper objects of mercy, unless they first know themselves to be miserable; and so, unless this be the case, it is impossible that they should come to God for mercy. They must be sensible that they are the children of wrath; that the law is against them, and that they are exposed to the curse of it; that the wrath of God abideth on them; and that he is angry with them every day while they are under the guilt of sin. They must be sensible that it is a very dreadful thing to be the object of the wrath of God; that it is a very awful thing to have him for their enemy; and that they cannot bear his wrath. They must he sensible that the guilt of sin makes them miserable creatures, whatever temporal enjoyments they have; that they can be no other than miserable, undone creatures, so long as God is angry with them; that they are without strength, and must perish, and that eternally, unless God help them. They must see that their case is utterly desperate, for anything that anyone else can do for them; that they hang over the pit of eternal misery; and that they must necessarily drop into it, if God have not mercy on them.

O wretched man that I am! who shall deliver me from the body of this death?
Romans 7:24

Righteous Forgiveness

If we confess our sins, he is faithful and just to forgive us our sins, and to cleanse us from all unrighteousness.

1 John 1:9

God may, through Christ, pardon the greatest sinner without any prejudice to the honor of his majesty. The honor of the divine majesty indeed requires satisfaction; but the sufferings of Christ fully repair the injury. Let the contempt be ever so great, yet if so honorable a person as Christ undertakes to be a Mediator for the offender, and suffers so much for him, it fully repairs the injury done to the Majesty of heaven and earth. The sufferings of Christ fully satisfy justice. The justice of God, as the supreme Governor and Judge of the world, requires the punishment of sin. The supreme Judge must judge the world according to a rule of justice. God doth not show mercy as a judge, but as a sovereign; therefore his exercise of mercy as a sovereign, and his justice as a judge, must be made consistent one with another; and this is done by the sufferings of Christ, in which sin is punished fully, and justice answered. . . . The law is no impediment in the way of the pardon of the greatest sin, if men do but truly come to God for mercy: for Christ hath fulfilled the law, he hath borne the curse of it, in his sufferings; "Christ hath redeemed us from the curse of the law, being made a curse for us; for it is written, Cursed is every one that hangeth on a tree" (Galatians 3:13).

Pursue Purity

Cleanse yourself from every external impurity of speech and behavior. Take heed that you never defile your hands in known wickedness. Break off all your sins by righteousness. And take heed that you do not give way to impure lusts that would entice to sinful actions. If you set about the work of cleansing yourself, but when a temptation comes then plunge yourself into the mire again, you never will be likely to become pure. But you must be steady in your reformation and the amendment of your ways and doings. Second, take heed you do not rest in external purity, but seek purity of heart in the ways of God's appointment. Seek it in a constant and diligent attendance on all God's ordinances. Third, be often searching your own heart, and seek and pray that you may see the filthiness of it. If ever you are made pure you must be brought to see that you are filthy. You must see the plague and pollution of your own heart. Fourth, beg of God that he would give you his Holy Spirit. It is the Spirit of God that purifies the soul. Therefore the Spirit of God is often compared to fire, and is said to baptize with fire. He cleanses the heart, as fire cleanses the metals; and burns up the filth and pollution of the mind, and is therefore called the Spirit of burning; "When the Lord shall have washed away the filth of the daughters of Zion, and shall have purged the blood of Jerusalem from the midst thereof by the spirit of judgment, and by the spirit of burning" (Isaiah 4:4).

Blessed are the pure in heart, for they shall see God.
Matthew 5:8

Cultivate Meekness

Better is the end of a thing than the beginning thereof: and the patient in spirit is better than the proud in spirit.
Ecclesiastes 7:8

If we would maintain peace, we must give place to wrath. When others are raging at us, we must be mild and gentle towards them. By this means, anger and strife mightily loses its force; it is quashed and deadened by this means more than any. Anger and wrath, if it find none in the object of like fire, that finds no fuel to work upon, will go out of itself. By stepping a little back when we are resisted, the blow of the enemy loses its force, as a woolsack stops and deadens a bullet sooner than an oak tree because it gives way. So a man of a meek and mild temper kills strife sooner than he that resists. Fire will never be quenched by fire; but if we would quench it, we must throw on water, its contrary. So neither will strife be quenched by strife, but by its contrary, meekness. "But I say unto you, That ye resist not evil" (Matthew 5:39); and in the nineteenth verse of our context, "Dearly beloved, avenge not yourselves, but rather give place unto wrath" (Romans 12:19).

If we would maintain peace, we must give place to wrath.

Spiritual Riches

As the covetous man desires earthly riches, so the regenerated person desires spiritual riches. He esteems grace in his soul as the best riches; he looks upon wisdom as better than gold and silver, and he is ambitious of the honor which is of God, to be a child of God and an heir of glory. And as the sensualist eagerly pursues sensual delights, he longs for those pleasures that are spiritual: the pleasure of seeing the glory of Christ, and enjoying his love and having communion with him; the pleasure and joys of the Holy Ghost that consist in the sweet and powerful exercise of grace, of faith and love, submission, thankfulness, charity, and brotherly kindness. And with respect to those appetites self-denial has nothing to do, but here they may give themselves an unbounded liberty.

Trust not in oppression, and become not vain in robbery: if riches increase, set not your heart upon them.
Psalm 62:10

He esteems grace in his soul as the best riches.

God's Pleasure

For he saith to Moses,
I will have mercy on
whom I will have
mercy, and I will have
compassion on whom
I will have
compassion.
Romans 9:15

If you were brought to see God's sovereignty, you would see that he might show you mercy if he pleased, as well as that he might refuse if he pleased. And that will raise a hope in you to see that God may show you mercy if he pleases. Self-righteous men under fear of hell are not fully convinced of either. They are not convinced that God may refuse them mercy; it seems to them very hard that he should cast them down into hell, and that he should have no regard to their good works. Nor yet are they convinced that God may show them mercy. They sometimes are ready to argue with themselves that they are so great sinners. God never will show mercy to them. They are afraid there are no hopes for them. They have affronted God so much, they fear he is irreconcilable. They think his honor requires that they should be punished. And thus they are tossed between two opinions: their hearts are all in a tumult, sometimes thinking that God ought to show them mercy for their works, and that it would be very hard if he didn't; and other times arguing that they are such great sinners that there are no hopes.

The Supreme Judge

God is the supreme judge of the world. He has power sufficient to vindicate his own right. As he has a right which cannot be disputed, so he has power which cannot be controlled. He is possessed of omnipotence, wherewith to maintain his dominion over the world. And he does maintain his dominion in the moral as well as the natural world. Men may refuse subjection to God as a lawgiver. They may shake off the yoke of his laws by rebellion. Yet they cannot withdraw themselves from his judgment. Although they will not have God for their lawgiver, yet they shall have him for their judge. The strongest of creatures can do nothing to control God, or to avoid him while acting in his judicial capacity. He is able to bring them to his judgment seat, and is also able to execute the sentence which he shall pronounce.

Lift up thyself, thou judge of the earth: render a reward to the proud.
Psalm 94:2

There was once a notable attempt made by opposition of power entirely to shake off the yoke of the moral government of God, both as lawgiver, and as judge. This attempt was made by the angels, the mightiest of creatures. But they miserably failed in it. God notwithstanding acted as their judge in casting those proud spirits out of heaven, and binding them in chains of darkness unto a further judgment, and a further execution. "He is wise in heart and mighty in strength: who hath hardened himself against him, and hath prospered?" (Job 9:4). Wherein the enemies of God deal proudly, he is above them. He ever has acted as judge in bestowing what rewards, and inflicting what punishments, he pleased on the children of men. And so he does still. He is daily fulfilling the promises and threatenings of the law, in disposing of the souls of the children of men, and so evermore will act.

> **Although they will not have God for their lawgiver, yet they shall have him for their judge.**

No Want of Power

The LORD hath made all things for himself: yea, even the wicked for the day of evil.
Proverbs 16:4

There is no want of power in God to cast wicked men into hell at any moment. Men's hands cannot be strong when God rises up. The strongest have no power to resist him, nor can any deliver out of his hands. He is not only able to cast wicked men into hell, but he can most easily do it. Sometimes an earthly prince meets with a great deal of difficulty to subdue a rebel, who has found means to fortify himself, and has made himself strong by the numbers of his followers. But it is not so with God. There is no fortress that is any defense from the power of God. Though hand join in hand, and vast multitudes of God's enemies combine and associate themselves, they are easily broken in pieces. They are as great heaps of light chaff before the whirlwind; or large quantities of dry stubble before devouring flames. We find it easy to tread on and crush a worm that we see crawling on the earth; so it is easy for us to cut or singe a slender thread that anything hangs by: thus easy is it for God, when he pleases, to cast his enemies down to hell. What are we that we should think to stand before him, at whose rebuke the earth trembles, and before whom the rocks are thrown down?

Self-Flatteries

hose that flatter themselves with hopes of living a great while longer in the world very commonly continue so to do till death comes. Death comes upon them when they expect it not; they look upon it as a great way off, when there is but a step between them and death. They thought not of dying at that time, nor at any-time near it. When they were young, they proposed to live a good while longer; and if they happen to live till middle age, they still maintain the same thought, that they are not yet near death; and so that thought goes along with them as long as they live, or till they are just about to die.

Have the gates of death been opened unto thee? or hast thou seen the doors of the shadow of death?
Job 38:17

The Sinking Soul

And he cried and said, Father Abraham, have mercy on me, and send Lazarus, that he may dip the tip of his finger in water, and cool my tongue; for I am tormented in this flame.

Luke 16:24

The nature of man desires happiness; it is the nature of the soul to crave and thirst after well-being; and if it be under misery, it eagerly pant after relief; and the greater the misery is, the more eagerly doth it struggle for help. But if all relief be withholden, all strength overborne, all support utterly gone; then it sinks into the darkness of death.

We can conceive but little of the matter; we cannot conceive what that sinking of the soul in such a case is. But to help your conception, imagine yourself to be cast into a fiery oven, or of a great furnace, where your pain would be as much greater than that occasioned by accidentally touching a coal of fire, as the heat is greater. Imagine also that your body were to lie there for a quarter of an hour, all the while full of quick sense; what horror would you feel at the entrance of such a furnace! And how long would that quarter of an hour seem to you! And after you had endured it for one minute, how overbearing would it be to you to think that you had it to endure the other fourteen!

But what would be the effect on your soul, if you knew you must lie there enduring that torment to the full for twenty-four hours! And how much greater would be the effect, if you knew you must endure it for a whole year; and how vastly greater still, if you knew you must endure it for a thousand years! O then, how would your heart sink, if you thought, if you knew, that you must bear it forever and ever! That there would be no end! That after millions of millions of ages, your torment would be no nearer to an end, than ever it was; and that you never, never should be delivered!

Lasting Peace

Our Lord Jesus Christ has bequeathed true peace and comfort to his followers. Christ is called the Prince of Peace (Isaiah 9:6). And when he was born into the world, the angels on that joyful and wonderful occasion sang, "Glory to God in the highest, on earth peace," because of that peace which he should procure for and bestow on the children of men: peace with God, and peace one with another, and tranquility and peace within themselves, which last is especially the benefit spoken of in the text. This Christ has procured for his followers, and laid a foundation for their enjoyment of it, in that he has procured for them the other two, viz., peace with God, and one with another. He has procured for them peace and reconciliation with God, and his favor and friendship, in that he satisfied for their sins and laid a foundation for the perfect removal of the guilt of sin, and the forgiveness of all their trespasses, and wrought out for them a perfect and glorious righteousness, most acceptable to God, and sufficient to recommend them to God's full acceptance, to the adoption of children, and to the eternal fruits of his fatherly kindness.

These things I have spoken unto you, that in me ye might have peace. In the world ye shall have tribulation: but be of good cheer; I have overcome the world. John 16:33

Christ's Glorious Return

*For the Lord himself
shall descend from
heaven with a shout,
with the voice of the
archangel, and with
the trump of God.*
1 Thessalonians
4:16

The saints on earth shall behold this glorious sight of their Savior coming in the clouds of heaven, with all his holy angels with him. The first notice that shall be given of this descent shall be in heaven, but soon after there shall be notice of it on earth. Christ shall be seen coming while he is yet at a great distance; every eye shall see him of both good and bad. And it will be the most joyful sight to the saints that ever they saw. The first notice of it will cause their hearts to overflow with joy and gladness, it will fill the hearts of the godly as full of joy as it will the wicked with terror and amazement. If the saints are then waked out of their sleep at midnight with this sound, that Christ appears in the clouds of heaven coming to judgment, it will be joyful news to them. It is probable many of the saints at that time will be found suffering persecution, for there are several things in Scripture which seem to declare that the time when Christ is coming shall be a time when wickedness shall exceedingly abound, and the saints shall be greatly persecuted. But this shall set them at liberty; then they may lift up their heads out of prisons and dungeons, and many out of galleys, and mines, and shall see their Redeemer drawing nigh. This sight will drive away their persecutors; it will put an end to all their cruelties, and set God's people at liberty. And then when all the kindred of the earth shall wail at the sight of Christ in the clouds of heaven, and wicked men everywhere shall be shrieking and crying with terrible amazement, the saints shall be filled with praise and transport.

Our Perishing Necessity

We are in a perishing necessity of seeking God's kingdom; without it we are utterly and eternally lost. Out of the kingdom of God is no safety; there is no other hiding place; this is the only city of refuge, in which we can be secure from the avenger that pursues all the ungodly. The vengeance of God will pursue, overtake, and eternally destroy them that are not in this kingdom. All that are without this enclosure will be swallowed up in an overflowing fiery deluge of wrath. They may stand at the door and knock, and cry, Lord, Lord, open to us, in vain; they will be thrust back; and God will have no mercy on them; they shall be eternally left of him. His fearful vengeance will seize them; the devils will lay hold of them; and all evil will come upon them; and there will be none to pity or help; their case will be utterly desperate, and infinitely doleful. It will be a gone case with them; all offers of mercy and expressions of divine goodness will be finally withdrawn, and all hope will be lost. God will have no kind of regard to their well-being; will take no care of them to save them from any enemy, or any evil; but himself will be their dreadful enemy, and will execute wrath with fury, and will take vengeance in an inexpressibly dreadful manner. Such as shall be in this case will be lost and undone indeed! They will be sunk down into perdition, infinitely below all that we can think. For who knows the power of God's anger? And who knows the misery of that poor worm, on whom that anger is executed without mercy?

The grass withereth, the flower fadeth: because the spirit of the LORD bloweth upon it: surely the people is grass.
Isaiah 40:7

Forsaking Sin

Let him eschew evil,
and do good; let him
seek peace, and ensue
it.
1 Peter 3:11

Let men pretend what they may; their hearts are not turned from sin if they do not forsake it. He is not converted who is not really come to a disposition utterly to forsake all ways of sin. If ever sinners have true hope and comfort, they must take a final leave of sin, as the children of Israel did of the Egyptians at the Red Sea. Persons may have a great deal of trouble from sin, and many conflicts and struggles with it, and seem to forsake it for a time, and yet not forsake it finally; as the children of Israel had with the Egyptians. They had a long struggle with them before they were freed from them. How many judgments did God bring upon the Egyptians, before they would let them go? And sometimes Pharaoh seemed as if he would let them go; but yet when it came to the proof he refused. And when they departed from Rameses doubtless they thought then they had got rid of them. They did not expect to see them anymore. But when they arrived at the Red Sea, and looked behind them, they saw them pursuing them. They found it a difficult thing wholly to get rid of them. But when they were drowned in the Red Sea, then they took an everlasting leave of them. . . . So sinners must not only part with sin for a little time, but they must forsake it forever, and be willing never to see or have anything to do with their old sinful ways and enjoyments.

Preciousness of Time

ime is very precious, because when it is past, it cannot be recovered. There are many things which men possess which, if they part with, they can obtain them again. If a man have parted with something which he had, not knowing the worth of it, or the need he should have of it, he often can regain it, at least with pains and cost. If a man have been overseen in a bargain, and have bartered away or sold something, and afterwards repents of it, he may often obtain a release, and recover what he had parted with. But it is not so with respect to time. When once that is gone, it is gone forever; no pains, no cost will recover it. Though we repent ever so much that we let it pass, and did not improve it while we had it, it will be to no purpose. Every part of it is successively offered to us, that we may choose whether we will make it our own, or not. But there is no delay. It will not wait upon us to see whether or no we will comply with the offer. But if we refuse, it is immediately taken away, and never offered more. As to that part of time which is gone, however we have neglected to improve it, it is out of our possession and out of our reach.

Redeeming the time, because the days are evil.
Ephesians 5:16

Comforts of Life

In the multitude of my thoughts within me thy comforts delight my soul.

Psalm 94:19

Consider that the comfort of life is in no measure in proportion to men's riches. No outward possession can be any way desirable otherwise than it contributes to a man's comfort, either here or hereafter. If our life is as comfortable both here and hereafter without riches as well, then everyone will own that we had as good be without it as with it. But the comfort even of this life and in temporal things is in no measure in proportion to a man's riches. There are many of those that are very rich that do not have so much comfort with all their possessions, with all their greatness and honor, and all the gratifications their money can procure, as many other men of more indifferent circumstances. They are no nearer to satisfaction for it; they don't crave the less for their having so much. Ecclesiastes 5:10, "He that loveth silver shall not be satisfied with silver; nor he that loveth abundance with increase;" and 4:8, "There is one alone, and there is not a second; yea, he hath neither child nor brother: yet is there no end of all his labour; neither is his eye satisfied with riches; neither saith he, For whom do I labour, and bereave my soul of good? This is also vanity, yea, it is a sore travail." When riches are increased, very often care and anxiety about what is possessed is increased; the mind is the more burdened with thoughts and concern about it. And as the wise man tells us, Ecclesiastes 4:6, "Better is an handful with quietness, than both the hands full with travail and vexation of spirit."

False Affections

alse affections, however persons may seem to be melted by them while they are new, yet have a tendency in the end to harden the heart. A disposition to some kind of passions may be established; such as imply self-seeking, self-exaltation, and opposition to others. But false affections, with the delusion that attends them, finally tend to stupefy the mind, and shut it up against those affections wherein tenderness of heart consists: and the effect of them at last is that persons in the settled frame of their minds become less affected with their present and past sins, and less conscientious with respect to future sins, less moved with the warnings and cautions of God's Word, or God's chastisements in his providence, more careless of the frame of their hearts, and the manner and tendency of their behavior, less quick-sighted to discern what is sinful, less afraid of the appearance of evil, than they were while they were under legal awakenings and fears of hell.

And the cares of this world, and the deceitfulness of riches, and the lusts of other things entering in, choke the word, and it becometh unfruitful.
Mark 4:19

Spiritually Ignorant

But the natural man receiveth not the things of the Spirit of God: for they are foolishness unto him: neither can he know them, because they are spiritually discerned.

1 Corinthians 2:14

The reason why natural men have no knowledge of spiritual things is because they have nothing of the Spirit of God dwelling in them. . . . for we are told that it is by the Spirit that these things are taught, and godly persons are called spiritual, because they have the Spirit dwelling in them. Hereby the sense again is confirmed, for natural men are in no degree spiritual; they have only nature and no Spirit. If they had anything of the Spirit, though not in so great a degree as the godly, yet they would be taught spiritual things, or things of the Spirit, in proportion to the measure of the Spirit that they had. The Spirit that searches all things would teach them in some measure. There would not be so great a difference that the one could perceive nothing of them, and that they should be foolishness to them, while to the other they appear divinely and remarkably wise and excellent.

A Spirit of Love

abor that there may be much of a spirit of love appearing in your behavior. If there be much of such a spirit appearing in you, it will be taking and winning to the unconverted. Unconverted persons are ready to have a prejudice against them that are accounted converted; but if they observe such a spirit of love in them not only one to another, but there seems evidently to be a spirit of hearty good will to the unconverted and to all; it will tend very much to abate of that prejudice, and to beget in them a good thought not only of them, but of godliness itself. Thus those that are converted should bring forth fruit meet for repentance.

And this commandment have we from him, That he who loveth God love his brother also.
1 John 4:21

Labor that there may be much of a spirit f love appearing in your behavior.

Holy Practice

According as he hath chosen us in him before the foundation of the world, that we should be holy and without blame before him in love.
Ephesians 1:4

oly practice is the aim of that eternal election which is the first ground of the bestowment of all true grace. Holy practice is not the ground and reason of election, as is supposed by the Arminians, who imagine that God elects men to everlasting life upon a foresight of their good works; but it is the aim and end of election. God does not elect men because he foresees they will be holy, but that he may make them, and that they may be holy. Thus, in election, God ordained that men should walk in good works, as says the apostle, "For we are his workmanship, created in Christ Jesus unto good works, which God hath before ordained that we should walk in them" (Ephesians 2:10). And again it is said that the elect are chosen to this very end: "He hath chosen us in him before the foundation of the world, that we should be holy, and without blame before him in love" (Ephesians 1:4). And so Christ tells his disciples, "I have chosen you, and ordained you, that ye should go and bring forth fruit, and that your fruit should remain" (John 15:16). Now God's eternal election is the first ground of the bestowment of saving grace. And some have such saving grace, and others do not have it, because some are from eternity chosen of God, and others are not chosen. And seeing that holy practice is the scope and aim of that which is the first ground of the bestowment of grace, this same holy practice is doubtless the tendency of grace itself. Otherwise it would follow that God makes use of a certain means to attain an end, which is not fitted to attain that end, and has no tendency to it.

Do Good to All

We are to do good both to the good and to the bad. This we are to do, as we would imitate our heavenly Father, for "he maketh his sun to rise on the evil and on the good, and sendeth rain on the just and on the unjust" (Matthew 5:43–45). The world is full of various kinds of persons, some good, and some evil; and we should do good to all. We should, indeed, especially "do good to them that are of the household of faith," or that we have reason, in the exercise of charity, to regard as saints. But though we should most abound in beneficence to them, yet our doing good should not be confined to them, but we should do good to all men, as we have opportunity. While we live in the world, we must expect to meet with some men of very evil properties, and hateful dispositions and practices. Some are proud, some immoral, some covetous, some profane, some unjust or severe, and some despisers of God. But any or all of these bad qualities should not hinder our beneficence, nor prevent our doing them good as we have opportunity. On this very account, we should the rather be diligent to benefit them, that we may win them to Christ, and especially should we be diligent to benefit them in spiritual things.

But I say unto you which hear, Love your enemies, do good to them which hate you.
Luke 6:27

God Is Not Like Us

God is not a man, that he should lie; neither the son of man, that he should repent: hath he said, and shall he not do it? or hath he spoken, and shall he not make it good?
Numbers 23:19

It is well for us that God is not as unfaithful to us as we are to him. We who are professing Christians are under solemn vows and engagements to be the Lord's and to serve him. Every time we come to the Lord's Supper we renew those vows in a most solemn manner. But how much unfaithfulness there is among professors towards God. And those who do sincerely give themselves to God at their conversion, how often they fail in point of faithfulness to their covenant God. God is not so towards those who are godly. God is engaged to them by promise, to keep them through faith to salvation, not to suffer them to be tempted above what they are able, to carry them on in a way of grace, to deliver them from all their enemies. He has promised that he will ever more take care of them and watch over them for good, that he will keep them from the power of the devil, that he will keep them out of hell and at last bring them to glory. God never fails in any one instance. The word has gone out of his mouth, and heaven and earth shall pass away before one jot or tittle of it shall fail. If we were not sure but that God's faithfulness towards us might fail, and was as liable to fail as men towards him, what a poor, doubtful case we would all be in!

God Hears Prayer

It is indeed a very wonderful thing that so great a God should be so ready to hear our prayers, though we are so despicable and unworthy. That he should give free access at all times to everyone, should allow us to be importunate without esteeming it an indecent boldness, [and] should be so rich in mercy to them that call upon him: that worms of the dust should have such power with God by prayer, that he should do such great things in answer to their prayers, and should show himself, as it were, overcome by them. This is very wonderful, when we consider the distance between God and us, and how we have provoked him by our sins, and how unworthy we are of the least gracious notice. It cannot be from any need that God stands in of us, for our goodness extends not to him. Neither can it be from anything in us to incline the heart of God to us. It cannot be from any worthiness in our prayers, which are in themselves polluted things. But it is because God delights in mercy and condescension. He is herein infinitely distinguished from all other Gods. He is the great fountain of all good, from whom goodness flows as light from the sun.

Blessed be the LORD, because he hath heard the voice of my supplications.
Psalm 28:6

Absent from the Lord

It was but a little that I passed from them, but I found him whom my soul loveth: I held him, and would not let him go, until I had brought him into my mother's house, and into the chamber of her that conceived me.

Song of Solomon 3:4

When we are absent from our dear friends, they are out of sight, but when we are with them, we have the opportunity and satisfaction of seeing them. So while the saints are in the body, and are absent from the Lord, he is in several respects out of sight, "Whom having not seen, ye love; in whom, though now ye see him not, yet believing" (1 Peter 1:8), etc. They have indeed, in this world, a spiritual sight of Christ, but they see through a glass darkly, and with great interruption, but in heaven they see him face to face (1 Corinthians 13:12). "The pure in heart are blessed; for they shall see God" (Matthew 5:8); their beatific vision of God is in Christ, who is that brightness or effulgence of God's glory, by which his glory shines forth in heaven, to the view of saints and angels there, as well as here on earth. This is the Sun of righteousness that is not only the light of this world, but is also the sun that enlightens the heavenly Jerusalem, by whose bright beams it is that the glory of God shines forth there, to the enlightening and making happy all the glorious inhabitants. "The glory of God doth lighten it, and the Lamb is the light thereof" (Revelation 21:23).

It Was for the Joy

hrist has done greater things than to create the world in order to obtain his bride and the joy of his espousals with her. For he became man for this end, which was a greater thing than his creating the world. For the Creator to make the creature was a great thing. But for him to become a creature was a greater thing. And he did a much greater thing still to obtain this joy; in that for this he laid down his life, and suffered even the death of the cross. For this he poured out his soul unto death. And he that is the Lord of the universe, God over all, blessed forevermore, offered up himself a sacrifice, in both body and soul, in the flames of divine wrath. Christ obtains his elect spouse by conquest. For she was a captive in the hands of dreadful enemies. Her Redeemer came into the world to conquer these enemies and rescue her out of their hands, that she might be his bride. And he came and encountered these enemies in the greatest battle that ever was beheld by men or angels. He fought with principalities and powers. He fought alone with the powers of darkness and all the armies of hell. Yea, he conflicted with the infinitely more dreadful wrath of God, and overcame in this great battle. And thus he obtained his spouse. Let us consider at how great a price Christ purchased his spouse. He did not redeem her with corruptible things, as silver and gold, but with his own precious blood. Yea, he gave himself for her. When he offered up himself to God in those extreme labors and sufferings, this was the joy that was set before him, that made him cheerfully to endure the cross, and despise the pain and shame in comparison of this joy; even that rejoicing over his church, as the bridegroom rejoices over the bride that the Father had promised him, and that he expected when he should present her to himself in perfect beauty and blessedness.

Looking unto Jesus the author and finisher of our faith; who for the joy that was set before him endured the cross, despising the shame, and is set down at the right hand of the throne of God.
Hebrews 12:2

Solely by Grace

That being justified by his grace, we should be made heirs according to the hope of eternal life.

Titus 3:7

The redeemed have all from the grace of God. It was of mere grace that God gave us his only-begotten Son. The grace is great in proportion to the excellency of what is given. The gift was infinitely precious, because it was of a person infinitely worthy, a person of infinite glory; and also because it was of a person infinitely near and dear to God. The grace is great in proportion to the benefit we have given us in him. The benefit is doubly infinite, in that in him we have deliverance from an infinite, because an eternal, misery, and do also receive eternal joy and glory. The grace in bestowing this gift is great in proportion to our unworthiness to whom it is given; instead of deserving such a gift, we merited infinitely ill of God's hands. The grace is great according to the manner of giving, or in proportion to the humiliation and expense of the method and means by which a way is made for our having the gift. He gave him to dwell amongst us; he gave him to us incarnate, or in our nature; and in the like though sinless infirmities. He gave him to us in a low and afflicted state; and not only so, but as slain, that he might be a feast for our souls.

Imitating God

ove to God disposes us to imitate him, and therefore disposes us to such longsuffering as he manifests. Longsuffering is often spoken of as one of the attributes of God. In Exodus 34:6, it is said, "And the LORD passed by before him, and proclaimed, The LORD, The LORD God, merciful and gracious, longsuffering," etc. And in Romans 2:4, the apostle asks, "Despisest thou the riches of his goodness and forbearance and longsuffering?" The longsuffering of God is very wonderfully manifest in his bearing innumerable injuries from men, and injuries that are very great and long-continued. If we consider the wickedness that there is in the world, and then consider how God continues the world in existence, and does not destroy it, but showers upon it innumerable mercies, the bounties of his daily providence and grace, causing his sun to rise on the evil and on the good, and sending rain alike on the just and on the unjust, and offering his spiritual blessings ceaselessly and to all, we shall perceive how abundant is his longsuffering toward us. And if we consider his longsuffering to some of the great and populous cities of the world, and think how constantly the gifts of his goodness are bestowed on and consumed by them, and then consider how great the wickedness of these very cities is, it will show us how amazingly great is his longsuffering. And the same longsuffering has been manifest to very many particular persons, in all ages of the world. He is longsuffering to the sinners that he spares, and to whom he offers his mercy, even while they are rebelling against him. And he is longsuffering toward his own elect people, many of whom long lived in sin, and despised alike his goodness and his wrath: and yet he bore long with them, even to the end, till they were brought to repentance, and made, through his grace, vessels of mercy and glory.

Seek ye the LORD, all ye meek of the earth, which have wrought his judgment; seek righteousness, seek meekness: it may be ye shall be hid in the day of the LORD's anger.
Zephaniah 2:3

Suffering without Love

And though I bestow all my goods to feed the poor, and though I give my body to be burned, and have not charity, it profiteth me nothing.
1 Corinthians 13:3

The apostle teaches us that not only our performances, but also our sufferings are of no avail without charity. Men are ready to make much of what they do, but more of what they suffer. They are ready to think it a great thing when they put themselves out of their way, or are at great expense or suffering, for their religion. The apostle here mentions a suffering of the most extreme kind, suffering even to death, and that one of the most terrible forms of death, and says that even this is nothing without charity. When a man has given away all his goods, he has nothing else remaining that he can give, but himself. And the apostle teaches that when a man has given all his possessions, if he then goes on to give his own body, and that to be utterly consumed in the flames, it will avail nothing, if it is not done from sincere love in the heart. The time when the apostle wrote to the Corinthians was a time when Christians were often called, not only to give their goods, but their bodies also, for Christ's sake. For the church then was generally under persecution. Multitudes were then or soon after put to very cruel deaths for the gospel's sake. But though they suffered in life, or endured the most agonizing death, it would be in vain without charity. What is meant by this charity has already been explained in the former lectures on these verses, in which it has been shown that charity is the sum of all that is distinguishing in the religion of the heart.

Godly Practice

e who sincerely prefers God to all other things in his heart will do it in his practice. For when God and all other things come to stand in competition, that is the proper trial what a man chooses; and the manner of acting in such cases must certainly determine what the choice is in all free agents, or those who act on choice. Therefore there is no sign of sincerity so much insisted on in the Bible as this, that we deny ourselves, sell all, forsake the world, take up the cross, and follow Christ whithersoever he goeth. Therefore, so run, not as uncertainly; so fight, not as those that beat the air; but keep under your bodies, and bring them into subjection. Act not as though you counted yourselves to have apprehended; but this one thing do, "forgetting those things which are behind, and reaching forth unto those things which are before, I press toward the mark for the prize of the high calling of God in Christ Jesus" (Philippians 3:13–14). "And besides this, giving diligence, add to your faith virtue; and to virtue knowledge; and to knowledge temperance; and to temperance patience; and to patience godliness; and to godliness brotherly kindness; and to brotherly kindness charity. For if these things be in you, and abound, they make you that ye shall neither be barren nor unfruitful in the knowledge of our Lord Jesus Christ" (2 Peter 1:5, etc.)

Ye are the light of the world. A city that is set on an hill cannot be hid.
Matthew 5:14

Practical Religion

*For whosoever shall do
the will of my Father
which is in heaven,
the same is my
brother, and sister,
and mother.*
Matthew 12:50

There are some who never have come to any determination in their own minds whether to embrace
religion in the practice of it. Religion consists not
merely, or chiefly, in theory or speculation, but in practice. It is a practical thing. The end of it is to guide and influence us in our practice. And considered in this view,
there are multitudes who never have come to a conclusion whether to embrace religion or not. It is probably
pretty general for men to design to be religious some
time or other before they die; for none intends to go to
hell. But they still keep it at a distance. They put it off
from time to time, and never come to any conclusion
which determines them in their present practice. And
some never so much as fix upon any time. They design
to be religious sometime before they die, but they know
not when.

**Religion consists
not merely, or
chiefly, in theory
or speculation,
but in practice.**

The City of God

eaven is likened in Scripture to a splendid and glorious city. Many men are ever surprised and amazed by the sight of a splendid city. We need not to be told how often heaven is called the holy city of God. Other cities are built by men, but this city, we are told, was built immediately by God himself. His hands reared up the stately mansions of this city, and his wisdom contrived them; "For he looked for a city which hath foundations, whose builder and maker is God" (Hebrews 11:10). Other cities that are royal cities, that is, the cities that are the seats of kings and where they keep their courts, are commonly, above all others, stately and beautiful; but heaven, we are told, is the royal city of God, where the King of heaven and earth dwells, and displays his glory.

The city of the living God.
Hebrews 12:22

The Gospel Feast

And he took bread, and gave thanks, and brake it, and gave unto them, saying, This is my body which is given for you: this do in remembrance of me.

Luke 22:19

The Lord's Supper is a representation of a spiritual gospel feast. It is very suitable to the gospel state of the church, the state wherein God's grace in providing for souls is so abundantly manifested, and this spiritual provision so plentifully bestowed, that there should be a feast appointed and observed in the church, showing forth that spiritual feast which God has provided in Jesus Christ for our souls with such great expense, and to signify and seal the covenant with agreement and friendship between God and his people. In this ordinance is represented, by the great cost which God has been at to provide this feast for us, the breaking of the body and shedding of the blood of Jesus Christ, in order that we have all spiritual blessings by the body and blood of Christ; and Christ did as it were submit himself to death, that he might give his body and blood to be our meat and drink, that we might have such food as would nourish and satisfy our souls.

Sacred Employment

et it be considered that the church on earth is the same society with those saints who are praising God in heaven. There is not one church of Christ in heaven, and another here upon earth. Though the one be sometimes called the church triumphant, and the other the church militant, yet they are not indeed two churches. By the church triumphant is meant the triumphant part of the church. And by the church militant, the militant part of it, for there is but one universal or catholic church; "My dove, my undefiled, is but one" (Song of Solomon 6:9). The glorious assembly and the saints on earth make but one family; "Of whom the whole family in heaven and earth is named" (Ephesians 3:15). Though some are in heaven, and some on earth, in very different circumstances, yet they are all united. For there is but one body, and one spirit, and one Lord Jesus Christ, one God and Father of all, who is above all, and through all, and in all. God hath in Christ united the inhabitants of heaven, and the holy inhabitants of this earth, and hath made them one; "That in the dispensation of the fulness of times he might gather together in one all things in Christ, both which are in heaven, and which are on earth; even in him" (Ephesians 1:10). Heaven is at a great distance from the earth. It is called a far country, yet the distance of place does not separate them so as to make two societies. For though the saints on earth, at present, are at a distance from heaven, yet they belong there. That is their proper home. The saints that are in this world are strangers here. And therefore the apostle reproved the Christians in his day for acting as though they belonged to this world; "Why, as though living in the world, are ye subject to ordinances" (Colossians 2:20)?

Let us come before his presence with thanksgiving, and make a joyful noise unto him with psalms.
Psalm 95:2

Paying Debts

*Provide things honest
in the sight of all
men.*
Romans 12:17

A way in which men unjustly withhold what is their neighbor's is in neglecting to pay their debts. Sometimes this happens because they run so far into debt that they cannot reasonably hope to be able to pay their debts; and this they do, either through pride and affectation of living above their circumstances, or through a grasping, covetous disposition, or some other corrupt principle. Sometimes they neglect to pay their debts from carelessness of spirit about it, little concerning themselves whether they are paid or not, taking no care to go to their creditor, or to send to him. And if they see him from time to time, they say nothing about their debts. Sometimes they neglect to pay their debts because it would put them to some inconvenience. The reason why they do it not, is not because they cannot do it, but because they cannot do it as conveniently as they desire. And so they rather choose to put their creditor to inconvenience by being without what properly belongs to him, than to put themselves to inconvenience by being without what doth not belong to them, and what they have no right to detain. In any of these cases they unjustly usurp the property of their neighbor.

A Precious Stone

o believers Christ is a precious stone: "Unto you therefore which believe he is precious." But to unbelievers he is a stone that is disallowed, and rejected, and set at nought. They set light by him, as by the stones of the street. They make no account of him, and they disallow him. When they come to build, they cast this stone away as being of no use, not fit for a foundation, and not fit for a place in their building. In the eighth verse the apostle tells the Christians to whom he writes that those unbelievers who thus reject Christ, and to whom he is a stone of stumbling, and rock of offense, were appointed to this. "And a stone of stumbling, and a rock of offense, even to them which stumble at the word, being disobedient: whereunto also they were appointed" (1 Peter 2:8). It was appointed that they should stumble at the word that Christ should be an occasion not of their salvation, but of their deeper damnation. And then in our text, he puts the Christians in mind how far otherwise God had dealt with them, than with those reprobates. They were a chosen generation. God had rejected the others in his eternal counsels, but themselves he had chosen from eternity. They were a chosen generation, a royal priesthood, a holy nation, a peculiar people.

How precious also are thy thoughts unto me, O God! how great is the sum of them!
Psalm 139:17

> To believers Christ is a precious stone.

Electing Love

Jacob have I loved, but
Esau have I hated.
Romans 9:13

od in election set his love upon those whom he elected; "The Lord hath appeared of old unto me, saying, Yea, I have loved thee with an everlasting love: therefore with lovingkindness have I drawn thee" (Jeremiah 31:3); "We love him, because he first loved us" (1 John 4:19). A God of infinite goodness and benevolence loves those that have no excellency to move or attract it. The love of men is consequent upon some loveliness in the object, but the love of God is antecedent to, and the cause of it. Believers were from all eternity beloved both by the Father and the Son. The eternal love of the Father appears in that he from all eternity contrived a way for their salvation, and chose Jesus Christ to be their Redeemer, and laid help upon him. It is a fruit of this electing love that God sent his Son into the world to die, it was to redeem those whom he so loved. "Herein is love, not that we loved God, but that he loved us, and sent his Son to be the propitiation for our sins" (1 John 4:10). It is a fruit of the eternal, electing love of Jesus Christ, that he was willing to come into the world, and die for sinners, and that he actually came and died, "I am crucified with Christ: nevertheless I live; yet not I, but Christ liveth in me: and the life which I now live in the flesh I live by the faith of the Son of God, who loved me, and gave himself for me" (Galatians 2:20). And so conversion, and glorification, and all that is done for a believer from the first to the last, is a fruit of electing love.

Bear with One Another

Love one another.
John 13:34

Christians ought to bear with one another . . . . they are all of one kindred, that they have a relation to other Christians which they have not to the rest of the world, being of a distinct race from them, but of the same race one with another. They are descended all along from the same progenitors; they are the children of the same universal church of God; they are all the children of Abraham; they are the seed of Jesus Christ; they are the offspring of God. And they are yet much more alike, than their being of the same race originally argues them to be: they are also immediately the children of the same Father. God hath begotten all by the same Word and Spirit. They are all of one family, and should therefore love as brethren, "Finally, be ye all of one mind, having compassion one of another, love as brethren, be pitiful, be courteous" (1 Peter 3:8).

God hath begotten all by the same Word and Spirit.

Great Labor and Care

Wherefore, my beloved, as ye have always obeyed, not as in my presence only, but now much more in my absence, work out your own salvation with fear and trembling.
Philippians 2:12

rue religion is a business of great labor and care. There are many commands to be obeyed, many duties to be done: duties to God, duties to our neighbor, and duties to ourselves. There is much opposition in the way of these duties from without. There is a subtle and powerful adversary laying all manner of blocks in the way. There are innumerable temptations of Satan to be resisted and repelled. There is great opposition from the world, innumerable snares laid, on every side, many rocks and mountains to be passed over, many streams to be passed through, and many flatteries and enticements from a vain world to be resisted. There is a great opposition from within; a dull and sluggish heart, which is exceedingly averse from that activity in religion which is necessary; a carnal heart, which is averse from religion and spiritual exercises, and continually drawing the contrary way; and a proud and a deceitful heart, in which corruption will be exerting itself in all manner of ways. So that nothing can be done to any effect without a most strict and careful watch, great labor and strife.

Debtors to Mercy

hose who truly come to God for mercy come as beggars, and not as creditors: they come for mere mercy, for sovereign grace, and not for anything that is due. Therefore, they must see that the misery under which they lie is justly brought upon them, and that the wrath to which they are exposed is justly threatened against them; and that they have deserved that God should *be* their enemy, and should *continue* to be their enemy. They must be sensible that it would be just with God to do as he hath threatened in his holy law, viz., make them the objects of his wrath and curse in hell to all eternity. They who come to God for mercy in a right manner are not disposed to find fault with his severity; but they come in a sense of their own utter unworthiness, as with ropes about their necks, and lying in the dust at the foot of mercy.

But as for me, I will come into thy house in the multitude of thy mercy: and in thy fear will I worship toward thy holy temple.
Psalm 5:7

> Those who truly come to God for mercy, come as beggars, and not as creditors.

The Great Physician

And when the woman saw that she was not hid, she came trembling, and falling down before him, she declared unto him before all the people for what cause she had touched him, and how she was healed immediately.
Luke 8:47

Christ is as able to help, and he is as ready to help under every kind of difficulty. Here is great encouragement for persons who are sick to look to Christ for healing, and for their near friends to carry their case to Christ; for how ready was Christ, when on earth, to help those that looked to him under such difficulties! And how sufficient did he appear to be for it, commonly healing by laying on his hand, or by speaking a word! And we read of his healing all manner of sickness and all manner of disease among the people. Persons under the most terrible and inveterate diseases were often healed. And Christ is the same still. And here is great encouragement for mourners to look to Christ for comfort. We read of Christ's pitying such, as in the case of the widow of Nain (Luke 7:12–13). And so he wept with those that wept, and groaned in spirit, and wept with compassion for Martha and Mary, when he saw their sorrow for the loss of their brother Lazarus (John 11:32, etc.). And he is the same still. He is as ready to pity those that are in affliction now as he was then.

He is as ready to pity those that are in affliction now as he was then.

The Best Mediator

he wisdom of God in choosing his eternal Son appears not only in that he is a fit person, but in that he was the only fit person of all persons, whether created or uncreated. No created person, neither man nor angel, was fit for this undertaking. . . . There are three uncreated persons of the Trinity, The Father, Son, and Holy Ghost. And Christ alone of these was a suitable person for a redeemer. It was not meet that the redeemer should be God the Father. Because he, in the divine economy of the persons of the Trinity, was the person that holds the rights of the Godhead, and so was the person offended, whose justice required satisfaction; and was to be appeased by a mediator. It was not meet it should be the Holy Ghost, for in being mediator between the Father and the saints, he is in some sense so between the Father and the Spirit. The saints, in all their spiritual transactions with God, act by the Spirit; or rather, it is the Spirit of God that acts in them. . . . And therefore it was meet that the mediator should not be either the Father or the Spirit, but a middle person between them both. It is the Spirit in the saints that seeks the blessing of God, by faith and prayer, and, as the apostle says, with groanings that cannot be uttered: "Likewise the Spirit also helpeth our infirmities: for we know not what we should pray for as we ought: but the Spirit itself maketh intercession for us with groanings that cannot be uttered" (Romans 8:26). The Spirit in the saints seeks divine blessings of God by and through a mediator. And therefore that mediator must not be the Spirit, but another person.

For there is one God, and one mediator between God and men, the man Christ Jesus.
1 Timothy 2:5

Wholly Repaired

Those who come to Christ do not need to be afraid of God's wrath for their sins; for God's honor will not suffer by their escaping punishment and being made happy. The wounded soul is sensible that he has affronted the majesty of God, and looks upon God as a vindicator of his honor; as a jealous God that will not be mocked, an infinitely great God that will not bear to be affronted, that will not suffer his authority and majesty to be trampled on, that will not bear that his kindness should be abused. A view of God in this light terrifies awakened souls. They think how exceedingly they have sinned, how they have sinned against light, against frequent and long-continued calls and warnings; and how they have slighted mercy, and been guilty of turning the grace of God into lasciviousness, taking encouragement from God's mercy to go on in sin against him; and they fear that God is so affronted at the contempt and slight which they have cast upon him, that he, being careful of his honor, will never forgive them, but will punish them. But if they go to Christ, the honor of God's majesty and authority will not be in the least hurt by their being freed and made happy. For what Christ has done has repaired God's honor to the full.

Born to Suffer

Our Lord Jesus Christ, in his original nature, was infinitely above all suffering, for he was "God over all, blessed for evermore;" but, when he became man, he was not only capable of suffering, but partook of that nature that is remarkably feeble and exposed to suffering. The human nature, on account of its weakness, is in Scripture compared to the grass of the field, which easily withers and decays. So it is compared to a leaf; and to the dry stubble; and to a blast of wind: and the nature of feeble man is said to be but dust and ashes, to have its foundation in the dust, and to be crushed before the moth. It was this nature, with all its weakness and exposedness to sufferings, which Christ, who is the Lord God omnipotent, took upon him. He did not take the human nature on him in its first, most perfect and vigorous state, but in that feeble forlorn state which it is in since the fall; and therefore Christ is called "a tender plant," and "a root out of a dry ground" (Isaiah 53:2). "For he shall grow up before him as a tender plant, and as a root out of a dry ground: he hath no form nor comeliness; and when we shall see him, there is no beauty that we should desire him." Thus, as Christ's principal errand into the world was suffering, so, agreeably to that errand, he came with such a nature and in such circumstances, as most made way for his suffering; so his whole life was filled up with suffering, he began to suffer in his infancy, but his suffering increased the more he drew near to the close of his life.

For he shall grow up before him as a tender plant, and as a root out of a dry ground.
Isaiah 53:2a

Godly Learning

The cloke that I left at Troas with Carpus, when thou comest, bring with thee, and the books, but especially the parchments.

2 Timothy 4:13

Seek not to grow in knowledge chiefly for the sake of applause, and to enable you to dispute with others, but seek it for the benefit of your souls, and in order to practice. If applause be your end, you will not be so likely to be led to the knowledge of the truth, but may justly, as often is the case of those who are proud of their knowledge, be led into error to your own perdition. This being your end, if you should obtain much rational knowledge, it would not be likely to be of any benefit to you, but would puff you up with pride: "Knowledge puffeth up" (1 Corinthians 8:1).

Seek to God that he would direct you, and bless you, in this pursuit after knowledge. This is the apostle's direction, "If any man lack wisdom, let him ask of God, that giveth to all men liberally, and upbraideth not" (James 1:5). God is the fountain of all divine knowledge: "The Lord giveth wisdom: out of his mouth cometh knowledge and understanding" (Proverbs 2:6). Labor to be sensible of your own blindness and ignorance, and your need of the help of God, lest you be led into error, instead of true knowledge: "If any man among you seemeth to be wise in this world, let him become a fool, that he may be wise" (1 Corinthians 3:18).

Seizing the Day

When men are dead they cease to bite and devour others; as it is said to have been of old a proverb among the Egyptians, "Dead men do not bite." There are many who will bite and devour as long as they live, but death tames them. Men could not be quiet or safe by them while alive, but none will be afraid of them when dead. The bodies of those that made such a noise and tumult when alive, when dead, lie as quietly among the graves of their neighbors as any others. Their enemies, of whom they strove to get their wills while alive, get their wills of them when they are dead. . . . The time will soon come when you who have for many years been at times warmly contending one with another will be very peaceable as to this world. Your dead bodies will probably lie quietly together in the same burying place. If you do not leave off contending before death, how natural will it be for others to have such thoughts as these when they see your corpses: What! Is this the man who used to be so busy in carrying on the designs of his party? Oh, now he has done. Now he hath no more any part in any of these things. . . . He will not sit any more to reproach and laugh at others. He is gone to appear before his Judge, and to receive according to his conduct in life.

The consideration of such things as these would certainly have a mighty effect among us, if we did not put far away the day of death. If we all acted every day as not depending on any other day, we should be a peaceful, quiet people.

Death and life are in the power of the tongue: and they that love it shall eat the fruit thereof.
Proverbs 18:21

The Serpent's Craftiness

Be sober, be vigilant; because your adversary the devil, as a roaring lion, walketh about, seeking whom he may devour.
1 Peter 5:8

The devil to gain his purposes poses under many transformations, and puts on many disguises. He manages all by deceit. If he acted openly and without disguise, and appeared what he is indeed, viz., a wicked, malicious, cruel spirit, he would frustrate his own ends, which are to oppose God, and to seek the ruin of men. If he appeared in his true shape, others would be aware of him, and would be upon their guard against him, and would not so readily fall in with his motions, and be influenced and led by him. When the devil first began his work in the world in tempting our first parents, it was under a transformation. He transformed himself into the shape of a serpent, or else actually entered into one of those animals, which he looked upon as the best disguise for his purpose at that time. So he frequently transforms himself into many other forms, as he thinks will best suit his occasions.

Conceit and Frailty

ow little do men think that they every moment depend on God. They are preserved, and kept alive, and kept out of hell. But how little do they think that it is God that keeps them. How little do they think how many evils they are liable to every day, unless God keeps them. And when they are seeking their own good and happiness, how little sensible are they of their absolute dependence on God. How is it the manner of men in such cases to be trying in their own strength. And when they are under conviction of their guilt, and the misery of a natural condition, how prone are men to be thinking that they can make themselves better, and can recommend themselves to God, or make some atonement for sin, when we can't do it, any more than we can create a world. How difficult a thing it is to convince men of the insufficiency of their own reason and abilities, to help them out of a natural state. These poor, feeble creatures look very big upon themselves. They little think how it is God that every day keeps them from falling into the most heinous wickedness imaginable, by the restraints that he lays on their corruptions, and how it is God that every moment keeps them from being destroyed by the devil, who, if God should give permission, would immediately fall upon them as a roaring lion. This arises from the grand conceit we naturally have of ourselves, and our ignorance of our own weakness.

For he knoweth our frame; he remembereth that we are dust.
Psalm 103:14

Virtuous and Holy Peace

*Behold, I will bring it
health and cure, and I
will cure them, and
will reveal unto them
the abundance of
peace and truth.*
Jeremiah 33:6

hrist's peace is a virtuous and holy peace. The peace that the men of the world enjoy is vicious. It is a vile stupidity that depraves and debases the mind, and makes men brutish. But the peace that the saints enjoy in Christ is not only their comfort, but it is a part of their beauty and dignity. The Christian tranquility, rest, and joy of real saints, are not only unspeakable privileges, but they are virtues and graces of God's Spirit, wherein the image of God in them does partly consist. This peace has its source in those principles that are in the highest degree virtuous and amiable, such as poverty of spirit, holy resignation, trust in God, divine love, meekness, and charity. The exercise of such blessed fruits of the Spirit as are spoken of (Galatians 5:22–23).

Christ's peace is
a virtuous and
holy peace.

Rivers of Water

The river that supplies the city of God is a full and never-failing stream; there is enough, and it never is dry. And they that trust in God, and whose hope the Lord is, they shall be like trees "planted by the waters, and that spreadeth out her roots, and shall not see when heat cometh, but her leaf shall be green; and shall not be careful in the year of drought, neither shall cease from yielding fruit" (Jeremiah 17:8). God has promised that he will never fail them, nor forsake them. The people that have God amongst them have the fountain of all good in the midst of them. There is a full fountain, indeed an inexhaustible and infinite fountain, enough for the supply of everyone, under all their circumstances and necessities; whatever anyone wants, he may go to this fountain, and there he may have a supply.

And he shall be like a tree planted by the rivers of water, that bringeth forth his fruit in his season; his leaf also shall not wither; and whatsoever he doeth shall prosper.
Psalm 1:3

The river that supplies the city of God is a full and never-failing stream.

Friendship with God

And the scripture was
fulfilled which saith,
Abraham believed
God, and it was im-
puted unto him for
righteousness: and he
was called the Friend
of God.
James 2:23

We ought to treat God as a dear friend. We ought to act towards him as those that have a sincere love and unfeigned regard to him; and so ought to watch and be careful against all occasions of that which is contrary to his honor and glory. If we have not a temper and desire so to do, it will show that, whatever our pretenses are, we are not God's sincere friends, and have no true love to him. If we should be offended at any that have professed friendship to us, if they have treated us in this manner, and were no more careful of our interest; surely God may justly be offended, that we are no more careful of his glory.

We ought to
treat God as a
dear friend.

Everlasting Mansions

The mansions in God's house above are everlasting mansions. Those that have seats allotted them there, whether of greater or lesser dignity, whether nearer or further from the throne, will hold them to all eternity. This is promised: "Him that overcometh I will make him a pillar in the temple of my God, and he shall go no more out" (Revelation 3:12). If it be worth the while to desire and seek high seats in the meetinghouse, where you are one day in a week, and where you shall never come but few days in all; if it be worth the while much to prize one seat above another in the house of worship only because it is the pew or seat that is ranked first in number, and to be seen here for a few days, how will it be worth the while to seek an high mansion in God's temple and in that glorious place that is the everlasting habitation of God and all his children! You that are pleased with your seats in this house because you are seated high or in a place that is looked upon honorable by those that sit round about, and because many can behold you, consider how short a time you will enjoy this pleasure. And if there be any that are not suited in their seats because they are too low for them, let them consider that it is but a very little while before it will [be] all one to you whether you have sat high or low here. But it will be of infinite and everlasting concern to you where your seat is in another world. Let your great concern be while in this world so to improve your opportunities in God's house in this world, whether you sit high or low, as that you may have a distinguished and glorious mansion in God's house in heaven, where you may be fixed in your place in that glorious assembly in an everlasting rest.

In my Father's house are many mansions: if it were not so, I would have told you. I go to prepare a place for you.
John 14:2

Mystical Union

If ye then be risen with Christ, seek those things which are above, where Christ sitteth on the right hand of God.

Colossians 3:1

As the wife is received to a joint possession of her husband's estate, and as the wife of a prince partakes with him in his princely possessions and honors, so the church, the spouse of Christ, when the marriage comes, and she is received to dwell with him in heaven, shall partake with him in his glory. When Christ rose from the dead, and took possession of eternal life, this was not as a private person, but as the public head of all his redeemed people. He took possession of it for them, as well as for himself, and they are "quickened . . . together with Christ, and . . . raised . . . up together." And so when he ascended into heaven, and was exalted to great glory there, this also was as a public person. He took possession of heaven, not only for himself, but his people, as their forerunner and head, that they might ascend also, and "sit together in heavenly places in Christ Jesus" (Ephesians 2:5, 6), and Christ writes upon them his new name, Revelation 3:12; i.e., he makes them partakers of his own glory and exaltation in heaven. His new name is that new honor and glory that the Father invested him with, when he set him on his own right hand, as a prince, when he advances anyone to new dignity in his kingdom, and gives him a new title. Christ and his saints shall be glorified together (Romans 8:17).

Desiring Riches

hose are said to have their hearts set upon riches that have a very high esteem of them and of the happiness that they yield, to whom wealth appears as the chief good which is sufficient to yield happiness to their souls. They have a notion, of them that are rich, that they are the happiest men, and none appear as miserable in their eyes as those that are poor and low in the world. They entertain vast expectations from riches. If they hope to be rich, they please themselves with imagining how much better out they shall be than other men, how much they shall be above them, and how much more they shall be accounted of and how much better [a] figure they shall make in the world.

Whoever imagines that happiness is to be found in anything, they set their hearts upon that thing: for all men's hearts are and will necessarily be upon happiness. There are many men in whose esteem earthly possessions and enjoyments have the place of the chief good. However they may say with the rest of professing Christians that happiness is not to be found in these things and that the enjoyment of God is the highest good, yet they are only words of course which they have been learned to speak by custom and education, and they have no sense at all of what they say, and they have a far higher notion of the happiness that arises from earthly good things than any others. Their souls are empty, and worldly enjoyments appear so big to them that they are of opinion that their souls can be filled with temporal riches.

Surely every man walketh in a vain shew: surely they are disquieted in vain: he heapeth up riches, and knoweth not who shall gather them.
Psalm 39:6

Saints Shall Persevere

And I give unto them eternal life; and they shall never perish, neither shall any man pluck them out of my hand.
John 10:28

hat the saints shall surely persevere will necessarily follow from this, that they have already performed the obedience which is the righteousness by which they have justification unto life; or it is already performed for them, and imputed to them: for that supposes that it is the same thing in the sight of God as if they had performed it. Now, when the creature has once actually performed and finished the righteousness of the law, he is immediately sealed and confirmed to eternal life. There is nothing to keep him off from the tree of life. But as soon as ever a believer has Christ's righteousness imputed to him, he has virtually finished the righteousness of the law.

It is evident the saints shall persevere, because they are already justified. Adam would not have been justified till he had fulfilled and done his work; and then his justification would have been a confirmation. It would have been an approving of him as having done his work, and as standing entitled to his reward. A servant that is sent out about a work is not justified by his master till he has done; and then the master views the work, and seeing it to be done according to his order, he then approves and justifies him as having done his work, and being now entitled to the promised reward; and his title to his reward is no longer suspended on anything remaining. So, Christ having done our work for us, we are justified as soon as ever we believe in him, as being, through what he has accomplished and finished, now already actually entitled to the reward of life. And justification carries in it not only remission of sins, but also being adjudged to life, or accepted as entitled by righteousness to the reward of life; as is evident, because believers are justified by communion with Christ in his justification.

Seeds of Hope

here is hope implied in the essence of justifying faith. Thus there is hope that I may obtain justification by Christ, though there is not contained in its essence a hope that I have obtained it. And so there is a trust in Christ contained in the essence of faith. There is a trust implied in seeking to Christ to be my Savior, in an apprehension that he is a sufficient Savior; though not a trust in him, as one that has promised to save me, as having already performed the condition of the promise. If a city was besieged and distressed by a potent enemy, and should hear of some great champion at a distance, and should be induced by what they hear of his valor and goodness, to seek and send to him for relief, believing what they have heard of his sufficiency, and thence conceiving hope that they may be delivered; the people, in sending, may be said to trust in such a champion; as of old the children of Israel, when they sent into Egypt for help, were said to trust in Egypt. It has by many been said that the soul's immediately applying Christ to itself as its Savior was essential to faith; and so that one should believe him to be his Savior. Doubtless, an immediate application is necessary. But that which is essential is not the soul's immediately applying Christ to itself so properly, as its applying itself to Christ.

Now the God of hope fill you with all joy and peace in believing, that ye may abound in hope, through the power of the Holy Ghost.
Romans 15:13

Selling Christ

*Buy the truth and sell
it not.*
Proverbs 23:23a

All natural men that hear of Christ and continue in unbelief are of the same spirit that the Gadarenes were of; they set their hearts on earthly things as they did, and are of the same mean, earthly, groveling disposition that they were of. They have the same contempt of Jesus Christ, and have no more love to him than they had. They set as mean and inferior things above him in their esteem and affection, as they did, and treat him after the same manner. They do also, as it were, love their swine above Christ; that is, they set more by the meanest and most sordid of earthly enjoyments, than they do by Christ. They sell Christ with all his glory and benefits for filthy lucre, and set more by a little worldly pelf or the filthy pleasure of gratifying some beastly lust, than they do by Christ, with all that he is or has done.

They love their
swine above
Christ.

Hardened Hearers

When Christ went through Samaria and had a little discourse with a woman, a harlot at a well, as he passed along, she believed from his word that she had heard that he was the Christ. And she went and told the men of the city, and we are told that many of the Samaritans of that city believed on him for the saying of the woman. And they went out in droves to Christ to the well and heard him themselves, and besought him that he would tarry with them. And he stayed but two days, and in that time many believed on him because of his word (John 5). But at Jerusalem and in Galilee, where he was so often preaching, working miracles for so long a time together, what little success had he.

Woe unto thee, Chorazin! woe unto thee, Bethsaida! for if the mighty works, which were done in you, had been done in Tyre and Sidon, they would have repented long ago in sackcloth and ashes.
Matthew 11:21

Seeing Christ's Glory

And he trembling and astonished said, Lord, what wilt thou have me to do?
Acts 9:6a

A true trusting in Jesus Christ always arises from a sight of the divine glory of Jesus Christ. But he that sees the divine glory will surely give up himself to the service of Jesus Christ. A sight of the divine glory of the Lord Jesus Christ will have such power upon the heart that it will change the heart and make it to be of a renewed and holy nature; and he that is of a renewed and holy nature cannot live in sin, for this reason, because it is exceeding contrary to that renewed nature. A man that sees the divine glory of the Lord Jesus Christ will give himself to this service; because he sees that he is worthy that he should do so. He is convinced that Christ is worthy to be served and obeyed in everything. He sees the unreasonableness and hatefulness of disobedience to so excellent and glorious a one.

> He is convinced that Christ is worthy to be served and obeyed in everything.

Blessed Security

hey that are in Christ shall never perish, for none shall pluck them out of his hand. They are delivered from all their dreadful misery, that indignation and wrath, tribulation and anguish, which shall come on ungodly men. They were naturally exposed to it, but they are delivered from it; their sins are all forgiven them. The handwriting is eternally blotted out. Their sins are all done away; God has cast them behind his back, and buried their sorrows in the depths of the sea, and they shall no more come into remembrance. They are most safe from misery, for they are built on Christ their everlasting rock. Who is he that condemns? It is Christ that died, yea, rather, is risen again, who is even at the right hand of God. They have the faithful promise of God for their security that is established as a sure witness in heaven. They have an interest in that covenant that is well ordered in all things and sure. "Neither death, nor life, nor angels, nor principalities, nor powers, nor things present, nor things to come, nor height, nor depth, nor any other creature, shall be able to separate them from the love of God which is in Christ Jesus" (Romans 8:38–39).

For the needy shall not alway be forgotten: the expectation of the poor shall not perish for ever.
Psalm 9:18

Eyewitnesses of Majesty

For we have not followed cunningly devised fables, when we made known unto you the power and coming of our Lord Jesus Christ, but were eyewitnesses of his majesty.

2 Peter 1:16

The beauty of Christ's body as seen by the bodily eyes will be ravishing and delightful, chiefly as it will express his spiritual glory. The majesty that will appear in Christ's body will express and show forth the spiritual greatness and majesty of the divine nature; the pureness and beauty of that light and glory will express the perfection of the divine holiness; the sweetness and ravishing mildness of his countenance will express his divine and spiritual love and grace. Thus it was when the three disciples beheld Christ at his transfiguration upon the mount. They beheld a wonderful outward glory in Christ's body, an inexpressible beauty in his countenance; but that outward glory and beauty delighted them principally as an expression of the divine excellencies of his mind, as we may see from their manner of speaking of it. It was the sweet mixture of majesty and grace in his countenance by which they were ravished.

Earthly Things

God never would distribute earthly enjoyments so plentifully amongst the wicked, while he commonly gives his own children but little, were it not that he knew that they were in themselves very worthless, a very man, worthless portion. What man in his wits would be willing to take up with that portion that God frequently allots to those that he hates most? If God did not see all those earthly things to be very worthless indeed, surely he would not be willing to give the very best of them to those that he hates; he would reserve some of the choicest for his favorites. But it is not so. He commonly gives the choicest of earthly things, the very cream of all that the earth can afford, to those that he hates, yea, to those that he hates with a peculiar hatred. He gives his children something of those things, so much as is necessary to carry them through their journey towards heaven.

Remove far from me vanity and lies: give me neither poverty nor riches; feed me with food convenient for me: lest I be full, and deny thee, and say, Who is the LORD? or lest I be poor, and steal, and take the name of my God in vain.
Proverbs 30:8–9

He gives his children so much as is necessary to carry them through their journey to heaven.

Justification

*For when we were yet
without strength, in
due time Christ died
for the ungodly.*
Romans 5:6

That justification respects a man as ungodly. This is evident by these words, "that justifies the ungodly"; which cannot imply less than that God, in the act of justification, has no regard to anything in the person justified, as godliness, or any goodness in him; but that immediately before this act, God beholds him only as an ungodly creature; so that godliness in the person to be justified is not so antecedent to his justification as to be the ground of it. When it is said that God justifies the ungodly, it is absurd to suppose that our godliness, taken as some goodness in us, is the ground of our justification; as, when it is said that Christ gave sight to the blind, to suppose that sight was prior to, and the ground of, that act of mercy in Christ; or as, if it should be said that such an one by his bounty has made a poor man rich, to suppose that it was the wealth of this poor man that was the ground of this bounty towards him and was the price by which it was procured.

Grace and Mercy

hrist is infinitely gracious and merciful. Though his justice is so strict with respect to all sin, and every breach of the law, yet he has grace sufficient for every sinner, and even the chief of sinners. And it is not only sufficient for the most unworthy to show them mercy, and bestow some good upon them, but to bestow the greatest good; yea, it is sufficient to bestow all good upon them, and to do all things for them. There is no benefit or blessing that they can receive so great but the grace of Christ is sufficient to bestow it on the greatest sinner that ever lived. And not only so, but so great is his grace, that nothing is too much as the means of this good. It is sufficient not only to do great things, but also to suffer in order to it; and not only to suffer, but to suffer most extremely even unto death, the most terrible of natural evils; and not only death, but the most ignominious and tormenting, and every way the most terrible that men could inflict; yea, and greater sufferings than men could inflict, who could only torment the body. He had sufferings in his soul that were the more immediate fruits of the wrath of God against the sins of those he undertakes for.

And he arose, and came to his father. But when he was yet a great way off, his father saw him, and had compassion, and ran, and fell on his neck, and kissed him.
Luke 15:20

He has grace sufficient for every sinner.

Christ's Last Suffering̊s

*For it became him, for
whom are all things,
and by whom are all
things, in bringing
many sons unto glory,
to make the captain of
their salvation perfect
through sufferings.*
Hebrews 2:10

Christ's holiness never so illustriously shone forth as it did in his last sufferings; and yet he never was to such a degree treated as guilty. Christ's holiness never had such a trial as it had then; and therefore never had so great a manifestation. When it was tried in this furnace, it came forth as gold, or as silver purified seven times. His holiness then above all appeared in his steadfast pursuit of the honor of God, and in his obedience to him. For his yielding himself unto death was transcendently the greatest act of obedience that ever was paid to God by any one since the foundation of the world. And yet then Christ was in the greatest degree treated as a wicked person would have been. He was apprehended and bound as a malefactor. His accusers represented him as a most wicked wretch. In his sufferings before his crucifixion, he was treated as if he had been the worst and vilest of mankind; and then, he was put to a kind of death, that none but the worst sort of malefactors were wont to suffer, those that were most abject in their persons, and guilty of the blackest crimes. And he suffered as though guilty from God himself, by reason of our guilt imputed to him; for he who knew no sin, was made sin for us; he was made subject to wrath, as if he had been sinful himself. He was made a curse for us. Christ never so greatly manifested his hatred of sin, as against God, as in his dying to take away the dishonor that sin had done to God; and yet never was he to such a degree subject to the terrible effects of God's hatred of sin, and wrath against it, as he was then. In this appears those diverse excellencies meeting in Christ, viz., love to God, and grace to sinners.

Absolute Sovereignty

When men are fallen, and become sinful, God by his sovereignty has a right to determine about their redemption as he pleases. He has a right to determine whether he will redeem any or not. He might, if he had pleased, have left all to perish, or might have redeemed all. Or, he may redeem some, and leave others; and if he doth so, he may take whom he pleases, and leave whom he pleases. To suppose that all have forfeited his favor, and deserved to perish, and to suppose that he may not leave any one individual of them to perish, implies a contradiction; because it supposes that such a one has a claim to God's favor, and is not justly liable to perish; which is contrary to the supposition. It is meet that God should order all these things according to his own pleasure. By reason of his greatness and glory, by which he is infinitely above all, he is worthy to be sovereign, and that his pleasure should in all things take place. He is worthy that he should make himself his end, and that he should make nothing but his own wisdom his rule in pursuing that end, without asking leave or counsel of any, and without giving account of any of his matters. It is fit that he who is absolutely perfect, and infinitely wise, and the Fountain of all wisdom, should determine everything that he effects by his own will, even things of the greatest importance. It is meet that he should be thus sovereign, because he is the first being, the eternal being, whence all other beings are. He is the Creator of all things; and all are absolutely and universally dependent on him; and therefore it is meet that he should act as the sovereign possessor of heaven and earth.

Jesus saith unto him, If I will that he tarry till I come, what is that to thee? follow thou me.
John 21:22

A Heavy Lead

And GOD saw that the wickedness of man was great in the earth, and that every imagination of the thoughts of his heart was only evil continually.
Genesis 6:5

Your wickedness makes you as it were heavy as lead, and to tend downwards with great weight and pressure towards hell; and if God should let you go, you would immediately sink and swiftly descend and plunge into the bottomless gulf, and your healthy constitution, and your own care and prudence, and best contrivance, and all your righteousness, would have no more influence to uphold you and keep you out of hell, than a spider's web would have to stop a falling rock. Were it not for the sovereign pleasure of God, the earth would not bear you one moment; for you are a burden to it; the creation groans with you; the creature is made subject to the bondage of your corruption, not willingly; the sun does not willingly shine upon you to give you light to serve sin and Satan; the earth does not willingly yield her increase to satisfy your lusts; nor is it willingly a stage for your wickedness to be acted upon; the air does not willingly serve you for breath to maintain the flame of life in your vitals, while you spend your life in the service of God's enemies. God's creatures are good, and were made for men to serve God with, and do not willingly serve to any other purpose, and groan when they are abused to purposes so directly contrary to their nature and end. And the world would spew you out, were it not for the sovereign hand of him who hath subjected it in hope. There are the black clouds of God's wrath now hanging directly over your heads, full of the dreadful storm, and big with thunder; and were it not for the restraining hand of God, it would immediately burst forth upon you. The sovereign pleasure of God, for the present, stays his rough wind; otherwise it would come with fury, and your destruction would come like a whirlwind, and you would be like the chaff of the summer threshing floor.

The Spirit's Wind

nd now you have an extraordinary opportunity, a day wherein Christ has thrown the door of mercy wide open, and stands in calling and crying with a loud voice to poor sinners; a day wherein many are flocking to him, and pressing into the kingdom of God. Many are daily coming from the east, west, north and south; many that were very lately in the same miserable condition that you are in, are now in a happy state, with their hearts filled with love to him who has loved them, and washed them from their sins in his own blood, and rejoicing in hope of the glory of God. How awful is it to be left behind at such a day! To see so many others feasting, while you are pining and perishing! To see so many rejoicing and singing for joy of heart, while you have cause to mourn for sorrow of heart, and howl for vexation of spirit! How can you rest one moment in such a condition? Are not your souls as precious as the souls of the people at Suffield, where they are flocking from day to day to Christ?

The wind bloweth where it listeth, and thou hearest the sound thereof, but canst not tell whence it cometh, and whither it goeth: so is every one that is born of the Spirit.
John 3:8

Christ has thrown the door of mercy wide open, and stands in calling and crying with a loud voice.

The Heart's Sense

And though after my
skin worms destroy
this body, yet in my
flesh shall I see God.
Job 19:26

There is a twofold knowledge of good of which God has made the mind of man capable. The first, that which is merely notional; as when a person only speculatively judges that anything is, by the agreement of mankind, called good or excellent, viz., that which is most to general advantage, and between which and a reward there is a suitableness, and the like. And the other thing is that which consists in the sense of the heart; as when the heart is sensible of pleasure and delight in the presence of the idea of it. In the former is exercised merely the speculative faculty, or the understanding, in distinction from the will or the disposition of the soul. In the latter, the will, or inclination, or heart are mainly concerned.

Thus there is a difference between having an opinion that God is holy and gracious, and having a sense of the loveliness and beauty of that holiness and grace. There is a difference between having a rational judgment that honey is sweet, and having a sense of its sweetness. A man may have the former that knows not how honey tastes; but a man cannot have the latter unless he has an idea of the taste of honey in his mind. So there is a difference between believing that a person is beautiful, and having a sense of his beauty. The former may be obtained by hearsay, but the latter only by seeing the countenance. When the heart is sensible of the beauty and amiableness of a thing, it necessarily feels pleasure in the apprehension. It is implied in a person's being heartily sensible of the loveliness of a thing, that the idea of it is pleasant to his soul; which is a far different thing from having a rational opinion that it is excellent.

Godly Conviction

A true sense of the divine excellency of the things of God's word doth more directly and immediately convince us of their truth; and that because the excellency of these things is so superlative. There is a beauty in them so divine and God-like, that it greatly and evidently distinguishes them from things merely human, or that of which men are the inventors and authors; a glory so high and great, that when clearly seen, commands assent to their divine reality. When there is an actual and lively discovery of this beauty and excellency, it will not allow of any such thought as that it is the fruit of men's invention. This is a kind of intuitive and immediate evidence. They believe the doctrines of God's word to be divine, because they see a divine, and transcendent, and most evidently distinguishing glory in them; such a glory as, if clearly seen, does not leave room to doubt of their being of God, and not of men.

Turn you at my reproof: behold, I will pour out my spirit unto you, I will make known my words unto you.
Proverbs 1:23

God's Word Sublime

How sweet are thy
words unto my taste!
yea, sweeter than
honey to my mouth!
Psalm 119:103

If Christ should now appear to anyone as he did on the mount at his transfiguration; or if he should appear to the world in his heavenly glory, as he will do at the day of judgment; without doubt, his glory and majesty would be such as would satisfy everyone that he was a divine person, and that religion was true: and it would be a most reasonable and well-grounded conviction too. And why may there not be that stamp of divinity, or divine glory, on the word of God, on the scheme and doctrine of the gospel, that may be in like matter distinguishing and as rationally convincing, provided it be but seen? It is rational to suppose that when God speaks to the world, there should be something in his word vastly different from men's word. Supposing that God never had spoken to the world, but we had notice that he was about to reveal himself from heaven, and speak to us immediately himself, or that he should give us a book of his own indicting; after what manner should we expect that he would speak? Would it not be rational to suppose that his speech would be exceeding different from men's speech, that there should be such an excellency and sublimity in his word, such a stamp of wisdom, holiness, majesty, and other divine perfections, that the word of men, yea, of the wisest of men, should appear mean and base in comparison of it? Doubtless it would be thought rational to expect this, and unreasonable to think otherwise. When a wise man speaks in the exercise of his wisdom, there is something in everything he says that is very distinguishable from the talk of a little child. So, without doubt, and much more, is the speech of God to be distinguished from that of the wisest of men.

Rejoicing in Beauty

Christ and his church rejoice in each other's beauty. The church rejoices in Christ's divine beauty and glory. She, as it were, sweetly solaces herself in the light of the glory of the Sun of righteousness; and the saints say one to another, as in Isaiah 2:5, "O house of Jacob, come ye, and let us walk in the light of the LORD." The perfections and virtues of Christ are as a perfumed ointment to the church, that make his very name to be to her as ointment poured forth; "Because of the savour of thy good ointments thy name is as ointment poured forth, therefore do the virgins love thee" (Song of Solomon 1:3). And Christ delights and rejoices in the beauty of the church, the beauty which he hath put upon her: her Christian graces are ointments of great price in his sight (1 Peter 3:4). And he is spoken of as greatly desiring her beauty (Psalms 45:11). Yea, he himself speaks of his heart as ravished with her beauty, "Thou hast ravished my heart, my sister, my spouse; thou hast ravished my heart with one of thine eyes, with one chain of thy neck" (Song of Solomon 4:9).

My beloved is mine, and I am his: he feedeth among the lilies.
Song of Solomon 2:16

Living by Christ's Life

For I am in a strait be-
twixt two, having a
desire to depart, and
to be with Christ;
which is far better.
Philippians 1:23

When the soul leaves the body, all these clogs and hindrances shall be removed, every separating wall shall be broken down, and every impediment taken out of the way, and all distance shall cease; the heart shall be wholly and forever attached and bound to him, by a perfect view of his glory. And the vital union shall then be brought to perfection; the soul shall live perfectly in and upon Christ, being perfectly filled with his spirit, and animated by his vital influences; living, as it were, only by Christ's life, without any remainder of spiritual death, or carnal life.

The soul shall live perfectly in and upon Christ, being filled with his spirit and animated by his vital influences.

The People's Prosperity

The prosperity of a people depends more on their rulers than is commonly imagined. As they have the public society under their care and power, so they have advantage to promote the public interest every way; and if they are such rulers as have been described, they are some of the greatest blessings to the public. Their influence has a tendency to promote wealth, and cause temporal virtue amongst them, and so unite them one to another in peace and mutual benevolence, and make them happy in society, each one the instrument of his neighbors' quietness, comfort, and prosperity; and by these means to advance their reputation and honor in the world; and which is much more, to promote their spiritual and eternal happiness. Therefore, the wise man says, "Blessed art thou, O land, when thy king is the son of nobles" (Ecclesiastes 10:17).

Hear the word of the LORD, ye rulers of Sodom; give ear unto the law of our God, ye people of Gomorrah.
Isaiah 1:10

Noah's Folly

Which sometime were disobedient, when once the longsuffering of God waited in the days of Noah, while the ark was a preparing, wherein few, that is, eight souls were saved by water.

1 Peter 3:20

oah's undertaking was of great difficulty, as it exposed him to the continual reproaches of all his neighbors for that whole one hundred and twenty years. None of them believed what he told them of a flood which was about to drown the world. For a man to undertake such a vast piece of work, under a notion that it should be the means of saving him when the world should be destroyed, it made him the continual laughingstock of the world. When he was about to hire workmen, doubtless all laughed at him, and we may suppose, that though the workmen consented to work for wages, yet they laughed at the folly of him who employed them. When the ark was begun, we may suppose that every one that passed by and saw such a huge hulk stand there laughed at it, calling it Noah's folly.

Lot's Wife

ot's wife looked back, because she remembered the pleasant things that she left in Sodom. She hankered after them; she could not but look back with a wishful eye upon the city, where she had lived in such ease and pleasure. Sodom was a place of great outward plenty; they ate the fat, and drank the sweet. The soil about Sodom was exceedingly fruitful; it is said to be as the garden of God (Genesis 13:10). And fulness of bread was one of the sins of the place (Ezekiel 16:49). Here Lot and his wife lived plentifully; and it was a place where the inhabitants wallowed in carnal pleasures and delights. But however much it abounded in these things, what were they worth now, when the city was burning? Lot's wife was very foolish in lingering in her escape, for the sake of things which were all on fire. So the enjoyments, the profits, and pleasures of sin, have the wrath and curse of God on them: brimstone is scattered on them; hell-fire is ready to kindle on them. It is not therefore worthwhile for any person to look back after such things.

Remember Lot's wife.
Luke 17:32

> Lot's wife was very foolish in lingering in her escape.

Honor the Sabbath

Neither carry forth a burden out of your houses on the sabbath day, neither do ye any work, but hallow ye the sabbath day, as I commanded your fathers.

Jeremiah 17:22

God appears in his word having abundantly more weight on this precept concerning the Sabbath, than on any precept of the ceremonial law. It is in the Decalogue, one of the ten commands, which were delivered by God with an audible voice. It was written with his own finger on the tablets of stone in the mount, and was appointed afterwards to be written on the tablets which Moses made. The keeping of the weekly Sabbath is spoken of by the prophets, as that wherein consists a great part or holiness of life; and is inserted among moral duties, "If thou turn away thy foot from the sabbath, from doing thy pleasure on my holy day; and call the sabbath a delight, the holy of the LORD, honourable; and shalt honour him, not doing thine own ways, nor finding thine own pleasure, nor speaking thine own words: then shalt thou delight thyself in the LORD; and I will cause thee to ride upon the high places of the earth, and feed thee with the heritage of Jacob thy father: for the mouth of the LORD hath spoken it" (Isaiah 58:13–14).

It was written in his own finger on the tablets of stone in the mount.

Possessing All Things

By virtue of the believer's union with Christ, he doth really possess all things. That we know plainly from Scripture: but it may be asked, "How he possesses all things; what is he the better for it; how is a true Christian so much richer than other men?" To answer this, I will tell you what I mean by possessing all things. I mean that God, three in one, all that he is, and all that he has, and all that he does, all that he has made or done, the whole universe, bodies and spirits, light, heaven, angels, men, and devils, sun, moon, stars, land, and sea, fish and fowls, all the silver and gold, all beings and perfections, as well as mere man, are as much the Christian's as the money in his pocket, the clothes he wears, or the house he dwells in, or the victuals he eats; yea, more properly his, more advantageously, more his than if he commanded all these things mentioned to be just in all respects as he pleased, at any time, by virtue of the union with Christ; because Christ who certainly doth here possess all things, is entirely his, so that he possesses it all, more than a wife the property of the best and dearest of husbands, more than the hand possesses what the head doth. All the universe is his, only he has not the trouble of managing it; but Christ, to whom it is no trouble to manage it, manages it for him a thousand times as much to his advantage as he could himself, if he had the managing of all the atoms in the universe.

According as his divine power hath given unto us all things that pertain unto life and godliness, through the knowledge of him that hath called us to glory and virtue.
2 Peter 1:3

Freed from Sin

And God shall wipe away all tears from their eyes; and there shall be no more death, neither sorrow, nor crying, neither shall there be any more pain: for the former things are passed away.

Revelation 21:4

The addition of happiness and glory made to the saints at the resurrection, it seems to me evident by the current of the Bible when it tells of those things, will be exceeding great. It is the marriage of the Lamb and the church; the state of things then is the state of perfection; all the state of the church before, both in earth and in heaven, is a growing state. Indeed, the spirits of just men made perfect will be perfectly free from sin and sorrow: will have inexpressible, inconceivable happiness and perfect contentment. But yet part of their happiness will consist in hope of what is to come. They will have as much happiness as they will desire in their existing state, because they will choose to have the addition at that time, and in that order, which God has designed; it will be every way most pleasing, and satisfying, and contenting to them that it should be so. Their having of perfect happiness does not exclude all increase, nor does it exclude all hope, for we do not know but they will increase in happiness forever. The souls of the saints may now have as much happiness as they, while separate, desire; and such happiness as so answers their nature in its present state, as to exclude all sort of uneasiness and disquietude; and yet part of that happiness, part of that sweet rest and contenting joy, consists in the sight of what is future. They do not desire that that addition should be now; they know that it will be most beautiful, most for God's glory, most for their own happiness, and most for the glory of the church, and every way most desirable, that it should be in God's order.

The Elect Angels

When Lucifer rebelled and set up himself as a head in opposition to God and Christ, and drew away a great number of the angels after him, Christ, the Son of God, manifested himself as an opposite head, and appeared graciously to dissuade and restrain by his grace the elect angels from hearkening to Lucifer's temptation, so that they were upheld and preserved from eternal destruction at this time of great danger by the free and sovereign distinguishing grace of Christ. Herein Christ was the Savior of the elect angels, for though he did not save them as he did elect men from the ruin they had already deserved, and were condemned to, and the miserable state they were already in, yet he saved them from eternal destruction they were in great danger of, and otherwise would have fallen into with the other angels. The elect angels joined with him, the glorious Michael, as their captain, while the other angels hearkened to Lucifer and joined with him, and then was that literally true that was fulfilled afterwards figuratively (Revelation 12).

And there was war in heaven: Michael and his angels fought against the dragon; and the dragon fought and his angels, and prevailed not; neither was their place found any more in heaven.
Revelation 12:7–8

Manifestation of Glory

According as he hath chosen us in him before the foundation of the world, that we should be holy and without blame before him in love.

Ephesians 1:4

God's electing a certain definite number from among fallen men from all eternity is a manifestation of his glory. It shows the glory of the divine sovereignty. God hereby declares himself the absolute disposer of the creature; he shows us how far his sovereignty and dominion extend, in eternally choosing some and passing by others, and leaving them to perish. God here appears in a majesty that is unparalleled. Those who can see no glory of dominion in this act have not attained to right apprehensions of God, and never have been made sensible of his glorious greatness. And here is especially shown the glory of divine grace, in God's having chosen his people to blessedness and glory long before they are born; in his choosing them out of the mass of mankind, from whom they were not distinguished, and in his love to them being prior to all that they have or do, being uninfluenced by any excellency of theirs, by the light of any labors or endeavors of theirs, or any respect of theirs towards him.

> God here appears in a majesty that is unparalleled.

The Same Spirit

he ministers of Christ should be persons of the same spirit that their Lord was of: the same spirit of humility and lowliness of heart; for the servant is not greater than his Lord. They should be of the same spirit of heavenly-mindedness, and contempt of the glory, wealth, and pleasures of this world: they should be of the same spirit of devotion and fervent love to God: they should follow the example of his prayerfulness; of whom we read from time to time of his retiring from the world, away from the noise and applauses of the multitudes, into mountains and solitary places, for secret prayer, and holy converse with his Father; and once of his rising up in the morning a great while before day, and going and departing into a solitary place to pray (Mark 1:35). And another time, of his going out into a mountain to pray, and continuing all night in prayer to God (Luke 6:12).

For I have given you an example, that ye should do as I have done to you. Verily, verily, I say unto you, The servant is not greater than his lord; neither he that is sent greater than he that sent him.
John 13:15–16

The World's Wonder

And as they were ston-
ing Stephen, he called
out, "Lord Jesus, re-
ceive my spirit."
Acts 7:59 (ESV)

The world was ready to wonder what strange principle it was that influenced Christians to expose themselves to so great sufferings, to forsake the things that were seen, and renounce all that was dear and pleasant, which was the object of sense. They seemed to the men of the world as if they were beside themselves, and to act as though they hated themselves; there was nothing in *their* view, that could induce them thus to suffer, or to support them under and carry them through such trials. But although there was nothing that the world saw, or that the Christians themselves ever saw with their bodily eyes, that thus influenced and supported them, yet they had a supernatural principle of love to something *unseen;* they loved Jesus Christ, for they saw him spiritually, whom the world saw not, and whom they themselves had never seen with bodily eyes.

They saw him
spiritually, whom
the world saw
not, and whom
they themselves
had never seen
with bodily eyes.

High Affections

Some are ready to condemn all high affection. If persons appear to have their religious affections raised to an extraordinary pitch, they are prejudiced against them, and determine that they are delusions, without further inquiry. But if, as before proved, true religion lies very much in religious affections, then it follows, that if there be a great deal of true religion, there will be great religious affections; if true religion in the hearts of men be raised to a great height, divine and holy affections will be raised to a great height.

Love is an affection, but will any Christian say men ought not to love God and Jesus Christ in a high degree? And will any say we ought not to have a very great hatred of sin, and a very deep sorrow for it? Or that we ought not to exercise a high degree of gratitude to God, for the mercies we receive of him, and the great things he has done for the salvation of fallen men? Or that we should not have very great and strong desires after God and holiness? Is there any who will profess that his affections in religion are great enough; and will say, "I have no cause to be humbled that I am no more affected with the things of religion than I am; I have no reason to be ashamed that I have no greater exercises of love to God, and sorrow for sin, and gratitude for the mercies which I have received?" Who is there that will go and bless God, that he is affected enough with what he has read and heard of the wonderful love of God to worms and rebels in giving his only-begotten Son to die for them, and of the dying love of Christ; and will pray that he may not be affected with them in any higher degree, because high affections are improper, and very unlovely in Christians, being enthusiastic, and ruinous to true religion!

Wherefore I say unto thee, Her sins, which are many, are forgiven; for she loved much: but to whom little is forgiven, the same loveth little.
Luke 7:47

Meekness and Forbearance

Seek ye the LORD, all ye meek of the earth, which have wrought his judgment; seek righteousness, seek meekness: it may be ye shall be hid in the day of the LORD's anger.

Zephaniah 2:3

God especially calls his people to the exercise of extraordinary meekness and mutual forbearance.

Christ appears as it were coming in his kingdom, which calls for great moderation in our behavior towards all men; "Let your moderation be known unto all men: The Lord is at hand" (Philippians 4:5). The awe of the Divine Majesty, that appears present or approaching, should dispose us to it, and deter us from the contrary. For us to be judging one another, and behaving with fierceness and bitterness one towards another, when he who is the searcher of all hearts, to whom we must all give an account, appears so remarkably present, is exceeding unsuitable. Our business at such a time should be at home, searching and condemning ourselves, and taking heed to our own behavior. If there be glorious prosperity to the church of God approaching, those that are the meekest will have the largest share in it. For, when Christ rides forth in his glory and his majesty it is "because of truth and meekness and righteousness" (Psalm 45:3–4).

The Future Harvest

The great works of God in the world during this whole space of time were all preparatory. There were many great changes and revolutions in the world, and they were all only the turning of the wheels of providence to make way for the coming of Christ, and what he was to do in the world; hither tended especially all God's great works towards his church. The church was under various dispensations of providence, and in very various circumstances, before Christ came; but all these dispensations were to prepare the way for his coming. God wrought salvation for the souls of men through all that space of time, though the number was very small to what it was afterwards; and all this was by way of anticipation. All the souls that were saved before Christ came, were only the earnests of the future harvest.

Be patient therefore, brethren, unto the coming of the Lord. Behold, the husbandman waiteth for the precious fruit of the earth, and hath long patience for it, until he receive the early and latter rain.
James 5:7

The Greatest Thing

Christ's incarnation was a greater and more wonderful thing than ever had yet come to pass. The creation of the world was a very great thing, but not as great as the incarnation of Christ. It was a great thing for God to make the creature, but not as great as for the Creator himself to become a creature. We have spoken of many great things that were accomplished between the fall of man and the incarnation of Christ: but God becoming man was greater than all. Then the greatest person was born that ever was or ever will be.

> The greatest person was born that ever was or ever will be.

God's Time, Not Ours

Remember that if ever God bestows mercy upon you, he will use his sovereign pleasure about the time when. He will bestow it on some in a little time and on others not till they have sought it long. If other persons are soon enlightened and comforted, while you remain long in darkness, there is no other way but for you to wait. God will act arbitrarily in this matter, and you cannot help it. You must even be content to wait, in a way of laborious and earnest striving, till his time comes. If you refuse, you will but undo yourself; and when you shall hereafter find yourself undone, and see that your case is past remedy, how will you condemn yourself for foregoing a great probability of salvation, only because you had not patience to hold out, and was not willing to be at the trouble of a persevering labor! And what will it avail before God or your own conscience to say that you could not bear to be obliged to seek salvation so long, when God bestowed it on others that sought it but for a very short time? . . . You must undertake the business of seeking salvation upon these terms, and with no other expectations than this, that if ever God bestows mercy it will be in his own time; and not only so, but also that when you have done all, God will not hold himself obliged to show you mercy at last.

To every thing there is a season, and a time to every purpose under the heaven.
Ecclesiastes 3:1

Dependent on God

That no flesh should glory in his presence.
1 Corinthians 1:29

We are dependent on God's power through every step of our redemption. We are dependent on the power of God to convert us, and give faith in Jesus Christ, and the new nature. It is a work of creation: "If any man be in Christ, he is a new creature" (2 Corinthians 5:17); We are "created in Christ Jesus" (Ephesians 2:10). The fallen creature cannot attain to true holiness, but by being created again: "And that ye put on the new man, which after God is created in righteousness and true holiness" (Ephesians 4:24). It is a raising from the dead: "Wherein also ye are risen with him through the faith of the operation of God, who hath raised him from the dead" (Colossians 2:12). Yea, it is a more glorious work of power than mere creation, or raising a dead body to life, in that the effect attained is greater and more excellent. That holy and happy being, and spiritual life, which is produced in the work of conversion, is a far greater and more glorious effect than mere being and life. And the state from whence the change is made, a death in sin, a total corruption of nature, and depth of misery, is far more remote from the state attained, than mere death or non-entity.

Natural Blindness

Christ is the Holy One of God. He is so holy that the heavens are not pure in his sight. He is possessed of all that holiness which is the infinite beauty and loveliness of the divine nature. But an unbeliever sets nothing by the holiness of Christ. Christ is the wisdom of God and the power of God (1 Corinthians 1:24). But an unbeliever sets nothing by his power and wisdom. The Lord Jesus Christ is full of grace and mercy: the mercy and love of God appear nowhere else so brightly and gloriously as they do in the face of Jesus Christ. But an unbeliever sets no value at all upon the infinite grace of Christ. Neither do unbelievers set anything by those excellent virtues which appeared in Christ's human nature when he was upon earth. He was holy, harmless, undefiled, and separate from sinners; he was meek and lowly of heart; he was patient under afflictions and injuries; when he was reviled, he reviled not again. But unbelievers set nothing by these things in Jesus Christ. They very often hear how excellent and glorious a person Christ is: they are told of his holiness, and grace, and condescension, and meekness, and have the excellencies of Christ plainly set forth to them; yet they set all at naught.

When they knew God, they glorified him not as God, neither were they thankful; but became vain in their imaginations, and their foolish heart was darkened.
Romans 1:21

Persevere in Holiness

Thy people shall be willing in the day of thy power, in the beauties of holiness from the womb of the morning: thou hast the dew of thy youth.

Psalm 110:3

any, when they think they are converted, seem to imagine that their work is done, and that there is nothing else needful in order to their going to heaven. Indeed perseverance in holiness of life is not necessary to salvation in the same way as the righteousness by which a right to salvation is obtained. Nor is actual perseverance necessary in order to our becoming interested in that righteousness by which we are justified. For as soon as ever a soul hath believed in Christ, or hath put forth one act of faith in him, it becomes interested in his righteousness, and in all the promises purchased by it. But persevering in the way of duty is necessary to salvation, as a concomitant and evidence of a title to salvation. There is never a title to salvation without it, though it be not the righteousness by which a title to salvation is obtained. It is necessary to salvation, as it is the necessary consequence of true faith. It is an evidence which universally attends uprightness, and the defect of it is an infallible evidence of the want of uprightness. There such as are good and upright in heart, are distinguished from such as fall away or turn aside: "Do good, O Lord, to those that be good, and to them that are upright in their hearts. As for such as turn aside unto their crooked ways, the LORD shall lead them forth with the workers of iniquity: but peace shall be upon Israel" (Psalm 125:4–5). It is mentioned as an evidence that the hearts of the children of Israel were not right with God, that they did not persevere in the ways of holiness; "A generation that set not their heart aright, and whose spirit was not stedfast with God" (Psalm 78:8).

The Tree of Life

This tree of life did as it were blossom in the sight of the angels when man was first created in an innocent, holy, pleasant, and happy state, and was that creature from whence this future fruit of the tree of life was to spring, the blossom out of which the fruit was to come. It was a fair and pleasant blossom, though weak and feeble, and proved a fading thing like a flower. When man fell, then the blossom faded and fell off; man came forth like a flower, and was cut down, but the blossom fell in order to the succeeding fruit. The fall of man made way for the incarnation of Christ, it gave occasion to the production and ripening of that fruit, and to its blessed consequences. Thus, though Christ is not the Savior of the angels, as he is of men, yet he is the tree of life to the angels, and the bread of life as truly as to men.

The fruit of the righteous is a tree of life; and he that winneth souls is wise.
Proverbs 11:30

When man fell, then the blossom faded and fell off.

Christ's Church

And the flood was forty days upon the earth; and the waters increased, and bare up the ark, and it was lift up above the earth.
Genesis 7:17

The company in Noah's ark was upon many accounts a type of the church of Christ. The ark did literally contain in it the church of God, for all flesh had corrupted their way before God, and true religion and piety seemed to be confined to Noah and his family. The ark was made for the salvation of the church, and for the saving the church from the destruction which the world was to undergo, and to which it was doomed, and of which all the rest of mankind were to be the subjects in an overflowing deluge of God's wrath. So Christ, God-man, mediator, was made for the salvation of his church, to save it from that destruction and woe that is denounced against this wicked world, and that deluge of wrath that will overwhelm all others. The way in which persons were saved by the ark was by taking warning from Noah the preacher of righteousness to fly from the wrath to come, and hearkening to the call, and flying for refuge to the ark, and getting into the ark. So the way by which we are saved by Christ is by flying from the deluge of God's wrath, and taking refuge in Christ, and being in him.

The Hiding Place

he ark was a refuge from storm, and from wind, the rain that poured down out of heaven in a very dreadful manner; it did not hurt those that were in the ark; so Christ is a hiding place from the wind, a covert from the tempest (Isaiah 32:2). He is a place of refuge, and a covert from storm and from wind (Isaiah 4:6); He is to his church a refuge from the storm, when the blast of the terrible ones is as a storm against the wall (Isaiah 25:4). He that is built in Christ, when the wind blows, the rain descends, and the floods come and beat upon his house, it will not fall (Matthew 7:25).

And God remembered Noah, and every living thing, and all the cattle that was with him in the ark: and God made a wind to pass over the earth, and the waters asswaged.
Genesis 8:1

> He is a place of refuge and a covert from storm and from wind.

An Unhappy Way

The secret things belong unto the LORD our God: but those things which are revealed belong unto us and to our children for ever, that we may do all the words of this law.
Deuteronomy 29:29

Don't perplex your mind with the secret decrees of God, and particularly about the eternal decrees of God with respect to yourself, prying into those secrets which are hidden from men and angels, laboring to unseal that book which is sealed with seven seals and which no man in heaven or earth is worthy or able to open or to look thereon. When men get into a way of perplexing their minds with such things, they are in a very unhappy way. The devil has them in a dismal snare. Therefore diligently avoid such a snare and let the revealed will of God be enough for you. Mind what God commands you, what counsels and direction he gives. Let your whole heart be intent upon those things. This is the way for you to prosper. But if you entangle and tease your mind with thoughts about the secret, eternal counsels of God, you will be out of the way of your duty and in the way to your own mischief and will expose yourself to ruin.

Great Delights

here is very great delight the Christian enjoys in the sight he has of the glory and excellency of God. How many arts and contrivances have men to delight the eye of the body. Men take delight in the beholding of great cities, splendid buildings, and stately palaces. And what delight is often taken in the beholding of a beautiful face. May we not well conclude that great delights may also be taken in pleasing the eye of the mind in seeing the most beautiful, the most glorious, the most wonderful Being in the world?

I beseech thee, shew me thy glory.
Exodus 33:18

> There is very great delight the Christian enjoys in the sight he has of the glory and excellency of God.

The Heart's Support

*Casting all your care
upon him; for he
careth for you.*
1 Peter 5:7

Christ is able to afford all that help that is needed . . .
His power and his wisdom are as sufficient as his
purpose, and answerable to his compassions. By
the bowels of his mercies, the love and tenderness of his
heart, he is disposed to help those that are in affliction;
and his ability is answerable to his disposition. He is able
to support the heart under the heaviest sorrows, and to
give light in the greatest darkness; he can divide the thick-
est cloud with beams of heavenly light and comfort; he is
one that gives songs in the night, and turns the shadow of
death into the morning; he has power to make up the loss
of those that are bereaved by the death of the most eminent minister. His own presence with the bereaved is sufficient; if the great Shepherd and Bishop of souls be
present, how much more is this than enough to supply
the want of any under shepherd! And then he is able to
furnish others with like gifts and graces for that work.

All of Grace

he doctrine of election shows that if those who are converted have earnestly sought grace and holiness, and in that way have obtained it, their obtaining it is not owing to their endeavors, but that it was the grace and mercy of God that caused them earnestly to seek conversion that they might obtain it. It shows also that faith itself is the gift of God, and that the saints persevering in a way of holiness unto glory is also the fruit of electing love. Believers' love to God is the fruit of God's love to them, and the giving of Christ, the preaching of the gospel, the appointing of ordinances, are all fruits of the grace of election. All the grace that is shown to any of mankind, either in this world or in the world to come, is comprised in the electing love of God.

But Noah found grace in the eyes of the LORD.
Genesis 6:8

Believers' love to God is the fruit of God's love to them.

Sacred Foretastes

The LORD recompense thy work, and a full reward be given thee of the LORD God of Israel, under whose wings thou art come to trust.

Ruth 2:12

When deeds of charity are done from right principles, God will give spiritual discoveries as a free reward. Though the goodness and excellency of the reward is infinitely greater than the wroth of what is given in charity, yet for Christ's sake it shall be accepted and shall receive such an exceeding great reward. For there is no man that gives a cup of water in Christ's name who loses his reward (Mark 9:41). For God rewards good persons, down, and shaken together, and running over (Luke 6:38). Yea, he rewards an hundredfold; yea, and much more than so. When we give to others earthly good things, God will reward us with heavenly good things. This Christ promises, "when thou makest a feast, call the poor, the maimed, the lame, the blind: and thou shalt be blessed; for they cannot recompense thee: but thou shalt be recompensed at the resurrection of the just" (Luke 14:13–14). And God often gives persons foretastes of those future rewards while here. Treasure is this way laid up in heaven and, therefore, heavenly blessings shall flow down from heaven upon them while they are here.

Helpless in Ourselves

od oftentimes makes use of men's own experience to convince them that they are helpless in themselves. When they first set out in seeking salvation, it may be they thought it an easy thing to be converted. They thought they should presently bring themselves to repent of their sins, and believe in Christ, and accordingly they strove in their own strength with hopes of success. But they were disappointed. And so God suffers them to go on striving to open their own eyes, and mend their own hearts. But they find no success. They have been striving to see for a long time, yet they are as blind as ever; and can see nothing. It is all Egyptian darkness. They have been striving to make themselves better; but they are bad as ever. They have often striven to do something which is good, to be in the exercise of good affections, which should be acceptable to God; but they have no success. And it seems to them, that instead of growing better, they grow worse and worse; their hearts are fuller of wicked thoughts than they were at first; they see no more likelihood of their conversion than there was at first. So God suffers them to strive in their own strength, till they are discouraged, and despair of helping themselves. The prodigal son first strove to fill his belly with the husks which the swine did eat. But when he despaired of being helped in that way, then he came to himself, and entertained thoughts of returning to his father's house.

He draweth also the mighty with his power: he riseth up, and no man is sure of life.
Job 24:22

Follow Paul

Be ye followers of me, even as I also am of Christ.

1 Corinthians 11:1

We should follow Paul in his earnestness in seeking his own salvation. He was not careless and indifferent in this matter; but the kingdom of heaven suffered violence from him. He did not halt between two opinions, or seek with a wavering, unsteady mind, but with the most full determination and strong resolution. He resolved, if it could by any means be possible, that he would attain to the resurrection of the dead. He does not say that he was determined to attain it, if he could, by means that were not very costly or difficult, or by laboring for it a little time, or only now and then, or without any great degree of suffering, or without great loss in his temporal interest. But if by any means he could do it, he would, let the means be easy or difficult. Let it be a short labor and trial, or a long one; let the cross be light or heavy; it was all one to his resolution. Let the requisite means be what they would, if it were possible, he would obtain it. He did not hesitate at worldly losses, for he tells us that he readily suffered the loss of all things, that he might win Christ, and be found in him, and in his righteousness (Philippians 3:8–9). It was not with him as it was with the young man that came kneeling to Christ to inquire of him what he should do to inherit eternal life, and when Christ said, Go and sell all that thou hast and give to the poor, he went away sorrowful. He was not willing to part with all. If Christ had bid him sell half, it may be he would have complied with it. He had a great desire to secure salvation. But the apostle Paul did not content himself with wishing. He was resolved, if it were possible, that he would obtain it. And when it was needful that he should lose worldly good, or when any great suffering was in his way, it was no cause of hesitation to him.

Heavenly Employment

ohn the beloved disciple had often visions of heaven, and in almost every instance had a vision of the inhabitants as praising God. . . . he tells us that he looked, and behold, a door was opened in heaven, and he was called up thither, and that he saw the throne of God and him that sat on the throne; and there he gives us an account how those that were round about the throne were praising God; the four living creatures rest not day nor night, saying, Holy, holy, holy Lord God Almighty, which was, and is, and is to come. And when those living creatures give glory and honor and thanks to him, the four and twenty elders fall down before him and worship him. Again . . . we have an account how they sing praises to Christ . . . we have an account how the hosts of heaven sing hallelujahs to God. By all which it most evidently appears that their work very much consists in praising God and Christ. We have but a very imperfect knowledge of the future state of blessedness, and of their employment: without doubt they have various employments there. We cannot reasonably question but they are employed in contributing to each other's delight. They shall dwell together in society. They shall also probably be employed in contemplating on God, his glorious perfections, and glorious works, and so gaining knowledge in these things. And doubtless they will be employed many ways which we know nothing of; but this we may determine, that much of their employment consists in praising God.

Heal me, O LORD, and I shall be healed; save me, and I shall be saved: for thou art my praise.
Jeremiah 17:14

Beautiful with Holiness

Give unto the LORD the glory due unto his name: bring an offering, and come before him: worship the LORD in the beauty of holiness.

1 Chronicles 16:29

It is a great pleasure for an intelligent and rational being to be excellent. Happiness and delight of soul arise always from the sight or apprehension of something that appears excellent. Thus even God himself has infinite delight in beholding his own infinite excellency, and for an excellent being there necessarily arises pleasure. Not the godly are pleased with proud and haughty thoughts of their own excellency, for they know they have nothing but what they received and that their excellency is wholly communicated to them by God. But the believer may rejoice, and does rejoice, to see the image of God upon their souls, to see the likeness of his dear Jesus. The saints in heaven, who have all remainders of pride taken away, do yet rejoice to see themselves made excellent by God and appearing beautiful with holiness. And if it be a great pleasure to see excellent things, it must be a sweet consideration to think that God of his grace has made me excellent and lovely. If they delight to see the loveliness of Jesus Christ, it must be a matter of delight to see that Christ has communicated of his loveliness to their souls.

The Wicked Hate His Holiness

The wicked dislike God because he is a holy God. This is the main foundation of the enmity that wicked men have against God. His perfect purity and holiness make them enemies to him, because from this perfection of his nature he necessarily hates sin, and so hates their sins, which they love, and he will not and cannot allow of any sin in them. They are utter enemies to such a holy God. And yet they would not like him if they supposed him to be an unholy being, or if they supposed him to be at all wanting in perfect holiness, for then he could not be depended upon. If he were unholy, they know that if he promised them anything they could have no certain dependence upon it, for an unholy being is liable to break his promises; if he were unholy they could have no dependence on his faithfulness, and therefore they would never be willing to give up themselves to him as their God, for they would not know how he would dispose of them, what he would do with them. If he were to obligate himself by covenant, yet they could have no dependence upon it: and therefore they would by no means accept of such a God to be their God, to rule over them, and dispose of them.

God judgeth the righteous, and God is angry with the wicked every day.
Psalm 7:11

The Narrow and the Broad

Because strait is the gate, and narrow is the way, which leadeth unto life, and few there be that find it.

Matthew 7:14

There are but two things which God offers to mankind for their portion: one is this world, with the pleasures and profits of sin, together with eternal misery ensuing; the other is heaven and eternal glory, with a life of self-denial and respect to all the commands of God. Many, as long as they live, come to no settled determination which of these to choose. They must have one or the other, they cannot have both; but they always remain in suspense, and never make their choice. They would fain have heaven and this world too; they would have salvation and the pleasures and profits of sin too. But considering heaven and the world, as God offers them, they will have neither. God offers heaven only with the self-denial and difficulty which are in the way to it; and they are not willing to have heaven on these conditions. God offers the world and the pleasures of sin to men not alone, but with eternal misery in connection with them; and so neither are they willing to have the world. They would fain divide heaven from the holiness and self-denial which are the way to it, and from the holiness which reigns in it, and then they would be glad to have heaven. They would fain divide sin from hell, and then they would fully determine forever to cleave to sin. But God will not make such a division for them. They must have one or the other of these for their portion, as God offers; and therefore they never make any choice at all.

Our Childlike Relation

Whis ascended into heaven, he was received to a glorious and peculiar joy and blessedness in the enjoyment of his Father, who, in his passion, hid his face from him; such an enjoyment as became the relation he stood in to the Father, and such as was a meet reward for the great and hard service he had performed on earth. Then God showed him the path of life, and brought him into his presence, where is fullness of joy, and to sit on his right hand, where there are pleasures for evermore, as is said of Christ (Psalm 16:11). Then the Father "made him most blessed forever." He "made him exceeding glad with his countenance," as in Psalm 21:6. The saints, by virtue of their union with Christ, and being his members, do in some sort partake of his childlike relation to the Father; and so are heirs with him of his happiness in the enjoyment of his Father; as seems to be intimated by the apostle, in Galatians 4:4–7. The spouse of Christ, by virtue of her espousals to that only begotten Son of God, is, as it were, a partaker of his filial relation to God, and becomes the king's daughter, and so partakes with her divine husband in his enjoyment of his Father and her Father, his God and her God.

That they all may be one; as thou, Father, art in me, and I in thee, that they also may be one in us: that the world may believe that thou hast sent me.
John 17:21

Surer Grounds

We have also a more sure word of prophecy; whereunto ye do well that ye take heed, as unto a light that shineth in a dark place, until the day dawn, and the day star arise in your hearts.

2 Peter 1:19

We have the truth upon surer grounds from God's testimony, than we could have it from the testimony of one rising from the dead. Suppose one should rise from the dead, and tell us of the dreadfulness of hell torments; how precarious a foundation would that be to build upon, in a matter of such importance, unless we consider it as confirmed by divine testimony. We should be uncertain whether there were not some delusion in the case. We know that it is impossible for God to lie; and we may know that the matter is just as he declares it to us. But if one should come from the dead, we could not be so sure that we were no way imposed upon. We could not be so sure that he who testified was not himself subject to some delusion. We could not be sure that the matter was not strained too high, and represented greater than it really is.

One coming from the dead could not, merely by force of his own testimony, make us sure that we should come to that place of torments if we did not repent and reform. And if there should come more witnesses than one from the dead, if there should be ever so many, yet there is no authority equal to that of God; there is no testimony of spirits from the invisible world which would be so indisputable and unquestionable as the divine testimony. How could we know, unless by some divine revelation, that they who should come from the dead had not come to deceive us? How could we know how wicked, or how good they were, and upon what views they acted?

Whereas we have the greatest ground to be assured that the First Being, and the Fountain of all being and perfection, is nothing but light and truth itself, and therefore that it is impossible he should deceive or be deceived.

Still a Great Work

The Christian's work is not done; but he finds still a great work to do, and great wants to be supplied. He sees himself still to be a poor, empty, helpless creature, and that he still stands in great and continual need of God's help. He is sensible that without God he can do nothing. A false conversion makes a man in his own eyes self-sufficient. He saith he is rich, and increased with goods, and hath need of nothing; and knoweth not that he is wretched, and miserable, and poor, and blind, and naked. But after a true conversion, the soul remains sensible of its own impotence and emptiness, as it is in itself, and its sense of it is rather increased than diminished. It is still sensible of its universal dependence on God for everything. A true convert is sensible that his grace is very imperfect; and he is very far from having all that he desires. Instead of that, by conversion are begotten in him new desires which he never had before. He now finds in him holy appetites, a hungering and thirsting after righteousness, a longing after more acquaintance and communion with God. So that he hath business enough still at the throne of grace; yea, his business there, instead of being diminished, is rather increased.

I press toward the mark for the prize of the high calling of God in Christ Jesus.
Philippians 3:14

Righteous Judgments

Doth God pervert judgment? or doth the Almighty pervert justice?

Job 8:3

It is not inconsistent with the mercy of God to inflict an eternal punishment on wicked men. It is an unreasonable and unscriptural notion of the mercy of God that he is merciful in such a sense that he cannot bear that penal justice should be executed. This is to conceive of the mercy of God as a passion to which his nature is so subject that God is liable to be moved, and affected, and overcome by seeing a creature in misery, so that he cannot bear to see justice executed: which is a most unworthy and absurd notion of the mercy of God, and would, if true, argue great weakness. It would be a great defect, and not a perfection, in the sovereign and supreme Judge of the world, to be merciful in such a sense that he could not bear to have penal justice executed. It is a very unscriptural notion of the mercy of God. The Scriptures everywhere represent the mercy of God as free and sovereign, and not that the exercises of it are necessary, so that God cannot bear justice should take place. The Scriptures abundantly speak of it as the glory of the divine attribute of mercy, that it is free and sovereign in its exercises; and not that God cannot but deliver sinners from misery. This is a mean and most unworthy idea of the divine mercy.

Christ Welcomes Sinners

Christ in times past has graciously received those that have come to him; he has made them welcome; he has embraced them in the arms of his love; he has admitted them to a blessed and eternal union with himself, and has given them a right to all the privileges of the sons of God; and he is the same still that he has been heretofore. We have an account in Scripture of many that came to him; we have an account in the history of Christ's life of many that accepted his calls, and we have an account in the book of the Acts of the Apostles, of multitudes that believed in him; but we read of none that ever were rejected by him. And we ourselves have seen many that we have reason to think Christ has accepted on their coming to him, many that have been great sinners, many that have been old hardened sinners, many that had been backsliders, and many that had been guilty of quenching the Spirit of God. And he is the same still; he is as ready to receive such sinners now as he was then. Christ never yet rejected any that came to him: he has always been the same in this respect; he is so now; and so he surely will be still.

Come unto me, all ye that labour and are heavy laden, and I will give you rest.
Matthew 11:28

Their Last Account

The Lord knoweth how to deliver the godly out of temptations, and to reserve the unjust unto the day of judgment to be punished.
2 Peter 2:9

he wicked must appear before their Judge to give their account. They will find no mountains or rocks to fall upon them that can cover them and hide them from the wrath of the Lamb . . . Many shall see their former neighbors and acquaintance, their companions, their brothers, and their wives taken and they left. They shall be summoned to go and appear before the judgment seat; and go they must, however unwilling; they must stand at Christ's left hand, in the midst of devils and wicked men. This shall again add still further amazement, and will cause their horror still to be in a further degree than ever. With what horror will that company come together! And then shall they be called to their account; then shall be brought to light the hidden things of darkness; then shall all the wickedness of their hearts be made known; then shall be declared the actual wickedness they have been guilty of; then shall appear their secret sins that they have kept hid from the eye of the world; then shall be manifested in their true light those sins that they used to plead for, and to excuse and justify. . . . All the world shall see it, and many shall rise up in judgment against them and condemn them; their companions whom they tempted to wickedness, others whom they have hardened in sin by their example, shall rise up against many of them; and the heathen that have had no advantages in comparison of them, and many of whom have yet lived better lives than they, shall rise up against them; and they shall be called to a special account; the Judge will reckon with them, they shall be speechless, they shall be struck dumb, their own consciences bearing testimony against them, and shall cry aloud against them, for they shall then see how great and terrible a God he is, against whom they have sinned. Then shall they stand at the left hand, while they see others whom they knew on earth sitting at the right hand of Christ in glory, shining forth as the sun, accepted of Christ, and sitting with him to judge and condemn them.

For Feeble Knees

hrist puts strength and a principle of new life into the weary soul that comes to him. The sinner, before he comes to Christ, is as a sick man that is weakened and brought low, and whose nature is consumed by some strong distemper: he is full of pain, and so weak that he cannot walk nor stand. Therefore, Christ is compared to a physician. . . . When he comes and speaks the word, he puts a principle of life into him that was before as dead: he gives a principle of spiritual life and the beginning of eternal life; he invigorates the mind with a communication of his own life and strength, and renews the nature and creates it again, and makes the man to be a new creature; so that the fainting, sinking spirits are now revived, and this principle of spiritual life is a continual spring of refreshment, like a well of living water. "Whosoever drinketh of the water that I shall give him shall never thirst; but the water that I shall give him shall be in him a well of water springing up into everlasting life" (John 4:14). Christ gives his Spirit that calms the mind, and is like a refreshing breeze of wind. He gives that strength whereby he lifts up the hands that hang down, and strengthens the feeble knees.

They that be whole need not a physician, but they that are sick.
Matthew 9:12b

Christ, Our Shelter

For thou hast been a shelter for me, and a strong tower from the enemy.
Psalm 61:3

God exercises his mercy towards his people, not for their sakes, but for Christ's sake, "for his name's sake." It is for his name's sake, in that it is for Christ's sake, in that God's "name is in him" (Exodus 23:21). He is that name of the Lord that is a strong tower, where God's people are safe. Even at the time when God seems to be about to pour out his wrath, this tower shelters them from his wrath. So that though it may in some sense be said that mercy overcame justice, and rejoices against judgment; yet in Christ Jesus justice rather willingly yields to mercy. Justice withdraws its hands, and goes away satisfied, without the blood of God's offending people, because it is satisfied in the blood of their surety. For in Christ Jesus, "Mercy and truth are met together; righteousness and peace have kissed each other" (Psalm 85:10).

God exercises his mercy towards his people, not for their sakes, but for Christ's sake.

Communion of Saints

What the primitive Christians meant by the communion of saints seems to be this, that believers or Christians (which at first were most commonly called saints) of the gentiles and all nations were equally partakers of the peculiar benefits and blessings of God's people. This was a great article of faith among them, and strongly opposed by the unbelieving Jews and by many of those that believed; which it is probable was the occasion of making it an article of the Creed. This seems to be the first meaning of the phrase, as with respect to this it is commonly used in the New Testament, which is by the apostles spoken of in an exalted manner as a very glorious discovery, doctrine, and blessing of the gospel, and is much insisted on by them.

That which we have seen and heard declare we unto you, that ye also may have fellowship with us: and truly our fellowship is with the Father, and with his Son Jesus Christ.
1 John 1:3

The Exodus

And the LORD said, I
have surely seen the af-
fliction of my people
which are in Egypt,
and have heard their
cry by reason of their
taskmasters; for I
know their sorrows.
Exodus 3:7

The redemption of the church of God out of Egypt
[is] the most remarkable of all in the Old Testament, the greatest pledge and forerunner of the
future redemption by Christ, and much more insisted on
in Scripture than any other of those redemptions. And indeed it was the greatest type of Christ's redemption of
any providential event whatsoever. This was by Jesus
Christ, for it was wrought by him who appeared to Moses
in the bush; the person that sent Moses to redeem that
people. But that was Christ, as is evident, because he is
called the angel of the Lord (Exodus 3:2–3). The bush represented the human nature of Christ, who is called the
branch. This bush grew on mount Sinai or Horeb, a word
that signifies a dry place, as the human nature of Christ
was a root out of a dry ground. The bush burning with
fire represented the sufferings of Christ, in the fire of
God's wrath. It burned and was not consumed; so Christ,
though he suffered extremely, yet perished not; but overcame at last, and rose from his sufferings. Because this
great mystery of the incarnation and sufferings of Christ
was here represented, therefore Moses says, I will turn
aside, and behold this great sight. A great sight he might
well call it, when there was represented God, manifest
in the flesh, suffering a dreadful death, and rising from
the dead.

The Destruction of Jerusalem

his destruction of Jerusalem was in all respects agreeable to what Christ had foretold of it (Matthew 24), as appeals by the account which Josephus gives of it, who was then present, who had a share in the calamity, and who wrote the history of their destruction. Many circumstances resembled the destruction of the wicked at the Day of Judgment; by his account, it was accompanied with many fearful sights in the heavens, and with a separation of the righteous from the wicked. Their city and temple were burnt, and razed to the ground; and the ground on which the city stood was ploughed, so that one stone was not left upon another (Matthew 24:2).

And Jesus said unto them, See ye not all these things? verily I say unto you, There shall not be left here one stone upon another, that shall not be thrown down.
Matthew 24:2

Strong Resolutions

*Who, when he had
found one pearl of
great price, went and
sold all that he had,
and bought it.*
Matthew 13:46

There are two things needful in a person, in order to these strong resolutions; there must be a sense of the great importance and necessity of the mercy sought, and there must also be a sense of opportunity to obtain it, or the encouragement there is to seek it. The strength of resolution depends on the sense which God gives to the heart of these things. Persons without such a sense may seem to themselves to take up resolutions; they may, as it were, force a promise to themselves, and say within themselves, "I will seek as long as I live, I will not give up till I obtain," when they do but deceive themselves. Their hearts are not in it; neither do they indeed take up any such resolution as they seem to themselves to do. It is the resolution of the mouth more than of the heart; their hearts are not strongly bent to fulfill what their mouth says. The firmness of resolution lies in the fulness of the disposition of the heart to do what is resolved to be done. Those who are pressing into the kingdom of God have a disposition of heart to do everything that is required, and that lies in their power to do, and to continue in it. They have not only earnestness, but steadiness of resolution: they do not seek with a wavering unsteady heart, by turns or fits, being off and on; but it is the constant bent of the soul, if possible, to obtain the kingdom of God.

God's Enemies

God, though the Creator of all things, yet has some enemies in the world. Men in general will own that they are sinners. There are few, if any, whose consciences are so blinded as not to be sensible they have been guilty of sin. And most sinners will own that they have bad hearts. They will own that they do not love God so much as they should do; that they are not as thankful as they ought to be for mercies; and that in many things they fail. And yet few of them are sensible that they are God's enemies. They do not see how they can be truly so called; for they are not sensible that they wish God any hurt, or endeavor to do him any. But we see that the Scripture speaks of them as enemies to God.

And you, that were sometime alienated and enemies in your mind by wicked works, yet now hath he reconciled.
Colossians 1:21

Types of the Messiah

And did all drink the same spiritual drink: for they drank of that spiritual Rock that followed them: and that Rock was Christ.

1 Corinthians 10:4

It is much more reasonably and credibly supposed that God should through the ages of the Old Testament be very much in typifying things pertaining to the Messiah and his salvation, not only in prophecies, but also in types; because we find in fact that, at the very beginning of God's revealing the Messiah to mankind, prophecies and types went together in the first prophecy of the Messiah, and the first proper prophecy that ever was in the world God foretold and typified the redemption both together when God said to the serpent: "I will put enmity between thee and the woman, and between thy seed and her seed; It shall bruise thy head, and thou shalt bruise his heel" (Genesis 3:15). This is undoubtedly a prediction of the Messiah's victory over Satan, and his suffering from Satan, and of the Messiah's people's victory and deliverance through him. And none can reasonably question but that here is also some respect had to that enmity there is between mankind and serpents, and the manner of serpents wounding mankind and of men's killing them; for God is here speaking concerning a beast of the field that was ranked with the cattle, as appears by the foregoing verse. And this state of things with respect to serpents was plainly ordered and established in these words. But if we suppose that both these things were intended in the same words, then undoubtedly one is spoken of and ordained as a representation of the other.

Gideon: A Type of Christ

he great agreement there also is between the story of Gideon's victory over the Midianites, and things spoken in the prophecies concerning the Messiah, is an argument that the former is typical of the latter. Gideon brought Israel out of the wilderness, and from the caves, rocks, and mountains, where they had had their abode. This agrees with Psalm 68:22, "The Lord said, I will bring again from Bashan!" And Psalm 89:12, "Tabor and Hermon shall rejoice in thy name." . . . and Isaiah 42:11, "Let the wilderness and the cities thereof lift up their voice, . . . let the inhabitants of the rock sing, let them shout from the tops of the mountains." And Canticles 2:14, "O my dove, that art in the clefts of the rock, let me see thy countenance."

I will . . . bring her into the wilderness, and speak comfortably unto her.
Hosea 2:14

Renounce Sinful Behavior

Let love be without dissimulation. Abhor that which is evil; cleave to that which is good.

Romans 12:9

Thoroughly renounce and forsake all ways of sinful behavior. For you have heard that hope and comfort are never to be expected till sin is slain or forsaken. He who is not thorough in his reformation cannot reasonably hope for comfort, how much soever he may abound in some particular duties. Persons who are under awakenings, and would seek a true hope of salvation, should in the first place see that they thoroughly renounce every wicked practice. They should search their ways, and consider what is wrong in them: what duties they have omitted, which ought to have been done; and what practices they have allowed, which ought to be forsaken; and should immediately reform, retaining no one way of sin, denying all ungodliness, omitting nothing which is required; and should see that they persevere in it, that it be not merely a temporary, short-lived restraint, but an everlasting renunciation. This is the way to have the troubler slain.

Persons who are under awakenings should thoroughly renounce every wicked practice.

A Burning and Shining Light

W hat Christ takes notice of in John, and declares concerning him, is that he was a burning and a shining light. He was a light to the church of Israel, to reveal the mind and will of God to them, after a long-continued dark season, and after they had been destitute of any prophet to instruct them for some ages; he arose on Israel, as the morning star, the forerunner of the Sun of righteousness, to introduce the dayspring, or dawning of the gospel day, to give light to them that till then had sat in the darkness of perfect night, which was the shadow of death; to give them the knowledge of salvation; as Zacharias his father declares at his circumcision, "And thou, child, shalt be called the prophet of the Highest: for thou shalt go before the face of the Lord to prepare his ways; to give knowledge of salvation unto his people by the remission of their sins, through the tender mercy of our God; whereby the dayspring from on high hath visited us, to give light to them that sit in darkness and in the shadow of death, to guide our feet into the way of peace" (Luke 1:76–79).

Ye sent unto John, and he bare witness unto the truth.
John 5:33

Sovereign Pleasure

*The LORD taketh plea-
sure in them that fear
him, in those that
hope in his mercy.*
Psalm 147:11

God exercises his sovereignty in the advantages he bestows upon particular persons. All need salvation alike, and all are, naturally, alike undeserving of it; but he gives some vastly greater advantages for salvation than others. To some he assigns their place in pious and religious families, where they may be well instructed and educated, and have religious parents to dedicate them to God, and put up many prayers for them. God places some under a more powerful ministry than others, and in places where there are more of the outpourings of the Spirit of God. To some he gives much more of the strivings and the awakening influences of the Spirit, than to others. It is according to his mere sovereign pleasure.

God exercises his
sovereignty in
the advantages
he bestows upon
particular
persons.

Absolutely Dependent

ence we learn how absolutely we are dependent on God in this great matter of the eternal salvation of our souls. We are dependent not only on his wisdom to contrive a way to accomplish it, and on his power to bring it to pass, but we are dependent on his mere will and pleasure in the affair. We depend on the sovereign will of God for everything belonging to it, from the foundation to the topstone. It was of the sovereign pleasure of God that he contrived a way to save any of mankind, and gave us Jesus Christ, his only begotten Son, to be our Redeemer. Why did he look on us; and send us a Savior, and not the fallen angels? It was from the sovereign pleasure of God. It was of his sovereign pleasure what means to appoint. His giving us the Bible, and the ordinances of religion, is of his sovereign grace. His giving those means to us rather than to others, his giving the awakening influences of his Spirit, and his bestowing saving grace, are all of his sovereign pleasure. When he says, "Let there be light in the soul of such an one," it is a word of infinite power and sovereign grace.

Is it any pleasure to the Almighty, that thou art righteous? or is it gain to him, that thou makest thy ways perfect?
Job 22:3

The Madness of Men

There went in two
and two unto Noah
into the ark, the male
and the female, as God
had commanded
Noah.
Genesis 7:9

God made the very beasts and birds of the old world to rebuke the madness of the men of that day: for they, even all sorts of them, fled to the ark while the door was yet open: which the men of that day refused to do; God hereby, thus signifying, that their folly was greater than that of the very brute creatures. Such folly and madness are you guilty of, who refuse to hearken to the warnings that are given you of the approaching flood of the wrath of God. You have been once more warned today, while the door of the ark yet stands open. You have, as it were, once again heard the knocks of the hammer and axe in the building of the ark, to put you in mind that a flood is approaching. Take heed therefore that you do not still stop your ears, treat these warnings with a regardless heart, and still neglect the great work which you have to do lest the flood of wrath suddenly come upon you, sweep you away, and there be no remedy.

Quiet Cheerfulness

I f a person has good evidence that his sins are forgiven, and that he is at peace with God, and is the object of God's love, and has within him the testimony of a good conscience; this is enough to give quietness and cheerfulness, wherever he is, and whatever he is about. It is enough to make hard labor easy, and he may well do whatsoever he does cheerfully that does to the Lord, and not to men. The exercise of religion would even sweeten young people's diversions, as it would regulate them according to the rules of wisdom and virtue, and would direct them to suitable and worthy ends, and make them subservient to excellent purposes. As has been said of earthly enjoyments and company, so it is true of diversions, that they are abundantly sweetest when virtue moderates and guides them.

He maketh me to lie down in green pastures: he leadeth me beside the still waters.
Psalm 23:2

> They are abundantly sweetest when virtue moderates and guides them.

Make Use of Prayer

Praying always with all prayer and supplication in the Spirit, and watching thereunto with all perseverance.
Ephesians 6:18

ake much use of prayer, seeing you have such a subtle and cruel enemy that so indefatigably seeks your ruin, and that so artfully disguises himself to deceive you. Keep close to God, and forsake him not. Be continually with him, near to him in the duty of prayer, that he would be your guard and your counselor; that he would defend you from the wiles of the devil; that he would instruct you, and undertake to be your counselor by the conduct of his own Holy Spirit; that he would enable you to discern the subtle devises of Satan, that you may escape his snares that he spreads for you. If you are one of them that dwells under the shadow of the Almighty, he will "deliver thee from the snare of the fowler" (Psalm 91:3).

Keep close to God, and forsake him not.

The Heart's Throne

He delights to exalt God in his own heart. He will not presume to sit in the throne of his own heart, but choose rather that God should sit there, and he himself at the footstool. The sinner, he sits in the throne of his own heart, he takes God's place, will be governed by none but himself; but the truly godly man, he invites God to sit in the highest place in his soul and delights to see him placed there, and instead of being against it, he wonders that God will even condescend so much as to take up his abode in his heart, although it be in the throne of it. He rejoices to see God possessing the best apartment in his heart, the best room of his soul, and greatly admires that the great Jehovah will ever so humble himself as to dwell there. Formerly, before he was converted, while he was yet a rebel against God, he would not admit God into his heart, proudly possessed the throne himself and held the scepter of his own soul; but since God has graciously enlightened him, how doth he immediately quit his seat, give place to God, and deliver up the scepter to him, and with pleasure cast himself down to the footstool, and finds vastly more pleasure now in the dust before God than he did before in the throne.

He that trusteth in his own heart is a fool: but whoso walketh wisely, he shall be delivered.
Proverbs 28:26

Abound in Prayer

Continue in prayer, and watch in the same with thanksgiving.
Colossians 4:2

Abound in earnest prayer to God that he would open your eyes, that you may behold the glorious and rich provision made for sinners in Jesus Christ. The souls of natural men are so blinded that they see no beauty or excellency in Christ. They do not see his sufficiency. They see no beauty in the work of salvation by him; and as long as they remain thus blind, it is impossible that they should close with Christ. The heart will never be drawn to an unknown Savior. It is impossible that a man should love that, and freely choose that, and rejoice in that, in which he sees no excellency. But if your eyes were opened to see the excellency of Christ, the work would be done. You would immediately believe on him; and you would find your heart going after him. It would be impossible to keep it back. But take heed that you do not entertain a wrong notion of what it is spiritually to see Christ. If you do, you may seek that which God never bestows. Do not think that spiritually to see Christ is to have a vision of him as the prophets had, to see him in some bodily shape, to see the features of his countenance. Do not pray or seek for any such thing as this. But what you are to seek is that you may have a sight of the glorious excellency of Christ, and of the way of salvation through him, in your heart. This is a spiritual sight of Christ. This is that for which you must cry to God day and night. God is the fountain of spiritual light. He opens the eyes of the blind. He commands the light to shine out of darkness. It is easy with God to enlighten the soul, and fill it with these glorious discoveries, though it is beyond the power of men and angels.

But for the Grace of God

Consider what a vast difference has God made between you and other men, how vastly different is your relative state from theirs, how much more has God done for you than for them. Seek therefore those things which are above, where God is. Will it not be a shame if one that is entitled to such glory conducts no better than a child of the devil? Consider it seriously; and let it not be asked with reference to you, What do you more than others? (Matthew 5:47). Other men love those that love them; other men do good to those that do good to them: walk worthy of the vocation wherewith ye are called; and let it appear that you are of a spirit more excellent than your neighbor; manifest more love, and more meekness, and more humility, with all lowliness and meekness, with longsuffering, forbearing one another in love; walk worthy of the Lord to all pleasing, strengthened with all might according to his glorious power unto all patience and longsuffering. Put ye on as the elect of God, holy and beloved, bowels of mercies, kindness, gentleness of mind, meekness, longsuffering, forbearing one another, forgiving one another; and let your light so shine before men, that they, seeing your good works, may glorify your Father who is in heaven. Seeing God has given you so much, God and men may well expect of you that you should be greatly distinguished in your life from other men.

For by grace are ye saved through faith; and that not of yourselves: it is the gift of God.
Ephesians 2:8

Pray for Others

Confess your faults one to another, and pray one for another, that ye may be healed. The effectual fervent prayer of a righteous man availeth much.

James 5:16

Christians ought to be earnest in their prayers and endeavors for the salvation of others. Christians are the followers of Christ, and they should follow him in this. We see . . . how great the labor and travail of Christ's soul was for others' salvation, and what earnest and strong cries to God accompanied his labors. Here he hath set us an example. Herein he hath set an example for ministers, who should as co-workers with Christ travail in birth with them till Christ be found in them; "My little children, of whom I travail in birth again until Christ be formed in you" (Galatians 4:19). They should be willing to spend and be spent for them. They should not only labor for them, and pray earnestly for them, but should, if occasion required, be ready to suffer for them, and to spend not only their strength, but their blood for them; "And I will very gladly spend and be spent for you; though the more abundantly I love you, the less I be loved" (2 Corinthians 12:15). Here is an example for parents, showing how they ought to labor and cry to God for the spiritual good of their children. You see how Christ labored and strove and cried to God for the salvation of his spiritual children; and will not you earnestly seek and cry to God for your natural children?

Common Grace

here are many in this world who are wholly destitute of saving grace, who yet have common grace. They have no true holiness, but nevertheless have something of that which is called moral virtue; and are the subjects of some degree of the common influences of the Spirit of God. It is so with those in general that live under the light of the gospel, and are not given up to judicial blindness and hardness. Yea, those that are thus given up, yet have some degree of restraining grace while they live in this world; without which the earth could not bear them, and they would in no measure be tolerable members of human society. But when any are damned, or cast into hell, as the devils are, God wholly withdraws his restraining grace, and all merciful influences of his Spirit whatsoever. They have neither saving grace nor common grace; neither the grace of the Spirit, nor any of the common gifts of the Spirit; neither true holiness, nor moral virtue of any kind. Hence arises the vast increase of the exercise of wickedness in the hearts of men when they are damned. And herein is the chief difference between the damned in hell, and unregenerate and graceless men in this world. Not that wicked men in this world have any more holiness or true virtue than the damned, or have wicked men, when they leave this world, any principles of wickedness infused into them: but when men are cast into hell, God perfectly takes away his Spirit from them, as to all its merciful common influences, and entirely withdraws from them all restraints of his Spirit and good providence.

That ye may be the children of your Father which is in heaven: for he maketh his sun to rise on the evil and on the good, and sendeth rain on the just and on the unjust.
Matthew 5:45

Sons of the Church

This is a great mystery: but I speak concerning Christ and the church.

Ephesians 5:32

That the sons of the church should be married to her as a young man to a virgin is a mystery not unlike many others held forth in the word of God concerning the relation between Christ and his people, and their relation to him and to one another. Christ is David's Lord and yet his Son, and both the Root and Offspring of David. Christ is a Son born and a Child given, and yet the everlasting Father. The church is Christ's mother, and yet his sister and brother. Ministers are the sons of the church, and yet are her fathers. The apostle speaks of himself as the father of the members of the church of Corinth, and also the mother of the Galatians, travailing in birth with them (Galatians 4:19).

Christ is a Son born and a Child given, and yet the everlasting Father.

Free Grace

The grace of God in bestowing this gift is most free. It was what God was under no obligation to bestow. He might have rejected fallen man, as he did the fallen angels. It was what we never did anything to merit; it was given while we were yet enemies, and before we had so much as repented. It was from the love of God who saw no excellency in us to attract it; and it was without expectation of ever being requited for it. And it is from mere grace that the benefits of Christ are applied to such and such particular persons. Those that are called and sanctified are to attribute it alone to the good pleasure of God's goodness, by which they are distinguished. He is sovereign, and hath mercy on whom he will have mercy.

But by the grace of God I am what I am: and his grace which was bestowed upon me was not in vain; but I laboured more abundantly than they all: yet not I, but the grace of God which was with me.
1 Corinthians 15:10

He is sovereign, and hath mercy on whom he will have mercy.

The Purchaser and the Price

Our blessings are what we have by purchase; and the purchase is made of God, the blessings are purchased of him, and God gives the purchaser; and not only so, but God is the purchaser. Yea, God is both the purchaser and the price; for Christ, who is God, purchased these blessings for us, by offering up himself as the price of our salvation. He purchased eternal life by the sacrifice of himself; "He offered up himself" (Hebrews 7:27); and, "He hath appeared to put away sin by the sacrifice of himself" (Hebrews 9:26). Indeed it was the human nature that was offered; but it was the same person with the divine, and therefore was an infinite price.

Yea, God is both the purchaser and the price.

Christ's Ascension

hrist appears gloriously exalted above all evil in his resurrection and ascension into heaven. When Christ rose from the dead, then it appeared that he was above death, which, though it had taken him captive, could not hold him. Then he appeared above the devil. Then this Leviathan that had swallowed him was forced to vomit him up again; as the Philistines that had taken captive the ark were forced to return it; Dagon being fallen before it, with his head and hands broken off, and only the stumps left. Then he appeared above our guilt: for he was justified in his resurrection. In his resurrection he appeared above all affliction. For though he had been subject to much affliction, and overwhelmed in it; he then emerged out of it, as having gotten the victory, never to conflict with any more sorrow.

He that descended is the same also that ascended up far above all heavens, that he might fill all things.
Ephesians 4:10

Christ appears gloriously exalted above all evil in his resurrection and ascension into heaven.

Exalted in Christ

*Nay, in all these
things we are more
than conquerors
through him that
loved us.*
Romans 8:37

What cause have they who have an interest in Christ to glory in their Redeemer! They are often beset with many evils, and many mighty enemies surround them on every side, with open mouths ready to devour them: over guilt, and over death. For as their Redeemer is mighty, and is so exalted above all evil, so shall they also be exalted in him. They are now, in a sense, so exalted; for nothing can hurt them. Christ carries them, as on eagle's wings, nigh out of the reach of all evils, so that they cannot come near them, to do them any real harm. And, in a little time, they shall be carried so out of their reach, that they shall not be able even to molest them anymore forever.

**Christ carries
them, as on
eagle's wings,
nigh out of the
reach of all evils.**

The Book of Instructions

God hath given us the Bible, which is a book of instructions. But this book can be of no manner of profit to us, any otherwise than as it conveys some knowledge to the mind: it can profit us no more than if it were written in the Chinese or Tartarian language, of which we know not one word. So the sacraments of the gospel can have a proper effect no other way than by conveying some knowledge. They represent certain things by visible signs. And what is the end of signs, but to convey some knowledge of the things signified? Such is the nature of man, that no object can come at the heart but through the door of the understanding: and there can be no spiritual knowledge of that of which there is not first a rational knowledge. It is impossible that any one should see the truth or excellency of any doctrine of the gospel who knows not what that doctrine is. A man cannot see the wonderful excellency and love of Christ in doing such and such things for sinners, unless his understanding be first informed how those things were done. He cannot have a taste of the sweetness and excellency of divine truth, unless he first have a notion that there is such a thing.

And ye shall know the truth, and the truth shall make you free.
John 8:32

The Way of Obedience

Know ye not, that to whom ye yield your-selves servants to obey, his servants ye are to whom ye obey; whether of sin unto death, or of obedience unto righteousness?
Romans 6:16

We should travel on in the way of obedience to all God's commands, even the difficult as well as the easy, denying all our sinful inclinations and interests. The way to heaven is ascending; we must be content to travel uphill, though it be hard and tiresome, and contrary to the natural bias of our flesh. We should follow Christ; the path he traveled was the right way to heaven. We should take up our cross and follow him, in meekness and lowliness of heart, obedience and charity, diligence to do good, and patience under afflictions. The way to heaven is a heavenly life; an imitation of those who are in heaven, in their holy enjoyments, loving, adoring, serving, and praising God and the Lamb. Even if we *could* go to heaven with the gratification of our lusts, we should prefer a way of holiness and conformity to the spiritual self-denying rules of the gospel.

We should follow Christ; the path he traveled was the right way to heaven.

Amazement and Horror

At the day of judgment, the saints in glory at Christ's right hand will see the wicked at the left hand in their amazement and horror, will hear the judge pronounce sentence upon them, saying, "Depart from me, ye cursed, into everlasting fire, prepared for the devil and his angels" (Matthew 25:41); and will see them go away into everlasting punishment. But the Scripture seems to hold forth to us, that the saints will not only see the misery of the wicked at the day of judgment, but . . . that the state of the damned in hell will be in the view of the heavenly inhabitants; that the two worlds of happiness and misery will be in view of each other. Though we know not by what means, nor after what manner, it will be; yet the Scriptures certainly lead us to think that they will some way or other have a direct and immediate apprehension of each other's state. The saints in glory will see how the damned are tormented; they will see God's threatenings fulfilled, and his wrath executed upon them (Matthew 25:41).

And in hell he lift up his eyes, being in torments, and seeth Abraham afar off, and Lazarus in his bosom.

Luke 16:23

A Deluge of Wrath

Kiss the Son, lest he be
angry, and ye perish
from the way, when
his wrath is kindled
but a little. Blessed are
all they that put their
trust in him.
Psalm 2:12

If a few drops of wrath do sometimes so distress the minds of men in this world, so as to be more dreadful than fire, or any bodily torment, how dreadful will be a deluge of wrath; how dreadful will it be, when all God's mighty waves and billows of wrath pass over them! Every faculty of the soul shall be filled with wrath, and every part of the body shall be filled with fire. After the resurrection the body shall be cast into that great furnace, which shall be so great as to burn up the whole world. These lower heavens, this air and this earth, shall all become one great furnace, a furnace that shall burn the earth, even to its very centre. In this furnace shall the bodies of the wicked lie to all eternity, and yet live, and have their sense of pain and torment not at all diminished. O, how full will the heart, the vitals, the brain, the eyes, the tongue, the hands, and the feet be of fire; of this fire of such an inconceivable fierceness! How full will every member, and every bone, and every vein, and every sinew, be of this fire! Surely it is a fearful thing to fall into the hands of the living God. Who can bear such wrath? A little of it is enough to destroy us.

Awakened Sinners

Sin is the disease of the soul, and such a disease as will, if the soul is not benumbed, cause exceeding pain. Sin brings guilt, and that brings condemnation and wrath. All this trouble arises from conviction of sin. Awakened sinners are convinced that they are sinful. Before, the sinner thought well of himself, or was not convinced that he was very sinful. But now he is led to reflect first on what he has done, how wickedly he has spent his time, what wicked acts or practices he has been guilty of. And afterwards in the progress of his awakenings he is made sensible of something of the sin and plague of his heart. They are made sensible of the guilt and wrath which sin brings. The threatenings of God's law are set home, and they are made sensible that God is angry, and that his wrath is dreadful. They are led to consider of the dreadfulness of that punishment which God has threatened. The affection or principle, which is wrought upon to cause this trouble, is fear. They are afraid of the punishment of sin, and God's wrath for it. They are commonly afraid of many things here in this world as the fruit of sin. They are afraid that God will not hear their prayers, that he is so angry with them, that he will never give them converting grace. They are afraid oftentimes that they have committed the unpardonable sin, or at least that they have been guilty of such sin as God will never pardon; that their day is past, and that God has given them up to judicial hardness of heart and blindness of mind. Or if they are not already, they are afraid they shall be.

Therefore snares are round about thee, and sudden fear troubleth thee.
Job 22:10

Infinite Riches

For whatsoever is born of God overcometh the world: and this is the victory that overcometh the world, even our faith.

1 John 5:4

They have a foundation of unspeakable comfort and joy, because of their riches. They have true and infinite riches. They are the possessors and heirs of something real and substantial, and that is worthy to be called by the name of riches. The things they possess are excellent, more precious than gold and than rubies; all the desirable things of this world cannot equal them, and they have enough of it. The riches that they have given them of God are inexhaustible. It is sufficient for them; there is no end of it. They have a fountain of infinite good for their comfort, and contentment, and joy; for God has given himself to them to be their portion, and he is a God of infinite glory. There is glory in him to engage their contemplation forever and ever, without ever being satiated. And he is also an infinite fountain of love; for God is love, yea, an ocean of love without shore or bottom! The glorious Son of God is theirs; that lovely one, who was from all eternity God's delight, rejoicing always before him. All his beauty is their portion, and his dying love is theirs, his very heart is theirs, and his glory and happiness in heaven are theirs, so far as their capacity will allow them to partake of it; for he has promised it to them, and has taken possession of it in their name. And the saints are also rich in the principle that is in them. They have inward riches which they carry about with them in their own hearts. They are rich in faith.

As Rivers of Water

he righteous shall be as "rivers of water in a dry place." This is an allusion to the deserts of Arabia, which was an exceedingly hot and dry country. One may travel there many days, and see no sign of a river, brook, or spring, nothing but a dry and parched wilderness; so that travelers are ready to be consumed with thirst, as the children of Israel were when they were in this wilderness, when they were faint because there was no water. Now when a man finds Jesus Christ, he is like one that has been traveling in those deserts till he is almost consumed with thirst, and who at last finds a river of cool and clear water. And Christ was typified by the river of water that issued out of the rock for the children of Israel in this desert: he is compared to a river, because there is such a plenty and fulness in him.

And a man shall be as an hiding place from the wind, and a covert from the tempest; as rivers of water in a dry place, as the shadow of a great rock in a weary land.

Isaiah 32:2

The righteous shall be as "rivers of water in a dry place."

Christ Weeps

Jesus wept.
John 11:35

He was one that wept with those that wept: and indeed it was mere pity that brought him into the world, and induced him not only to shed tears but to shed his blood: he poured out his blood as water on the earth, out of compassion to the poor, miserable children of men. And when do we ever read of any one person coming to him when on earth, with a heavy heart, or under any kind of sorrow or distress for pity or help, but what met with a kind and compassionate reception? And he has the same compassion now he is ascended into glory: there is still the same encouragement for bereaved ones to go and spread their sorrows before him.

He has the same compassion now he is ascended into glory.

Walk Worthily

Let Christians take heed so to walk, that they may not dishonor their pedigree. You are of a very honorable race, more honorable by far than if you were the offspring of kings, and had royal blood in your veins; you are a heavenly offspring, the seed of Jesus Christ, the children of God. They that are of noble race are wont to value themselves highly upon the honor of their families, to dwell on their titles, their coats of arms, and their ensigns of honor, and to recount the exploits of their illustrious forefathers. How much more careful should you be of the honor of your descent, that you in nothing behave yourself unworthy of the great God, the eternal and omnipotent King of heaven and earth, whose offspring you are!

That ye might walk worthy of the Lord unto all pleasing, being fruitful in every good work, and increasing in the knowledge of God.
Colossians 1:10

> You are of a very honorable race, more honorable by far than if you were the offspring of kings.

Unspeakable Grace

In whom we have redemption through his blood, the forgiveness of sins, according to the riches of his grace.

Ephesians 1:7

God is the sovereign disposer of his own favor and blessing: he may bestow it on whom he pleases, and in what way he pleases. None of us can challenge any right in God's grace. We have to a great degree deserved the contrary of him. He might in our first state of innocence bestow his favors and bounties just in what way he pleased; he might appoint what conditions he would, as he was absolute Lord over us. Much more now since we have sinned and his justice has infinite demands upon us, it is wonderful, unspeakable grace that he is willing to be gracious to us in any way.

God is the sovereign disposer of his own favor and blessing.

Living by Faith

t is God's design that his people here should live by faith and not by sight; whereas if God bestowed grace upon men in a miraculous manner when they never used any means, then there would not be that exercise for faith that there is now in believing that God is the author of all grace. God now works secretly upon men's hearts; his power is inward and not seen by the world, and oftentimes not by him that is the subject of it but by faith. But if men should be taken in a moment, in their full career in sin, in gross ignorance and darkness and heathenism, without the preaching or hearing of the gospel or reading the Word or any outward instruction, or using any means themselves or any other using any means with them: if all that had the grace of God bestowed on them had it so, and should be at once taken and instructed and made to believe, and be under the government of the doctrines of the gospel, then it would cease to be a matter of faith that these things were not from ourselves.

For therein is the righteousness of God revealed from faith to faith: as it is written, The just shall live by faith.
Romans 1:17

Seeing God Exalted

The LORD liveth; and blessed be my rock; and let the God of my salvation be exalted.
Psalm 18:46

he godly delight in seeing God exalted. They love to see God reigning on the throne of his glory, exalted up on high. They love to have him do whatever is his will and pleasure in the armies of heaven and amongst the inhabitants of the earth. They love that he should do just what he pleases. They rejoice in it, that God is the governor of the world; it is a happy and joyful consideration to them that God reins. This was spoken of as what is a joyful piece of news to the godly. "How beautiful upon the mountains are the feet of him that bringeth good tidings, that publisheth peace; that bringeth [good tidings of] good, that publisheth salvation; that saith unto Zion, Thy God reigneth" (Isaiah 52:7).

> The godly delight in seeing God exalted.

God's Righteous Ways

I t is most evident by the works of God that his understanding and power are infinite. For he that has made all things out of nothing, and upholds, and governs, and manages all things every moment, in all ages, without growing weary, must be of infinite power. He must also be of infinite knowledge; for if he made all things, and upholds and governs all things continually, it will follow that he knows and perfectly sees all things, great and small, in heaven and earth, continually at one view; which cannot be without infinite understanding. Being thus infinite in understanding and power, he must also be perfectly holy; for unholiness always argues some defect, some blindness. Where there is no darkness or delusion, there can be no unholiness. It is impossible that wickedness should consist with infinite light. God being infinite in power and knowledge, he must be self-sufficient and all-sufficient. Therefore it is impossible that he should be under any temptation to do anything amiss; for he can have no end in doing it. When any are tempted to do amiss, it is for selfish ends. But how can an all-sufficient Being, who wants nothing, be tempted to do evil for selfish ends? So that God is essentially holy, and nothing is more impossible than that God should do amiss.

Shall not the Judge of all the earth do right?
Genesis 18:25

He must also be perfectly holy.

Miracles

But when that which is perfect is come, then that which is in part shall be done away.
1 Corinthians 13:10

t was not God's design that miracles should always be continued in the world. Miracles are only for the introducing the true religion into the world, to accompany the revelation and first promulgating the Word of God by them to whom it was revealed by inspiration, to confirm to the world that it was a divine revelation; but now, when the true religion is long since introduced and the canon of the Scripture completed, the use of miracles in the church ceases.

Miracles are only for the introducing the true religion into the world.

Heat and Light

oly affections are not heat without light; but evermore arise from some information of the understanding, some spiritual instruction that the mind receives, some light or actual knowledge. The child of God is graciously affected, because he sees and understands something more of divine things than he did before, more of God or Christ, and of the glorious things exhibited in the gospel. He has a clearer and better view than he had before, when he was not affected; either he receives some new understanding of divine things, or has his former knowledge renewed after the view was decayed; "Every one that loveth . . . knoweth God" (1 John 4:7); "I pray, that your love may abound yet more and more in knowledge and in all judgment" (Philippians 1:9) . . . Knowledge is the key that first opens the hard heart, enlarges the affections, and opens the way for men into the kingdom of heaven.

They have a zeal of God, but not according to knowledge.
Romans 10:2

Wonderful Wisdom

But we speak the wisdom of God in a mystery, even the hidden wisdom, which God ordained before the world unto our glory.
1 Corinthians 2:7

God showed a wonderful wisdom in his gradual revelation of the gospel in the world. First, darkly in types. And revealing first to the Jews, and then rejecting them and revealing to the Gentiles; and afterwards calling the Jews again, and with them bringing in the fullness of the Gentiles. Which wisdom was so wonderful that [it] made the Apostle cry out, as Romans 11:33–36, "O the depth of the riches both of the wisdom and knowledge of God! how unsearchable are his judgments, and his ways past finding out! For who hath known the mind of the Lord? or who hath been his counsellor? Or who hath first given to him, and it shall be recompensed unto him again? For of him, and through him, and to him, are all things: to whom be glory for ever. Amen."

For who hath known the mind of the Lord?

Ascribing Glory to God

The godly loves to attribute to God the glory of what he is, what he has, and what he does. The believer delights in giving the praise of all that he has, all that he is, and all that he enjoys to God, in acknowledging that it comes from him; and that it is all the fruit of his benignity, and is not owing to himself; that it is not owing to his own strength to get it, or to his own merit to deserve it, but alone to the mercy of God in being willing to give it, and to his power in procuring it. Thus he loves to give God the glory of all his temporal things, even his common enjoyments. He is not as some are, living continually on the bounty of God and not considering who they are owing to, nor sincerely once praising him for them. But especially is the joy of his heart to give God all the glory of his spiritual enjoyments: he loves to give him the whole praise of his redemption and salvation, admires of God's goodness in electing him from all eternity, admires that he should be, of his distinguishing goodness, chosen out from amongst so many to be made the vessel of honor and subject of glory. He wonders at God's goodness in sending his Son to redeem him. He likewise admires at his grace in calling of him to Christ by his Holy Spirit. He delights to acknowledge that his conversion is not at all owing in any respect to himself, but to the grace of God alone.

He staggered not at the promise of God through unbelief; but was strong in faith, giving glory to God.
Romans 4:20

> The godly loves to attribute to God the glory of what he is.

Christ's Testament

By so much was Jesus made a surety of a better testament.
Hebrews 7:22

The covenant between Christ and his children is like a will or testament also in this respect, that it becomes effectual, and a way is made for putting it in execution, no other way than by his death; as the apostle observes it is with a will or testament among men. "For a testament is of force after men are dead" (Hebrews 9:17). For though the covenant of grace indeed was of force before the death of Christ, yet it was of force no otherwise than by his death; so that his death then did virtually intervene; being already undertaken and engaged. As a man's heirs come by the legacies bequeathed to them no otherwise than by the death of the testator, so men come by the spiritual and eternal inheritance no otherwise than by the death of Christ. If it had not been for the death of Christ they never could have obtained it.

Seeing Christ's Glory

When the saints shall see Christ's glory and exaltation in heaven, it will indeed possess their hearts with the greater admiration and adoring respect, but will not awe them into any separation, but will serve only to heighten their surprise and joy, when they find Christ condescending to admit them to such intimate access, and so freely and fully communicating himself to them. So that if we choose Christ for our friend and portion, we shall hereafter be so received to him, that there shall be nothing to hinder the fullest enjoyment of him, to the satisfying the utmost cravings of our souls. We may take our full swing at gratifying our spiritual appetite after these holy pleasures. Christ will then say, as in Song of Solomon 5:1, "Eat, O friends; drink, yea, drink abundantly, O beloved." And this shall be our entertainment to all eternity! There shall never be any end of this happiness, or anything to interrupt our enjoyment of it, or in the least to molest us in it!

Beloved, now are we the sons of God, and it doth not yet appear what we shall be: but we know that, when he shall appear, we shall be like him; for we shall see him as he is.
1 John 3:2

Spiritual Light

But the natural man receiveth not the things of the Spirit of God: for they are foolishness unto him: neither can he know them, because they are spiritually discerned.
1 Corinthians 2:14

This spiritual and divine light does not consist in any impression made upon the imagination. It is no impression upon the mind, as though one saw anything with the bodily eyes: it is no imagination or idea of an outward light or glory, or any beauty of form or countenance, or a visible luster or brightness of any object. The imagination may be strongly impressed with such things; but this is not spiritual light. Indeed when the mind has a lively discovery of spiritual things, and is greatly affected by the power of divine light, it may, and probably very commonly doth, much affect the imagination; so that impressions of an outward beauty or brightness may accompany those spiritual discoveries. But spiritual light is not that impression upon the imagination, but an exceeding different thing from it. Natural men may have lively impressions on their imaginations; and we cannot determine. But the devil, who transforms himself into an angel of light, may cause imaginations of an outward beauty, or visible glory, and of sounds and speeches, and other such things; but these are things of a vastly inferior nature to spiritual light.

Death's Impotency

eath not only cannot destroy a Christian, but it cannot hurt him; Christ carries him on eagle wings aloft on high, out of the reach of death. Death, with respect to him, is disarmed of his power: and every Christian may say, "O death, where is thy sting?" Death was once indeed a terrible enemy, but now he has become weak. He spent all his strength on Christ; in killing him, he killed himself; he was conquered then, and has now no power to hurt his followers. Death is now but the shadow of what he would have been if Christ had not conquered him; he was once a lion, but now he is but a lamb. A good man may indeed be harassed with fears of death, and may be much terrified when going through the valley of the shadow of death, but that is no just ground of any terror, and if the saints are terrified, it is only through their infirmity and darkness. As a child is frightened in the dark where there is no danger, because he is a child, so a good man may be affrighted at the terrible looks of death. But he will find this awful appearance to be only a shadow, that can look terribly, but can do nothing terrible. Death may, through the weakness of the saints, trouble them, and exercise them, but he cannot destroy the ground they have for comfort and support. When death comes to a wicked man, all those things on which he built his comfort fail, their foundation is overflown with a flood (Job 22:16). But the foundation of the peace and comfort of the godly man is not shaken at such a time.

O death, where is thy sting?
1 Corinthians 15:55

Dear to the Father

Christ is a person so dear to the Father, that those who are in Christ need not be at all jealous of being accepted upon his account. If Christ is accepted they must of consequence be accepted, for they are in Christ, as members, as parts, as the same. They are the body of Christ, his flesh and his bones. They that are in Christ Jesus are one spirit; and therefore, if God loves Christ Jesus, he must of necessity accept of those that are in him, and that are of him. But Christ is a person exceedingly dear to the Father; the Father's love to the Son is really infinite. God necessarily loves the Son; God could as soon cease to be, as cease to love the Son. He is God's elect, in whom his soul delights; he is his beloved Son, in whom he is well pleased; he loved him before the foundation of the world, and had infinite delight in him from all eternity. A terrified conscience, therefore, may have rest here, and abundant satisfaction that he is safe in Christ, and that there is not the least danger but that he shall be accepted, and that God will be at peace with him in Christ.

The Way to Glory

nd this is the way to be advanced to glory hereafter. Yea, the lower you lay yourself by humility in this world, the higher will you be exalted
in glory in the other. This is so well-pleasing to God, that
it not only draws the eyes of God, yea, holds his eyes
fixed as if it were with admiration, and holds the King in
the galleries; yea, this grace of humility, this link of the
chain of the graces of the spouse, not only ravishes his
heart and brings light, communion, and all spiritual blessings down upon the believer in this world: but even
causes the gates of heaven and the arms of God to open,
and attracts the rivers of pleasure, and causes the tree of
life to bend to yield her fruit and all the blessing of Jerusalem above to flow in upon him.

*Humble yourselves
therefore under the
mighty hand of God,
that he may exalt
you in due time.*
1 Peter 5:6

The lower you
lay yourself by
humility in this
world, the higher
will you be
exalted in glory
in the other.

Wrought by the Spirit

For as many as are led by the Spirit of God, they are the sons of God.
Romans 8:14

ence we may learn that a godly temper is undoubtedly wrought by the Spirit of God. How much is it against man's natural disposition to love to abase himself. It is quite contrary to it. It is therefore quite beyond the powers of nature to bring man to this temper and fix it in him. This must undoubtedly be the supernatural work of the Spirit of God: for what else can ever bring a man to love to lay himself low that God may be exalted? Surely none else but he who made the soul of man, can thus alter and change and put a new nature into it so contrary to that disposition which is natural to all men universally. Yea, there is hardly any disposition stronger in man by nature than that which is contrary to this, even a disposition to exalt themselves. But the godly are of such a temper as not only to abase themselves, but to love and delight so to do, and to take great pleasure in it. Therefore here are the undoubted marks of the finger of God, and plain evidences of the effects of his Holy Spirit powerfully working in man's heart.

High Affections

They who condemn high affections in others are certainly not likely to have high affections themselves. And let it be considered that they who have but little religious affection have certainly but little religion. And they who condemn others for their religious affections, and have none themselves, have no religion. There are false affections, and there are true. A man's having much affection does not prove that he has any true religion: but if he has no affection, it proves that he has no true religion. The right way is not to reject all affections, nor to approve all: but to distinguish between them, approving some and rejecting others; separating between the wheat and the chaff, the gold and the dross, the precious and the vile.

Wherefore I say unto thee, Her sins, which are many, are forgiven; for she loved much: but to whom little is forgiven, the same loveth little.
Luke 7:47

Come to Christ

Come unto me, all ye that labour and are heavy laden, and I will give you rest.
Matthew 11:28

ome to Christ, and accept of salvation in this way. You are invited to come to Christ, heartily to close with him and trust in him for salvation: and if you do so, you shall have the benefit of this glorious contrivance. You shall have the benefit of all; as much as if the whole had been contrived for you alone. God has already contrived everything that is needful for your salvation; and there is nothing wanting but your consent. Since God has taken this matter of the redemption of sinners into his own hand, he has made thorough work of it; he has not left it for you to finish. Satisfaction is already made, righteousness is already wrought out: death and hell are already conquered. The Redeemer has already taken possession of glory, and keeps it in his hands to bestow on them who come to him. There were many difficulties in the way, but they are all removed. The Savior has already triumphed over all, and is at the right hand of God, to give eternal life to his people. Salvation is ready brought to your door; and the Savior stands, knocks, and calls that you would open to him, that he might bring it in to you. There remains nothing but your consent. All the difficulty now remaining is with your own heart. If you perish now, it must be wholly at your door. It must be because you would not come to Christ that you might have life; and because you virtually choose death rather than life.

You are invited to come to Christ.

Seeking the Lord

Certainly that expression of seeking the Lord is very commonly used to signify . . . that God himself is the great good desired and sought after; that the blessings pursued are God's gracious presence, the blessed manifestations of him, union and intercourse with him; or, in short, God's manifestations and communications of himself by his Holy Spirit. Thus the psalmist desired God, thirsted after him, and sought him. "O God, thou art my God; early will I seek thee. . . . My flesh longeth for thee in a dry and thirsty land, where no water is; to see thy power and thy glory, so as I have seen thee in the sanctuary. . . . My soul followeth hard after thee" (Psalm 63:1, 2, 8). "Whom have I in heaven but thee? and there is none upon earth that I desire beside thee" (Psalm 73:25). The psalmist earnestly pursued after GOD, his soul thirsted after him; he stretched forth his hands unto him (Psalm 143:6). And therefore it is in Scripture the peculiar character of the saints, that they are those who seek God. "This is the generation of them that seek him" (Psalm 24:6). "Your heart shall live that seek God" (Psalm 69:32). If the expression in the text be understood agreeably to this sense, then by seeking the Lord of hosts, we must understand a seeking, that God who had withdrawn, or as it were hid himself for a long time, would return to his church, and grant the tokens and fruits of his gracious presence, and those blessed communications of his Spirit to his people, and to mankind on earth, which he had often promised, and which his church had long waited for.

But if from thence thou shalt seek the LORD thy God, thou shalt find him, if thou seek him with all thy heart and with all thy soul.
Deuteronomy 4:29

God Will Vindicate

*Consume them in
wrath, consume them,
that they may not be:
and let them know
that God ruleth in
Jacob unto the ends of
the earth.*
Psalm 59:13

God will make all men to know the truth of those great things which he speaks of in his word, one way or another; for he will vindicate his own truth. He has undertaken to convince all men. They who will not be convinced in this world, by the gentle and gracious methods which God uses with them now, shall be convinced hereafter by severe means. If they will not be convinced for salvation, they shall be convinced by damnation. God will make them know that he is the Lord. And he will make them know that he bears rule.

He will make
them know that
he bears rule.

Improving the Time

Improve well your time of leisure from worldly business. Many persons have a great deal of such time, and all have some. If men be but disposed to it, such time may be improved to great advantage. When we are most free from cares for the body, and business of an outward nature, a happy opportunity for the soul is afforded. Therefore spend not such opportunities unprofitably, nor in such a manner that you will not be able to give a good account thereof to God. Waste them not away wholly in unprofitable visits, or useless diversions or amusements. Diversion should be used only in subservience to business. So much, and no more, should be used, as doth most fit the mind and body for the work of our general and particular callings. You have need to improve every talent, advantage, and opportunity to your utmost, while time lasts; for it will soon be said concerning you, according to the oath of the angel in Revelation 10:5–6: "And the angel which I saw stand upon the sea and upon the earth lifted up his hand to heaven, and sware by him that liveth for ever and ever, who created heaven, and the things that therein are, and the earth, and the things that therein are, and the sea, and the things which are therein, that there should be time no longer."

Thou carriest them away as with a flood; they are as a sleep: in the morning they are like grass which groweth up.
Psalm 90:5

Convinced of the Truth

Whom having not seen, ye love; in whom, though now ye see him not, yet believing, ye rejoice with joy unspeakable and full of glory.

1 Peter 1:8

All gracious persons have a solid, full, thorough, and effectual conviction of the truth of the great things of the gospel. They no longer halt between two opinions; the great doctrines of the gospel cease to be any longer doubtful things, or matters of opinion, which, though probable, are yet disputable; but with them, they are points settled and determined, as undoubted and indisputable; so that they are not afraid to venture their all upon their truth. Their conviction is an effectual conviction; so that the great, spiritual, mysterious, and invisible things of the gospel have the influence of real and certain things upon them; they have the weight and power of real things in their hearts; and accordingly rule in their affections, and govern them through the course of their lives. With respect to Christ's being the Son of God, and Savior of the world, and the great things he has revealed concerning himself, and his Father, and another world, they have not only a predominating opinion that these things are true, and so yield their assent, as they do in many other matters of doubtful speculation; but they see that it is ready so: their eyes are opened, so that they see that really Jesus is the Christ, the Son of the living God. And as to the things which Christ has revealed, of God's eternal purposes and designs, concerning fallen man, and the glorious and everlasting things prepared for the saints in another world, they see that they are so indeed: and therefore these things are of great weight with them, and have a mighty power upon their hearts, and influence over their practice, in some measure answerable to their infinite importance.

Seek Another Disposition

To all such as depend on their own righteousness, be exhorted to let go of your hold. You see how far distant you are from the spirit of such as are in a state of salvation. They don't delight and pride themselves in their own goodness and the goodness of their works, but delight in the contrary. They are not endeavoring to dress themselves in the apparel of their own goodness, but come in beggar's rags before God: for they come to beg a garment of him, even the righteousness of Christ. They had rather be saved freely, upon the account of mere goodness and pity, than for the works that they do; they delight in such a way of salvation. They love to have their hearts broken for their sin. They love to lie low and in the dust, and take no pleasure in self-exalting thoughts. Wherefore by this such may see how far they are from a godly disposition. Let them be exhorted therefore not to hope for salvation in the state they are in for the present, but seek another disposition of mind, and get into another state.

For Christ is the end of the law for righteousness to every one that believeth.
Romans 10:4

Evangelical Repentance

Bring forth therefore
fruits meet for
repentance.
Matthew 3:8

Evangelical repentance, being active conversion, is not to be treated of as a particular grace, properly and entirely distinct from faith, as by some it seems to have been. What is conversion, but the sinful, alienated soul's closing with Christ, or the sinner's being brought to believe in Christ? That exercise of soul in conversion that respects sin cannot be excluded out of the nature of faith in Christ: there is something in faith, or closing with Christ, that respects sin, and that is evangelical repentance. That repentance, which in Scripture is called repentance for the remission of sins, is that very principle or operation of the mind itself that is called faith, so far as it is conversant about sin. Justifying faith in a Mediator is conversant about two things: it is conversant about sin or evil to be rejected and to be delivered from, and about positive good to be accepted and obtained by the Mediator; as conversant about the former of these, it is evangelical repentance, or repentance for remission of sins. Surely they must be very ignorant, or at least very inconsiderate, of the whole tenor of the gospel, who think that the repentance by which remission of sins is obtained can be completed, as to all that is essential to it, without any respect to Christ, or application of the mind to the Mediator, who alone has made atonement for sin. Surely so great a part of salvation as remission of sins is not to be obtained without looking or coming to the great and only Savior. It is true, repentance, in its more general abstracted nature, is only a *sorrow* for sin, and forsaking of it, which is a duty of natural religion; but evangelical repentance, or repentance for remission of sins has more than this essential to it; a dependence of soul on the Mediator for deliverance from sin is of the essence of it.

Dwelling with God

We naturally desire not only to see those whom we love, but to converse with them. Provision is made for this also, that we should have spiritual conversation with God while in this world; and that we should be hereafter admitted to converse with Christ in the most intimate manner possible. Provision is made in this way of salvation, that we should converse with God much more intimately than otherwise it would have been possible for us; for now Christ is incarnate, is in our nature: he is become one of us, whereby we are under advantages for an immensely more free and intimate converse with him, than could have been, if he had remained only in the divine nature; and so in a nature infinitely distant from us. We naturally desire not only to converse with those whom we greatly love, but to dwell with them. Provision, through Christ, is made for this. It is purchased and provided that we should dwell with God in his own house in heaven, which is called our Father's house; to dwell forever in God's presence, and at his right hand.

And Enoch walked with God: and he was not; for God took him.
Genesis 5:24

Conforming to the Beloved

*We love him, because
he first loved us.*
1 John 4:19

Love naturally inclines to a conformity to the beloved; to have those excellencies, upon the account of which he is beloved, copied in himself. Provision is made in this way of salvation, that we may be conformed to God; that we shall be transformed into the same image. "We all, with open face beholding as in a glass the glory of the Lord, are changed into the same image from glory to glory" (2 Corinthians 3:18). And that hereafter we shall see him as he is, and be like him. It is the natural desire of love to do something for the beloved, either for his pleasure or honor. Provision is made for this also in this way of salvation; that we should be made instruments of glorifying God, and promoting his kingdom here, and of glorifying him to all eternity.

We shall be
transformed into
the same image.

Christ's Satisfaction

The he satisfaction of Christ is as sufficient for the removal of the greatest guilt, as the least. All the sins of those who truly come to God for mercy, let them be what they will, are satisfied for, if God be true who tells us so; and if they be satisfied for, surely it is not incredible that God should be ready to pardon them. So that Christ having fully satisfied for all sin, or having wrought out a satisfaction that is sufficient for all, it is now no way inconsistent with the glory of the divine attributes to pardon the greatest sins of those who in a right manner come unto him for it. God may now pardon the greatest sinners without any prejudice to the honor of his holiness. The holiness of God will not suffer him to give the least countenance to sin, but inclines him to give proper testimonies of his hatred of it. But Christ having satisfied for sin, God can now love the sinner, and give no countenance at all to sin, however great a sinner he may have been. It was a sufficient testimony of God's abhorrence of sin that he poured out his wrath on his own dear Son when he took the guilt of it upon himself. Nothing can more show God's abhorrence of sin than this. If all mankind had been eternally damned, it would not have been so great a testimony of it. God may, through Christ, pardon the greatest sinner without any prejudice to the honor of his majesty. The honor of the divine majesty indeed requires satisfaction; but the sufferings of Christ fully repair the injury.

The blood of Jesus Christ his Son cleanseth us from all sin.
1 John 1:7

Using the Means

So then faith cometh by hearing, and hearing by the word of God.
Romans 10:17

All encouragement that a person may take from their own diligence and constancy in the use of the means [of grace] is not self-righteousness, because God has revealed that this is the ordinary way wherein he meets with men and blesses them. Persons may think and have God's Word for their foundation that they are in a far more likely way to obtain salvation in their using means than if they used none, and in their diligent use than if they were slothful and partial, and so may take encouragement from their own endeavors.

Indeed, for sinners to take encouragement as though God were under any obligation to them for their use of means, either naturally or by promise, is self-righteousness. But the godly that faithfully and with a true heart use means may assuredly expect success from God's promise, that in that way they shall grow in grace.

They shall grow in grace.

Spiritual Darkness

I f you live very much in spiritual darkness, and without the comfortable presence of God, it may be this is the cause. If you complain that you have but little sweet communion with God, that you seem to be left and deserted of God, that God seems to hide his face from you, and but seldom gives you the sweet views of his glory and grace, that you seem to be left very much to grope in darkness, and to wander in a wilderness; perhaps you have wondered what is the matter; you have cried to God often that you might have the light of his countenance, but he heareth you not; and you have sorrowful days and nights upon this account. But if you have found, by what hath been said, that you live in some way of sin, it is very probable that is the cause, that is the root of your mischief, that is the Achan, the troubler that offends God, and causes him to withdraw, and brings so many clouds of darkness upon your souls. You grieve the Holy Spirit by the way in which you live; and that is the reason that you have no more comfort from him.

When I looked for good, then evil came unto me: and when I waited for light, there came darkness.
Job 30:26

Flee from the Wrath to Come

You have often been exhorted to flee from the "wrath to come." This devouring fire, these everlasting burnings, of which we have been speaking, are the wrath to come. You hear of this fire, of these burnings, and of that fearfulness which will seize and surprise sinners in Zion hereafter; and O what reason have you of thankfulness that you only hear of them, that you do not as yet feel them, and that they have not already taken hold of you! They are, as it were, following you, and coming nearer and nearer every day. Those fierce flames are already kindled in the wrath of God; yea, the fierceness and wrath of Almighty God burn against you; it is ready for you: that pit is prepared for you, with fire and much wood, and the wrath of the Lord, as a stream of brimstone, doth kindle it.

Lot was with great urgency hastened out of Sodom, and commanded to make haste, and fly for his life, and escape to the mountains, lest he should be consumed in those flames which burned up Sodom and Gomorrah. But that burning was a mere spark to that devouring fire, and those everlasting burnings, of which you are in danger. Therefore improve the present opportunity.

Hating Sin

s sin in its own nature is infinitely hateful, so in its natural tendency it is infinitely dreadful. It is the tendency of all sin eternally to undo the soul. Every sin naturally carried hell in it! Therefore, all sin ought to be treated by us as we would treat a thing that is infinitely terrible. If any one sin, yea, the least sin, does not necessarily bring eternal ruin with it, this is owing to nothing but the free grace and mercy of God to us, and not to the nature and tendency of sin itself. But certainly, we ought not to take the less care to avoid sin, or all that tends to it, for the freeness and greatness of God's mercy to us, through which there is hope of pardon; for that would be indeed a most ungrateful and vile abuse of mercy. Were it made known to us, that if we ever voluntarily committed any particular act of sin, we should be damned without any remedy or escape, should we not exceedingly dread the commission of such? Should we not be very watchful and careful to stand at the greatest distance from that sin; and from everything that might expose us to it; and that has any tendency to stir up our lusts, or to betray us to such an act of sin? Let us then consider, that though the next voluntary act of known sin shall not necessarily and unavoidably issue in certain damnation, yet it will certainly deserve it. We shall thereby really deserve to be cast off, without any remedy or hope; and it can only be owing to free grace that it will not certainly and remedilessly be followed with such a punishment. And shall we be guilty of such a vile abuse of God's mercy to us, as to take encouragement from it, the more boldly to expose ourselves to sin?

The fear of the LORD is to hate evil: pride, and arrogancy, and the evil way, and the froward mouth, do I hate.
Proverbs 8:13

True Godliness

According as his divine power hath given unto us all things that pertain unto life and godliness, through the knowledge of him that hath called us to glory and virtue.

2 Peter 1:3

The inward principle is a communication of God, a participation of the divine nature, Christ living in the heart, the Holy Spirit dwelling there in union with the faculties of the soul as an internal vital principle, exerting His own proper nature in the exercise of these faculties. This is sufficient to show us why true grace should have such activity, power, and efficacy. No wonder that which is divine is powerful and effectual; for it has omnipotence on its side. If God dwells in the heart, and is vitally united to it, he will show that he is God by the efficacy of his operation. Christ is not in the heart of a saint as in a sepulcher, or as a dead Savior who does nothing, but as in his temple, and as one who is alive from the dead. For in the heart where Christ savingly is, there he lives, and exerts himself after the power of that endless life that he received at his resurrection. Thus every saint is a subject of the benefit of Christ's sufferings, and is made to know and experience the power of his resurrection. The Spirit of Christ, which is the immediate spring of grace in the heart, is all life, all power, all act. Hence saving affections, though oftentimes they do not make so great a noise and show as others, yet have in them a secret solidity, life, and strength, whereby they take hold of and carry away the heart, leading it into a kind of captivity, gaining a full and steadfast determination of the will of God and holiness.

An Occasion of Glory

B y this contrivance for our redemption, God's greatest dishonor is made an occasion of his greatest glory. Sin is a thing by which God is greatly dishonored; the nature of its principle is enmity against God, and contempt of him. And man, by his rebellion, has greatly dishonored God. But this dishonor, by the contrivance of our redemption, is made an occasion of the greatest manifestation of God's glory that ever was. Sin, the greatest evil, is made an occasion of the greatest good. It is the nature of a principle of sin that it seeks to dethrone God: but this is hereby made an occasion of the greatest manifestation of God's royal majesty and glory that ever was. By sin man has slighted and despised God: but this is made an occasion of his appearing the more greatly honorable. Sin casts contempt upon the authority and law of God: but this, by the contrivance of our redemption, is made the occasion of the greatest honor done to that same authority, and to that very law. It was a greater honor to the law of God that Christ was subject to it, and obeyed it, than if all mankind had obeyed it. It was a greater honor to God's authority that Christ showed such great respect, and such entire subjection to it, than the perfect obedience of all the angels in heaven. Man by his sin showed his enmity against the holiness of God: but this is made an occasion of the greatest manifestation of God's holiness. The holiness of God never appeared to so great a degree, as when God executed vengeance upon his own dear Son.

Who is this King of glory? The Lord strong and mighty.
Psalm 24:8

Qualities of the Heart

But I have trusted in thy mercy; my heart shall rejoice in thy salvation.
Psalm 13:5

Whatever controversies and variety of opinions there are about the nature of virtue, yet all mean by it something beautiful, or rather some kind of beauty or excellency. It is not all beauty that is called virtue; for instance, not the beauty of a building, but some beauty belonging to beings that have perception and will. It is not all beauty of mankind that is called virtue; for instance, not the external beauty of the countenance, but it is a beauty that has its original seat in the mind. Yet, perhaps not everything that may be called a beauty of mind is properly called virtue. There is a beauty of understanding and speculation. But virtue is the beauty of those qualities and acts of the mind that are of a moral nature, that is, such as are attended with desert or worthiness of praise or blame. Things of this sort belong to the disposition and will, or the heart. Therefore, I shall not depart from the common opinion when I say that virtue is the beauty of the qualities and exercises of the heart, or those actions which proceed from them. So then when it is inquired what it is which renders any habit, disposition, or exercise of the heart truly beautiful, what I mean by true virtue is that which belongs to the heart of an intelligent being. It is plain by the Holy Scriptures that virtue most essentially consists in love.

Consolation in Praise

I t may be matter of great comfort to you that you are to spend your eternity with the saints in heaven, where it is so much their work to praise God. The saints are sensible what cause they have to praise God, and oftentimes are ready to say they long to praise him more, and that they never can praise him enough. This may be a consolation to you, that you shall have a whole eternity in which to praise him. They earnestly desire to praise God better. This, therefore, may be your consolation, that in heaven your heart shall be enlarged, you shall be enabled to praise him in an immensely more perfect and exalted manner than you can do in this world. You shall not be troubled with such a dead, dull heart, with so much coldness, so many clogs and burdens from corruption, and from an earthly mind; with a wandering, unsteady heart; with so much darkness and so much hypocrisy. You shall be one of that vast assembly that praise God so fervently, that their voice is "as the voice of many waters, and as the voice of mighty thunderings." You long to have others praise God, to have every one praise him. There will be enough to help you, and join you in praising him, and those that are capable of doing it ten thousand times better than saints on earth. Thousands and thousands of angels and glorified saints will be around you, all united to you in the dearest love, all disposed to praise God, not only for themselves, but for his mercy to you.

Praise ye the LORD. *Praise ye the* LORD *from the heavens: praise him in the heights.*
Psalm 148:1

The Judgment

In this world, ministers and their people often meet together to hear of and wait upon an unseen Lord. But at the judgment, they shall meet in his most immediate and visible presence. Ministers, who now often meet their people to preach to them the King eternal, immortal, and invisible, to convince them that there is a God and declare to them what manner of being he is; and to convince them that he governs and will judge the world, and that there is a future state of rewards and punishments; and to preach to them a Christ in heaven, at the right hand of God, in an unseen world; shall then meet their people in the most immediate sensible presence of this great God, Savior, and Judge, appearing in the most plain, visible, and open manner, with great glory, with all his holy angels, before them and the whole world. They shall not meet them to hear about an absent Christ, an unseen Lord, and future Judge; but to appear before that Judge, being set together in the presence of that supreme Lord, in his immense glory and awful majesty, of whom they have heard so often in their meetings together on earth.

Divine Cordials

Christ has purchased all that persons need under bereavement. He has purchased all that miserable men stand in need of under all their calamities, and comfort under every sort of affliction. And therefore that his invitation to those that "Labour and are heavy laden," with either natural or moral evil: he has purchased divine cordials and supports for those hearts that are ready to sink: he has purchased all needed comfort and help for the widow and the fatherless: he has purchased a sanctified improvement and fruit of affliction for all such as come to him and spread their sorrows before him. He has purchased those things that are sufficient to make up their loss, that are bereaved of a great blessing in an eminent minister of the gospel. It is he that has purchased those divine blessings, those influences and fruits of the Spirit of God, that the work of the ministry is appointed to be the means of. Faithful ministers themselves are the fruits of his purchase; and he has purchased all those gifts and graces whereby ministers do become faithful, eminent, and successful. And therefore when he "ascended up on high, he . . . gave gifts unto men" (Ephesians 4:8). So that he has purchased all that is needed to make up for the loss that is sustained by the death of an eminent minister.

Is there no balm in Gilead; is there no physician there? why then is not the health of the daughter of my people recovered?
Jeremiah 8:22

The Prayer of Faith

And the prayer of faith shall save the sick, and the Lord shall raise him up; and if he have committed sins, they shall be forgiven him.

James 5:15

As to particular temporal blessings for which we pray, it is no argument that he is not a prayer-hearing God because he bestows them not upon us, for it may be that God sees the things for which we pray not to be best for us. If so, it would be no mercy in him to bestow them upon us, but a judgment. Such things, therefore, ought always to be asked with submission to the divine will. God can answer prayer, though he does not bestow the very thing for which we pray. He can sometimes better answer the lawful desires and good end we have in prayer another way. If our end be our own good and happiness, God can perhaps better answer that end in bestowing something else than in the bestowment of that very thing which we ask. And if the main good we aim at in our prayer be attained, our prayer is answered, though not in the bestowment of the individual thing which we sought. And so that may still be true which was before asserted, that God always hears the prayer of faith. God never once failed of hearing a sincere and believing prayer; and those promises forever hold good, "Ask, and it shall be given you; seek, and ye shall find; knock, and it shall be opened unto you: for every one that asketh receiveth; and he that seeketh findeth; and to him that knocketh it shall be opened" (Matthew 7:7–8).

Longing for God

A godly man prefers God before anything else that might be in heaven. Not only is there nothing actually in heaven which is in his esteem equal with God; but neither is there any of which he can conceive as possible to be there, which by him is esteemed and desired equally with God. Some suppose quite different enjoyments to be in heaven from those which the Scriptures teach us. The Mohammedans, for instance, suppose that in heaven are to be enjoyed all manner of sensual delights and pleasures. Many things which Mahomet has feigned are to the lusts and carnal appetites of men the most agreeable that he could devise, and with them he flattered his followers. But the true saint could not contrive one more agreeable to his inclination and desires than such as is revealed in the Word of God; a heaven of enjoying the glorious God and the Lord Jesus Christ. There he shall have all sin taken away, and shall be perfectly conformed to God, and shall spend an eternity in exalted exercises of love to him, and in the enjoyment of his love. If God were not to be enjoyed in heaven, but only vast wealth, immense treasures of silver, and gold, great honor of such kind as men obtain in this world, and a fullness of the greatest sensual delights and pleasures; all these things would not make up for the want of God and Christ, and the enjoyment of them there. If it were empty of God, it would indeed be an empty melancholy place. The godly have been made sensible as to all creature-enjoyments, that they cannot satisfy the soul; and therefore nothing will content them but God. Offer a saint what you will, [but] if you deny him God, he will esteem himself miserable. God is the center of his desires; and as long as you keep his soul from its proper center, it will not be at rest.

Whom have I in heaven but thee? and there is none upon earth that I desire beside thee.
Psalm 73:25

Godly Self-Love

So ought men to love their wives as their own bodies. He that loveth his wife loveth himself.
Ephesians 5:28

It is not a thing contrary to Christianity that a man should love himself, or, which is the same thing, should love his own happiness. If Christianity did indeed tend to destroy a man's love to himself, and to his own happiness, it would therein tend to destroy the very spirit of humanity; but the very announcement of the gospel, as a system of peace on earth and goodwill toward men (Luke 2:14), shows that it is not only not destructive of humanity, but in the highest degree promotive of its spirit. That a man should love his own happiness is as necessary to his nature as the faculty of the will is; and it is impossible that such a love should be destroyed in any other way than by destroying his being. The saints love their own happiness. Yea, those that are perfect in happiness, the saints and angels in heaven, love their own happiness; otherwise that happiness which God hath given them would be no happiness to them; for that which anyone does not love he cannot enjoy any happiness in.

Integrity

ntegrity . . . signifies "wholeness," intimating that where this sincerity exists, God is sought, and religion is chosen and embraced with the whole heart, and adhered to with the whole soul. Holiness is chosen with the whole heart. The whole of duty is embraced, and entered upon most cordially, whether it have respect to God or to man, whether it be easy or difficult, whether it have reference to little things or great. There is a proportion and fullness in the character. The whole man is renewed. The whole body and soul and spirit are sanctified. Every member is yielded to the obedience of Christ. All the parts of the new creature are brought into subjection to his will. The seeds of all holy dispositions are implanted in the soul, and they will more and more bear fruit in the performance of duty and for the glory of God.

Let integrity and uprightness preserve me; for I wait on thee.
Psalm 25:21

The whole body and soul and spirit are sanctified.

Lampposts

Let your light so shine before men, that they may see your good works, and glorify your Father which is in heaven.
Matthew 5:16

I t is the spirit and temper of the godly to delight to exalt God amongst men. They are glad when God is highly esteemed in the world; it rejoices them when they hear God spoken highly of. And they'll do all that they can to beget such an high esteem of God in the minds of men. They'll leave no stone unturned, that, if possible, they may be the means of bringing of it about, that God shall be highly thought of by others as well as themselves. And how is the Christian glad when his endeavors succeed, how his heart rejoices when he can give a lift towards the rearing up of the kingdom of God amongst men. He will exalt God amongst men by endeavoring all that possibly he can in his place and station, that sin and wickedness may decay and holiness and religion flourish and prosper, by endeavoring by his best strength and wisdom to reclaim persons from wicked courses, that men may be brought over to Jesus Christ and to live a holy life. He with delight will exalt God amongst men by showing his regard unto the worship and ordinances of God by his regard to his public worship, his holy Sabbath and his ministers.

A Heaven of Holiness

The heaven I desired was a heaven of holiness; to be with God, and to spend my eternity in divine love and holy communion with Christ. My mind was very much taken up with contemplations on heaven, and the enjoyments there; and living there in perfect holiness, humility, and love: And it used at that time to appear a great part of the happiness of heaven, that there the saints could express their love to Christ. It appeared to me a great clog and burden, that what I felt within, I could not express as I desired. The inward ardor of my soul seemed to be hindered and pent up, and could not freely flame out as it would. I used often to think how in heaven this principle should freely and fully vent and express itself. Heaven appeared exceedingly delightful, as a world of love; and that all happiness consisted in living in pure, humble, heavenly, divine love.

O God, thou art terrible out of thy holy places: the God of Israel is he that giveth strength and power unto his people. Blessed be God.
Psalm 68:35

> **All happiness consisted in living in pure, humble, heavenly, divine love.**

Excellent in the Earth

In that day shall the branch of the LORD be beautiful and glorious, and the fruit of the earth shall be excellent and comely for them that are escaped of Israel.

Isaiah 4:2

A humble disposition is attractive unto God. When God sees a person of such an excellent disposition, it draws the eyes of God upon you; and not only so, but draws him down from heaven into his heart. It brings the influences of his Holy Spirit into the soul. God will delight to take up his abode in such a soul and fill it with comfort. He has said, "Though the Lord be high, yet hath he respect unto the lowly" (Psalm 138:6); "With him also that is of a contrite and humble spirit, to revive the spirit of the humble, and to revive the heart of the contrite ones" (Isaiah 57:15). . . . This is the way to have the guidance of his Holy Spirit in all your way. God has said that the meek he will guide in his way. "The meek will he guide in judgment: and the meek will he teach his way" (Psalm 25:9).

Religious Affections

I f true religion lies much in the affections, hence we may learn what great cause we have to be ashamed and confounded before God that we are no more affected with the great things of religion. It appears, from what has been said, that this arises from our having so little true religion. God has given to mankind affections for the same purpose as that for which he has given all the faculties and principles of the human soul, viz., that they might be subservient to man's chief end, and the great business for which God has created him, that is, the business of religion. And yet how common is it among mankind that their affections are much more exercised and engaged in other matters than in religion! In matters which concern men's worldly interest, their outward delights, their honor and reputation, and their natural relations, their hearts are tender and sensible, easily moved, deeply impressed, much concerned, very sensibly affected, and greatly engaged. But how insensible and unmoved are most men about the great things of another world! How dull are their affections! How heavy and hard their hearts in these matters! Here their love is cold, their desires languid, their zeal low, and their gratitude small. How they can sit and hear of the infinite height, and depth, and length, and breadth of the love of God in Christ Jesus; of his giving his infinitely dear Son to be offered up a sacrifice for the sins of men; and all this for enemies, to redeem them from deserved, eternal burnings, and to bring to unspeakable and everlasting joy and glory; and yet be cold, heavy, insensible, and regardless! Where are the exercises of our affections proper, if not here? Can anything be set in our view, greater and more important? anything more wonderful and surprising? or that more nearly concerns our interest? Can we suppose that the wise Creator implanted such principles in our nature as the affections, to lie still on such an occasion as this?

I will praise thee, O LORD, with my whole heart; I will shew forth all thy marvellous works.
Psalm 9:1

Glorious in Salvation

hose very attributes which seemed to require man's destruction are more glorious in his salvation than they would have been in his destruction. The revenging justice of God is a great deal more manifested in the death of Christ than it would have been if all mankind had been sufferers to all eternity. If man had remained under the guilt and imputation of sin, the justice of God would not have had such a trial, as it had, when his own Son was under the imputation of sin. If all mankind had stood guilty, and justice had called for vengeance upon them, that would not have been such a trial of the inflexibleness and unchangeableness of the justice of God, as when his own Son, who was the object of his infinite love, and in whom he infinitely delighted, stood with the imputation of guilt upon him. This was the greatest trial that could be, to manifest whether God's justice was perfect and unchangeable, or not; whether God was so just that he would not upon any account abate of what justice required; and whether God would have any respect to persons in judgment. So the majesty of God appears much more in the sufferings of Christ than it would have done in the eternal sufferings of all mankind. The majesty of a prince appears greater in the just punishment of great personages under the guilt of treason, than of inferior persons. The sufferings of Christ have this advantage over the eternal sufferings of the wicked, for impressing upon the minds of the spectators a sense of the dread majesty of God, and his infinite hatred of sin; viz., that the eternal sufferings of the wicked never will be seen actually accomplished, and finished; whereas they have seen that which is equivalent to those eternal sufferings actually fulfilled and finished in the sufferings of Christ.

The Neglect of Prayer

he neglect of the duty of prayer seems to be inconsistent with supreme love to God also upon another account, and that is, that it is against the will of God so plainly revealed. True love to God seeks to please God in everything, and universally to conform to his will. . . . Thus restraining prayer before God is not only inconsistent with the love, but also with the fear of God. Consider how living in such neglect is inconsistent with leading an holy life. We are abundantly instructed in scripture that true Christians do lead an holy life; that without holiness no man shall see the Lord (Hebrews 12:14); and that everyone that has this hope in him, purifies himself, even as Christ is pure (1 John 3:3). In Proverbs 16:17, it is said, "The highway of the upright is to depart from evil," that is, it is, as it were, the common beaten road in which all the godly travel. . . . It is spoken of in Romans 8:1 as the character of all believers that they walk not after the flesh, but after the spirit. But how is a life, in a great measure prayerless, consistent with a holy life? To lead an holy life is to lead a life devoted to God; a life of worshipping and serving God; a life consecrated to the service of God. But how doth he lead such a life who doth not so much as maintain the duty of prayer? How can such a man be said to walk by the Spirit and to be a servant of the Most High God? A holy life is a life of faith. The life that true Christians live in the world they live by the faith of the Son of God. But who can believe that man lives by faith who lives without prayer, which is the natural expression of faith? Prayer is as natural an expression of faith as breathing is of life; and to say a man lives a life of faith, and yet lives a prayerless life, is every whit as inconsistent and incredible, as to say that a man lives without breathing. A prayerless life is so far from being an holy life, that it is a profane life. He that lives so, lives like the heathen, who calls not on God's name; he that lives a prayerless life, lives without God in the world.

The transgression of the wicked saith within my heart, that there is no fear of God before his eyes.
Psalm 36:1

The Lamb of God

An admirable conjunction of excellencies will be manifest in Christ's acts at the last judgment. He then, above all other times, will appear as the Lion of the tribe of Judah, in infinite greatness and majesty, when he shall come in the glory of his Father, with all the holy angels, and the earth shall tremble before him, and the hills shall melt. This is he that shall sit on a great white throne, before whose face the earth and heaven shall flee away (Revelation 20:11). He will then appear in the most dreadful and amazing manner to the wicked. The devils tremble at the thought of that appearance; and when it shall be, the kings, and the great men, and the rich men, and the chief captains, and the mighty men, and every bondman, and every freeman, shall hide themselves in the dens, and in the rocks of the mountains, and shall cry to the mountains and rocks to fall on them, to hide them from the face and wrath of the Lamb. And none can declare or conceive of the amazing manifestations of wrath in which he will then appear towards these; or the trembling and astonishment, the shrieking and gnashing of teeth, with which they shall stand before his judgment seat, and receive the terrible sentence of his wrath. And yet he will at the same time appear as a Lamb to his saints; he will receive them as friends and brethren, treating them with infinite mildness and love. There shall be nothing in him terrible to them; but towards them he will clothe himself wholly with sweetness and endearment. The church shall be then admitted to him as his bride; that shall be her wedding day. The saints shall all be sweetly invited to come with him to inherit the kingdom, and reign in it with him to all eternity.

Natural Men Hate God

natural men . . . are enemies in the natural relish of their souls. They have an inbred distaste and disrelish of God's perfections. God is not such a being as they would have. Though they are ignorant of God; yet from what they hear of him, and from what is manifest by the light of nature, they do not like him. By his being endowed with such attributes as he is, they have an aversion to him. They hear God is an infinitely holy, pure, and righteous Being, and they do not like him upon this account; they have no relish of such qualifications: they take no delight in contemplating them. It would be a mere task, a bondage to a natural man, to be obliged to set himself to contemplate those attributes of God. They see no manner of beauty or loveliness, nor taste any sweetness, in them. And on account of their distaste of these perfections, they dislike all his other attributes. They have greater aversion to him because he is omniscient and knows all things; and because his omniscience is a holy omniscience. They are not pleased that he is omnipotent, and can do whatever he pleases; because it is a holy omnipotence. They are enemies even to his mercy, because it is a holy mercy. They do not like his immutability, because by this he never will be otherwise than he is, an infinitely holy God.

Let God arise, let his enemies be scattered: let them also that hate him flee before him.
Psalm 68:1

Grow in Holiness

Thy testimonies are very sure: holiness becometh thine house, O LORD, for ever.
Psalm 93:5

We ought to be continually growing in holiness; and in that respect coming nearer and nearer to heaven. We should be endeavoring to come nearer to heaven, in being more heavenly; becoming more and more like the inhabitants of heaven, in respect of holiness and conformity to God; the knowledge of God and Christ; in clear views of the glory of God, the beauty of Christ, and the excellency of divine things, as we come nearer to the beatific vision. We should labor to be continually growing in divine love, that this may be an increasing flame in our hearts, till they ascend wholly in this flame, in obedience and a heavenly conversation; that we may do the will of God on earth as the angels do in heaven; in comfort and spiritual joy; in sensible communion with God and Jesus Christ. Our path should be as "the shining light, that shines more and more to the perfect day." We ought to be hungering and thirsting after righteousness; after an increase in righteousness. "As newborn babes, desire the sincere milk of the word, that ye may grow thereby" (1 Peter 2:2). The perfection of heaven should be our mark: "This one thing I do, forgetting those things which are behind, and reaching forth unto those things that are before, I press toward the mark for the prize of the high calling of God in Christ Jesus" (Philippians 3:13–14).

The perfection of heaven should be our mark.

A Friend Forever

You may greatly comfort yourself that you have an unchangeable friend in Christ Jesus. Constancy is justly looked upon as a most necessary and most desirable qualification in a friend; that he be not fickle, and so that his friendship cannot be depended on as that of a steady sure friend. How excellent his friendship is you may learn from his manner of treating his disciples on earth, whom he graciously treated as a tender father his children; meekly instructing them, most friendlily conversing with them, and being ready to pity them, and help them, and forgive their infirmities. And then you may consider this doctrine, and how it thence appears that he is the same still that he was then, and ever will be the same.

From the unchangeableness of your Savior, you may be assured of your continuance in a state of grace. As to yourself, you are so changeable, that, if left to yourself, you would soon fall utterly away; there is no dependence on your unchangeableness; but Christ is the same, and therefore, when he has begun a good work in you he will finish it; as he has been the author, he will be the finisher of your faith. Your love to Christ is in itself changeable; but his to you is unchangeable, and therefore he will never suffer your love to him utterly to fail. The apostle gives this reason why the saints' love to Christ cannot fail, viz., that his love to them never can fail.

His mouth is most sweet: yea, he is altogether lovely. This is my beloved, and this is my friend, O daughters of Jerusalem.
Song of Solomon 5:16

Loving Your Neighbor

And to love him with all the heart, and with all the understanding, and with all the soul, and with all the strength, and to love his neighbour as himself, is more than all whole burnt offerings and sacrifices.
Mark 12:33

To love our neighbor as ourselves is the sum of the moral law respecting our fellow creatures; and to help them, and to contribute to their relief, is the most natural expression of this love. It is vain to pretend to a spirit of love to our neighbors when it is grievous to us to part with anything for their help when under calamity. They who love only in word, and in tongue, and not in deed, have no love in truth. Any profession without it is a vain pretence. To refuse to give to the needy is unreasonable because we therein do to others contrary to what we would have others to do to us in like circumstances. We are very sensible of our own calamities; and when we suffer, are ready enough to think that our state requires the compassion and help of others; and are ready enough to think it hard if others will not deny themselves in order to help us when in straits.

To refuse to give to the needy is unreasonable.

Christ Pursues Sinners

Christ himself is now seeking your salvation. He seeks it by . . . appointing men to make it their business to seek it; he seeks it by them; they are his instruments, and they beseech you in Christ's stead, to be reconciled to God. He seeks it, in commanding your neighbors to seek it. Christ is represented in Scripture as wooing the souls of sinners. He uses means to persuade them to choose and accept of their own salvation. He often invites them to come to him that they may have life, that they may find rest to their souls; to come and take of the water of life freely. He stands at the door and knocks; and ceases not, though sinners for a long time refuse him. He bears repeated repulses from them, and yet mercifully continues knocking, saying. "Open to me, that I may come in and sup with you, and you with me." At the doors of many sinners he stands thus knocking for many years together. Christ is become a most importunate suitor to sinners, that he may become their sovereign. He is often setting before them the need they have of him, the miserable condition in which they are, and the great provision that is made for the good of their souls; and he invites them to accept of this provision, and promises it shall be theirs upon their mere acceptance.

For the Son of man is come to seek and to save that which was lost.
Luke 19:10

Escape Temptation

Flee also youthful lusts: but follow righteousness, faith, charity, peace, with them that call on the Lord out of a pure heart.
2 Timothy 2:22

It is evident that we ought not only to avoid sin, but things that expose and lead to sin; because this is the way we act in things that pertain to our temporal interest. Men avoid not only those things that are themselves the hurt or ruin of their temporal interest, but also the things that tend or expose to it. Because they love their temporal lives, they will not only actually avoid killing themselves, but they are very careful to avoid those things that bring their lives into danger; though they do not certainly know but they may escape.

They are careful not to pass rivers and deep waters on rotten ice, though they do not certainly know that they shall fall through and be drowned. They will not only avoid those things that would be in themselves the ruin of their estates, as setting their own houses on fire, and burning them up with their substance; taking their money and throwing it into the sea, but they carefully avoid those things by which their estates are exposed. . . . If a man be sick of a dangerous distemper, he is careful to avoid everything that tends to increase the disorder; not only what he knows to be mortal, but other things that he fears may be prejudicial to him. Men are in this way wont to take care of their temporal interest. And therefore, if we are not as careful to avoid sin, as we are to avoid injury in our temporal interest, it will show a regardless disposition with respect to sin and duty; or that we do not much care though we do sin against God. God's glory is surely of as much importance and concern as our temporal interest. Certainly we should be as careful not to be exposed to sin against the Majesty of heaven and earth, as men are wont to be of a few pounds; yea, the latter are but mere trifles, compared with the former.

Prayer and Praise

We ought also to follow the example of the apostle in his abounding in prayer and praise. He was very earnest, and greatly engaged in those duties, and continued in them, as appears from many passages: "First, I thank my God through Jesus Christ for you all, that your faith is spoken of throughout the whole world. For God is my witness, whom I serve with my spirit in the gospel of his Son, that without ceasing I make mention of you always in my prayers" (Romans 1:8–9); "Wherefore I also, after I heard of your faith in the Lord Jesus, and love unto all the saints, cease not to give thanks for you, making mention of you in my prayers" (Ephesians 1:15–16); "We give thanks to God and the Father of our Lord Jesus Christ, praying always for you" (Colossians 1:3); "We give thanks to God always for you all, making mention of you in our prayers; remembering without ceasing your work of faith and labour of love, and patience of hope in our Lord Jesus Christ, in the sight of God and our Father" (1 Thessalonians 1:2–3).

Be careful for nothing; but in every thing by prayer and supplication with thanksgiving let your requests be made known unto God.
Philippians 4:6

Growing in Grace

But grow in grace, and in the knowledge of our Lord and Saviour Jesus Christ. To him be glory both now and for ever. Amen.

2 Peter 3:18

Conversion is a great and glorious work of God's power, at once changing the heart, and infusing life into the dead soul; though the grace then implanted more gradually displays itself in some than in others. But as to fixing on the precise time when they put forth the very first act of grace, there is a great deal of difference in different persons; in some it seems to be very discernible when the very time was; but others are more at a loss. In this respect, there are very many who do not know, even when they have it, that it is the grace of conversion, and sometimes do not think it to be so till a long time after. Many, even when they come to entertain great hopes that they are converted, if they remember what they experienced in the first exercises of grace, they are at a loss whether it was any more than a common illumination; or whether some other more clear and remarkable experience which they had afterwards, was not the first of a saving nature. The manner of God's work on the soul, sometimes especially, is very mysterious; and it is with the kingdom of God as to its manifestation in the heart of a convert, as is said, "So is the kingdom of God, as if a man should cast seed into the ground; and should sleep, and rise night and day, and the seed should spring and grow up, he knoweth not how. For the earth bringeth forth fruit of herself; first the blade, then the ear, after that the full corn in the ear" (Mark 4:26–28).

A Life-Long Pursuit

This business of seeking salvation never ends till life ends. They that undertake this laborious, careful, expensive, self-denying business must not expect to rest from their labors till death shall have put an end to them. The long continuance of the work which Noah undertook was what especially made it a great undertaking. This also was what made the travel of the children of Israel through the wilderness appear so great to them, that it was continued for so long a time. Their spirits failed, they were discouraged, and had not a heart to go through with so great an undertaking.

But such is this business that it runs parallel with life, whether it be longer or shorter. Although we should live to a great age, our race and warfare will not be finished till death shall come. We must not expect that an end will be put to our labour, and care, and strife by any hope of a good estate which we may obtain. Past attainments and past success will not excuse us from what remains for the future, nor will they make future constant labor and care not necessary to our salvation.

One thing have I desired of the LORD, that will I seek after; that I may dwell in the house of the LORD all the days of my life, to behold the beauty of the LORD, and to enquire in his temple.
Psalm 27:4

Above the Stars

Heaven is far above the stars. So it is said that Christ ascended far above all heavens. "He that descended is the same also that ascended up far above all heavens, that he might fill all things" (Ephesians 4:10), that is, far above all the heaven that we see. This is the mount Zion, the city of the living God, the heavenly Jerusalem, and hither the angels conduct the souls of the saints when they leave their earthly tabernacles. When they come there, they shall be received with a joyful welcome, the doors of this glorious city are opened to them, and they shall have entrance given to them into heaven, as an inheritance to which they have a right. "Blessed are they that do his commandments, that they may have right to the tree of life, and may enter in through the gates into the city" (Revelation 22:14). And then shall open to view that glorious world, that beautiful city, and delightful paradise, which they had often before heard of, and thought of, and desired; then they shall see it, and possess it as their own. There they shall be welcomed and joyfully received by that glorious company that dwell there, by the angels, and by the saints that went to heaven before them. There was joy among them at their conversion, and now also will there be joy among them when they are brought home to glory. To have one that was dear to them before, because a child of the same family and a disciple of the same Lord, brought home from a strange country to come and dwell with them for ever; how will their fellow citizens and brethren in heaven be glad for them, and rejoice with them, and embrace them, when they come there to join them in their praises of God and the Lamb!

The Prayers of the Humble

od will love to exalt and help to honor such. Luke 14:11, "He that humbleth himself shall be exalted." It seems that this disposition it is that more peculiarly attracts the Almighty's bounty, is the only way [to] have God as a Father to us in this world, to keep us in all our ways, to provide for us, to keep us from evils and dangers, and to be our comforter in afflictions and the answerer of our prayers: for God takes most pleasure in the prayer of the humble (Psalm 10:17).

Better it is to be of an humble spirit with the lowly, than to divide the spoil with the proud.
Proverbs 16:19

God takes most pleasure in the prayer of the humble.

The Son's Radiance

*Thou art beautiful, O
my love, as Tirzah,
comely as Jerusalem,
terrible as an army
with banners.*
Song of Solomon
6:4

Immediately after my conversion, God's excellency began to appear to me in everything: in the sun, in the moon, in the stars, in the waters, and in all nature. The Son of God created the world for this very end, to communicate to us through it a certain image of his own excellency, so that when we are delighted with flowery meadows and gentle breezes we may see in all that only the sweet benevolence of Jesus Christ.

When we behold the fragrant rose and the snow-white lily, we are to see his love and his purity. The green trees and the song of the birds, what are they but the emanation of his infinite joy and benignity? The crystal rivers and the murmuring streams, what are they but the footsteps of his favor and grace and beauty? When we behold the brightness of the sun, the golden edges of the evening cloud, and the beauteous rainbow spanning the whole heaven, we but behold some adumbration of his goodness and glory.

And, without any doubt, this is the reason that Christ is called the Sun of Righteousness, the Morning Star, the Rose of Sharon, the Lily of the Valley, the Apple Tree among the trees of the wood, a bundle of myrrh, a doe, and a young hart. But we see the most proper image of Jesus Christ when we behold the intellectual and spiritual beauty of the mind and heart of a truly holy man.

No Security for the Wicked

It is no security to wicked men for one moment that there are no visible means of death at hand. It is no security to a natural man that he is now in health, and that he does not see which way he should now immediately go out of the world by any accident, and that there is no visible danger in any respect in his circumstances. The manifold and continual experience of the world in all ages shows this is no evidence that a man is not on the very brink of eternity, and that the next step will not be into another world. The unseen, unthought-of ways and means of persons going suddenly out of the world are innumerable and inconceivable. Unconverted men walk over the pit of hell on a rotten covering, and there are innumerable places in this covering so weak that they will not bear their weight, and these places are not seen. The arrows of death fly unseen at noonday; the sharpest sight cannot discern them. God has so many different unsearchable ways of taking wicked men out of the world and sending them to hell, that there is nothing to make it appear that God had need to be at the expense of a miracle, or go out of the ordinary course of his providence, to destroy any wicked man, at any moment. All the means that there are of sinners going out of the world are so in God's hands, and so universally and absolutely subject to his power and determination, that it does not depend at all the less on the mere will of God, whether sinners shall at any moment go to hell, than if means were never made use of, or at all concerned in the case.

As a dream when one awaketh; so, O Lord, when thou awakest, thou shalt despise their image.
Psalm 73:20

God's Wonders

And it shall come to pass in the last days, saith God, I will pour out of my Spirit upon all flesh: and your sons and your daughters shall prophesy, and your young men shall see visions, and your old men shall dream dreams.
Acts 2:17

God is pleased again to put out his Spirit upon us. And he is doing great things amongst us. God is indeed come again, the same great God who so wonderfully appeared among us some years ago, and who has since, for our sins, departed from us, left us so long in so dull and dead a state, and has let sinners alone in their sins, so that there have been scarcely any sins to be seen of any such work as conversion. That same God is now come again. He is really come in like manner, and begins, as he did before, gloriously to manifest his mighty power, and the riches of his grace. He brings sinners out of darkness into marvelous light. He rescues poor captive souls out of the hands of Satan. He saves persons from the devouring fire. He plucks one and another as brands out of the burnings. He opens the prison doors and knocks off their chains and brings out poor prisoners.

He brings sinners out of darkness into marvelous light.

Degrees of Suffering

The Scripture teaches that the wicked will suffer different degrees of torment, according to the different aggravations of their sins. "Whosoever is angry with his brother without a cause shall be in danger of the judgment: and whosoever shall say to his brother, Raca, shall be in danger of the council: but whosoever shall say, Thou fool, shall be in danger of hell fire" (Matthew 5:22). Here Christ teaches us that the torments of wicked men will be different in different persons, according to the different degrees of their guilt. It shall be more tolerable for Sodom and Gomorrah, for Tyre and Sidon, than for the cities where most of Christ's mighty works were wrought. Again, our Lord assures us that he that knows his Lord's will, and prepares not himself, nor does according to his will, shall be beaten with many stripes. But he that knows not, and commits things worthy of stripes, shall be beaten with few stripes. These several passages of Scripture infallibly prove that there will be different degrees of punishment in hell, which is utterly inconsistent with the supposition that the punishment consists in annihilation, in which there can be no degrees.

But it shall be more tolerable for Tyre and Sidon at the judgment, than for you.
Luke 10:14

Saints Shall Rise

All the saints shall mount up, as with wings, to meet the Lord in the air, and to be forever with him. After the dead in Christ are risen, and the living saints changed, then they will be prepared to go to Christ, and to meet the bridegroom. The world will be about to be destroyed, and the wicked shall be in dreadful amazement, but the saints shall be delivered. "And at that time shall Michael stand up, the great prince which standeth for the children of thy people: and there shall be a time of trouble, such as never was since there was a nation even to that same time: and at that time thy people shall be delivered, every one that shall be found written in the book" (Daniel 12:1). They shall take an everlasting farewell of this evil world where there is so much sin, and where they have met with so much trouble, and they shall be caught up in the clouds, and there they shall meet their glorious Redeemer; and a joyful meeting it will be. They shall go to Christ, never any more to be separated from him.

Bearing Injuries

We should improve what our friends say to us and of us, when they from friendship tell us of anything which they observe amiss in us. It is most imprudent, as well as most unchristian, to take it amiss, and resent it, when we are thus told of our faults. We should rather rejoice in it, that we are shown our spots. Thus also we should improve what our enemies say of us. If they from an ill spirit reproach and revile us to our faces, we should consider it, so far as to reflect inward upon ourselves, and inquire whether it be not so, as they charge us. For though what is said, be said in a reproachful, reviling manner, yet there may be too much truth in it . . . so when we hear of others talking against us behind our backs, though they do very ill in so doing, yet the right improvement of it will be to reflect upon ourselves, and consider whether we indeed have not those faults which they lay to our charge. This will be a more Christian and a more wise improvement of it than to be in a rage, to revile again, and to entertain an ill will towards them for their evil-speaking. This is the most wise and prudent improvement of such things. Hereby we may get good out of evil. And this is the surest way to defeat the designs of our enemies in reviling and back-biting us. They do it from ill will, and to do us an injury; but in this way we may turn it to our own good.

Examine me, O LORD, and prove me; try my reins and my heart.
Psalm 26:2

Hopes of Heaven

Therefore my heart is glad, and my glory rejoiceth: my flesh also shall rest in hope.
Psalm 16:9

Christ not only delivers from fears of hell and of wrath, but he gives hopes of heaven, and the enjoyment of God's love. He delivers from inward tumults and inward pain from that guilt of conscience which is as a worm gnawing within, and he gives delight and inward glory. He brings us out of a wilderness of pits, and drought, and fiery flying spirits; and he brings us into a pleasant land, a land flowing with milk and honey. He delivers us out of prison, and lifts us off from the dunghill, and he sets us among princes, and causes us to inherit the throne of glory. Wherefore, if anyone is weary, if any is in prison, if anyone is in captivity, if anyone is in the wilderness, let him come to the blessed Jesus, who is as the shadow of a great rock in a weary land. Delay not, arise and come away.

Delay not, arise and come away.

Gratitude

This temper to love to exalt God and debase self arises from gratitude. The believer considers what God has done for him, considers on his wonderful mercy the greatness and the multitude, and a principle of gratitude makes him delight to exalt God for it. He considers how God has humbled himself, that is, condescended to have mercy on him and help him. Therefore gratitude makes him delight to do that which is not condescension but his bounden duty, even to humble for sin, and lay himself in the dust for it.

He considers how Jesus Christ, who is God, humbled himself and left heaven and lived in ignominy upon earth, and became obedient unto death, even the death of the cross, for him. Therefore gratitude moves him to humble himself and to love to lay himself low before God, seeing his Son made himself so low for him as to be in the form of a servant and a malefactor. Therefore seek to be affected with those wonderful instances of the goodness of God, and let not your heart be as a stone; be not more ungrateful than the beasts, and you will find that abhorrence of yourself, and those high thoughts of God, as will make you delight to exalt and honor him, and to lay yourself low.

Enter into his gates with thanksgiving, and into his courts with praise: be thankful unto him, and bless his name.
Psalm 100:4

Always Open

I will therefore that
men pray every where,
lifting up holy hands,
without wrath and
doubting.
1 Timothy 2:8

God sits on a throne of grace, and there is no veil to hide this throne and keep us from it. The veil is rent from the top to the bottom. The way is open at all times, and we may go to God as often as we please. Although God be infinitely above us, yet we may come with boldness. "Let us therefore come boldly unto the throne of grace, that we may obtain mercy, and find grace to help in time of need" (Hebrews 4:16). How wonderful is it that such worms as we should be allowed to come boldly at all times to so great a God! Thus God indulges all kinds of persons, of all nations: "with all that in every place call upon the name of Jesus Christ our Lord, both theirs and ours; grace be unto you" (1 Corinthians 1:2–3). Yea, God allows the most vile and unworthy: the greatest sinners are allowed to come through Christ. And he not only allows, but encourages and frequently invites them, yea, and manifests himself as delighting in being sought to by prayer. "The prayer of the upright is his delight" (Proverbs 15:8), and in the Song 2:14 we have Christ saying to the spouse, "O my dove, . . . let me hear thy voice; for sweet is thy voice." The voice of the saints in prayer is sweet unto Christ; he delights to hear it. He allows them to be earnest and importunate, yea, to the degree as to take no denial, and as it were to give him no rest, and even encouraging them so to do.

Clothed with Love

God and Christ appear in the gospel revelation as being clothed with love; as sitting as it were on a throne of mercy and grace, a seat of love, encompassed about with the sweet beams of love. Love is the light and glory that is round about the throne on which God is seated. This seems to be intended in the vision the apostle John, that loving and loved disciple, had of God in the isle of Patmos, "And there was a rainbow round about the throne, in sight like unto an emerald" (Revelation 4:3), that is, round about the throne on which God was sitting. So that God appeared to him as he sat on his throne, as encompassed with a circle of exceeding sweet and pleasant light, like the beautiful colors of the rainbow, and like an emerald, which is a precious stone of exceeding pleasant and beautiful color—thus representing that the light and glory with which God appears surrounded in the gospel, is especially the glory of his love and covenant grace, for the rainbow was given to Noah as a token of both of these. Therefore, it is plain that this spirit, even a spirit of love, is the spirit that the gospel revelation does especially hold forth motives and inducements to; and this is especially and eminently the Christian spirit—the right spirit of the gospel.

He that loveth not knoweth not God; for God is love.
1 John 4:8

Suffering for Christ

And if children, then heirs; heirs of God, and joint-heirs with Christ; if so be that we suffer with him, that we may be also glorified together.

Romans 8:17

It is a frequent thing for the apostle Paul to mention suffering in the cause of Christ as a fruit of Christian love; and therefore it is not probable that he would omit so great a fruit of love in this place, where he is professedly reckoning up all the important fruits of love or charity. It is common for the apostle elsewhere to mention suffering in the cause of religion as a fruit of love or charity. So he does in 2 Corinthians 5:14, where, after speaking of what he had undergone in the cause of Christ, on account of which others were ready to say he was beside himself, he gives as the reason of it, that the love of Christ constrained him. And so, again, in Romans 5:3–5, he gives it as a reason why he was willing to glory in tribulations, that the love of God was shed abroad in his heart by the Holy Ghost. And still again, he declares, that neither tribulation, nor distress, nor persecution, nor famine, nor nakedness, nor peril, nor sword, should be able to separate him from the love of Christ (Romans 8:35). Now, since suffering in the cause of Christ is so great a fruit of charity, and so often spoken of elsewhere by the apostle, it is not likely that he would omit it here, where he is professedly speaking of the various fruits of charity.

The Betraying Kiss

en who attend ordinances, and yet willingly live in wicked practices, treat Christ in the same manner that the Jews did. They come to public worship, and pretend to pray to him, to sing his praises, to sit and hear his word; they come to the sacrament, pretending to commemorate his death. Thus they kneel before him, and say, Hail, King of the Jews; yet at the same time they live in ways of wickedness, which they know Christ hath forbidden, of which he hath declared the greatest hatred, and which are exceedingly to his dishonor. Thus they buffet him, and spit in his face. They do as Judas did, who came to Christ saying, Hail, Master, and kissed him, at the same time betraying him into the hands of those who sought his life.

But Jesus said unto him, Judas, betrayest thou the Son of man with a kiss?
Luke 22:48

They do as Judas did.

As This Little Child

Whosoever therefore shall humble himself as this little child, the same is greatest in the kingdom of heaven.

Matthew 18:4

The tenderness of the heart of a true Christian is elegantly signified by our Savior, in his comparing such a one to a little child. The flesh of a little child is very tender: so is the heart of one that is new-born. This is also represented in what we are told of Naaman's cure of his leprosy, by his washing in Jordan, by the direction of the prophet; which was undoubtedly a type of the renewing of the soul, by washing in the laver of regeneration. We are told that "then went he down, and dipped himself seven times in Jordan, according to the saying of the man of God: and his flesh came again like unto the flesh of a little child" (2 Kings 5:14). Not only is the flesh of a little child tender, but his mind is tender. A little child has his heart easily moved, wrought upon, and bowed: so is a Christian in spiritual things. A little child is apt to be affected with sympathy, to weep with them that weep, and cannot well bear to see others in distress: so it is with a Christian (John 11:35; Romans 12:15; 1 Corinthians 12:26). A little child is easily won by kindness: so is a Christian. A little child is easily affected with grief at temporal evils, his heart is melted, and he falls a-weeping; thus tender is the heart of a Christian, with regard to the evil of sin. A little child is easily affrighted at the appearance of outward evils, or anything that threatens its hurt: so is a Christian apt to be alarmed at the appearance of moral evil, and anything that threatens the hurt of the soul. A little child when it meets enemies, or fierce beasts, is not apt to trust its own strength, but flies to its parents for refuge; so a saint is not self-confident in engaging spiritual enemies, but flies to Christ.

Increase in Humility

e exhorted to increase more and more in this temper and disposition. It is an excellent and heavenly temper; it is that which makes you shine much brighter than other sort of men, who are sinners and hypocrites. Be not lifted up at any thoughts of your own goodness or worthiness; give God all the praise, "For who maketh thee so to differ from another? and what hast thou that thou didst not receive?" (1 Corinthians 4:7). When you do good works, do not be elated in your own minds, but let God have the praise. Seek not the applause and commendation of men. Let God have the praise, and you shall have praise from him hereafter. Delight in having your heart broken for sin, delight in humbling yourself at the foot of mercy and let it be your delight to exalt God in your heart and by your acknowledgments.

When men are cast down, then thou shalt say, There is lifting up; and he shall save the humble person.
Job 22:29

Let it be your delight to exalt God in your heart.

A Farewell

*The grace of our Lord
Jesus Christ be with
you all. Amen.*
Romans 16:24

ear children, I leave you in an evil world, which is full of snares and temptations. God only knows what will become of you. The Scripture has told us that there are but few saved, and we have abundant confirmation of it from what we see. This we see, that children die as well as others. Multitudes die before they grow up, and of those that grow up, comparatively few ever give good evidence of saving conversion to God. I pray God to pity you, and take care of you, and provide for you the best means for the good of your souls, and that God himself would undertake for you to be your heavenly Father, and the mighty Redeemer of your immortal souls. Do not neglect to pray for yourselves. Take heed you are not of the number of those who cast off fear and restrain prayer before God. Constantly pray to God in secret, and often remember that great day when you must appear before the judgment seat of Christ, and meet your minister there, who has so often counseled and warned you.

Do not neglect to pray for yourselves.

Sources of Readings

Readers who wish to explore further the readings in this collection will find most of them in Hendrickson's two-volume edition *The Works of Jonathan Edwards*. Other selections can be found in *The Works of Jonathan Edwards* (vols. 10, 13, 14, 16, 19) published by Yale University Press. The unpublished transcripts used for this devotional are housed in The Beinecke Manuscript and Rare Book Room at Yale University, and are courtesy of *The Works of Jonathan Edwards*, Yale University.